Eighty Not Out
Memoirs of a Bad Mixer

Elizabeth McCullough

BLACKSTAFF PRESS

First published in 2012 by
Blackstaff Press
4c Sydenham Business Park
Belfast BT3 9LE
with the assistance of
The Arts Council of Northern Ireland

Typeset by CJWT Solutions, St Helens, England
Printed in Great Britain by the MPG Books Group

A CIP catalogue record for this book
is available from the British Library

ISBN 978-0-85640-887-8

www.blackstaffpress.com

www.blackstaffpress.com/ebooks

She thought of the narrowness of the limits within which a human soul may speak and be understood by its nearest mental kin, of how soon it reaches that solitary land of the individual experience, in which no fellow footfall is ever heard.

Olive Schreiner, *The Story of an African Farm* (1883)

Contents

Maps

Acknowledgements

To all persons involved in aid projects throughout Africa. Irrespective of profession, the challenges faced are similar. My own experience relates to working with my husband, Fergus, whose expertise was in the field of debilitating diseases such as Guinea-worm disease (dracunculiasis), and bilharziasis (schistosomiasis).

In memory of Dr Vivian Gotto, former reader in zoology, Queen's University, Belfast, who, while terminally ill, wrote a Foreword for my book *Late Developer: A Greenhorn in Ghana 1960–65*. He was my husband's mentor during the preparation of his M.Sc. thesis; the men shared an interest in parasitic diseases, and both were fanatical tennis players. Vivian took satisfaction in his role as fairy godmother when, in 1955, Fergus returned to Queen's from Ghana to write his Ph.D. thesis. I had just been appointed university photographer.

A tribute to my husband, Fergus, who died aged sixty-nine on May Day 1995: his early death was caused by haemolytic anaemia, a condition often found in patients who have suffered multiple attacks of malaria. Also to our three children, Katharine, Mary and Michael, who suffered anguish during the years 1977–87 when my alcoholism reached, in AA jargon, 'rock bottom'.

For anyone whose life has been affected, directly or indirectly, by the disease of alcoholism. In gratitude to AA groups in Geneva and Ferney-Voltaire, which agonised over my lamentably slow progress towards sobriety: in particular Canadian Ted Hooper, who lived long enough to see his conviction, that I would make it in the end, fulfilled. To these should be added Ed, my counsellor at Broadway Lodge in 1981, whom I traced as recently as February 2012; now 77, he lives in Tenerife.

For Donald Gilchrist, FRCS, who cared for my husband after his heart attack in 1971. We were stationed at Mwanza, on the southern shores of Lake Victoria, and the nearest cardiologist was in Nairobi. Donald provided moral as well as medical support at a critical time in all our lives. Most of his professional career was spent working in remote mission hospitals under adverse conditions; the same age as me, he now lives in a retirement home in Lancashire.

For my friend Judge Lillian Fisher, first met on the foothills of Kilimanjaro in 1969, who encouraged me to write, and with whom I have corresponded ever since – she becoming PC and e-mail literate long before me. With her husband, Bernie, she visited us in France in the eighties, and we stayed with them in Arizona in 1993. Lillian, now ninety, remains an active Democrat; the local press will no longer publish her letters, but she knew and mourns for all who died, or were injured, in the shooting in Tucson on 8 January 2011.

To John and Rosemary McMahon, doctors who devoted a great part of their lives to the field of public health, nutrition and parasitic diseases. A close friend since we first met in 1967, Rosemary lost a protracted and painful battle with arthritis in October 2010; John, who cared for her when she was not in hospital, now lives in a Quaker retirement home near their daughter and grandson in Sidcot, Somerset; their two sons and a granddaughter are in Australia.

For Val Corey and Joy MacDonald, who acted as proofreaders in the early days, and to Ken Ford who has cheerfully taken many packets to the post office since October 2009, when I finished writing this book. To Bob Jones, who has helped with photographs and never fails to sort out problems stemming from my incompetence. Gratitude to Maura Pringle at Queen's University, recruited only recently, on the advice of Noel Mitchel, to draw the maps: she has done a superlative job. Thanks to Patsy Horton and Helen Wright at Blackstaff Press and Hilary Bell, who edited the MS, for their infinite patience on finding yet another bunch of ill-coordinated overnight thoughts in the morning inbox.

Lastly, for Dodi, who will be eighty-seven on 30 June, and Arthur Norris, who married my aunt Rosemary in 1957 and who will celebrate his ninety-eighth birthday on 10 July.

Prologue
Minus Nine Months

Half of me has been waiting nearly six years for a determined sperm to reach and pierce my defences. Assuming each ovary in the dark cavern I inhabit first began to produce eggs ripe for fertilisation some eighteen years ago, and taking into account my place in the queue, the number of eggs lost every month, the ageing factor and the fact that an infusion of sperm arrives seldom, the chances of my ever joining the human race had been rapidly dwindling. Now, this August of the Dublin Horse Show, I am an entity. Last night he returned, less inebriated than usual, and injected a host of lively swimmers, one of which – or is it whom? – penetrated my outer layer. Was there an element of wanting to punish my mother in the violence of the final thrust? Given luck, wholesome nourishment and little disturbance, I should join the common herd in April.

Already I know more than is good for me and am impatient with my mother, who, not realising she is pregnant, subjects me to jolts and knocks while she canters her horse and jumps fences. Finally, after four months, something was applied to the wall outside, and I heard heavy breathing and stern voices. Thereafter, the routine has been more restful, although not without occasional interference, provoking more raised voices and my mother's accelerated heartbeat. Sometimes she plays the piano, which is soothing, but more often she does mad things like going for a swim. I am used to being in a watery cocoon, but sounds indicate a violent environment with slaps and swoops more alarming than the horse-jumping. The worst was a flight in a noisy aeroplane – embryos have sensitive ears, and mine popped quite painfully.

1

I am impatient to join the world, even though its inhabitants seem to be in perpetual dispute, if only to voice my own views – 'shoving your oar in' was my mother's term for such precocious participation.

1
Derry to Greenisland

What a relief, the comfortable little bag had become claustrophobic; now, after the initial shock, I am getting used to the light. Competent hands wiped me free of messy substances, cut the pulsating cord linking me to my mother, and swaddled me tightly, before laying me in a cot beside her bed. It would have been nice to have been taken into her arms, but the competent hands were busy making comforting noises as they washed and wiped. A mass of wavy auburn hair lay on the pillows surrounding a beautiful but exhausted face: she did not even glance in my direction. I was further hurt when a pink-faced young man with fair curly hair peered into my cot before remarking to my mother: 'Well done, Dorothy, old thing – what a pity it's a girl.' The nurse looked affronted as he left without kissing my mother. It is a nice room with a large window overlooking a rock garden, small pond and a lawn that graduates to fields, where two horses are grazing. An avenue of beech trees, surrounded by clusters of daffodils, leads to a busy main road. Distant voices come from other parts of what seems to be quite a large house. There are small panes of coloured glass at the top of the window – I like this room but wish someone would lay me on my mother's somewhat flat chest.

She seems to be sleeping, so I provoke some action by the only means I can, and begin a relentless wail. It feels good; I am surprised how strong my lungs are and how it brings instant results. The nurse appears, lifts me out of the cot and puts me on my mother's chest near a dark swollen nipple. The nurse says something about the milk coming down and breasts needing stimulus from a hungry infant. She grasps my head too firmly for comfort and forces it onto the nipple, squashing my nose and making it hard to breathe; my mother's involvement in this operation is minimal, but after all, we are both beginners at this

3

game. They squeeze, and I chomp away until something nice enters my mouth, but not enough. They change me to the other side – same sequence. We are both tired and doze off in the weak afternoon sunlight, which throws multicoloured patterns through the stained glass onto the counterpane.

There is a lot of talk over the next few days about the milk being there, but the flow is inhibited by my mother's state of mind. She is encouraged not to be so tense and to enjoy the baby. I am frustrated and perpetually hungry; she is awash with apprehension. They decide to change to bottle-feeding: this is horrible – a smelly rubber teat instead of that comforting breast; a thin substance to swallow, after which I get griping spasms and often vomit the lot when they try to wind me.

My mother asks the kindly family doctor questions about my health prospects, and in particular, the risk posed by heredity. Ahead of his time, the doctor says that alcoholism is a disease, which seems to run in families, but that being female should be an advantage. Conveniently, he chooses to ignore the often outlandish behaviour of my paternal grandmother, Eileen, and her elder sister, Charlotte, who is incarcerated in Letterkenny Asylum. My father refers to the institution as the loony bin and says they put the wrong one away. The sisters and their two brothers had been brought up in Waterford by austere, unadorned, grey-stuff-clad, Plymouth Brethren grandparents. The fate of the children's parents is not recorded: no paintings or photographs remain – they might as well have never existed. My grandmother's two nephews, Homer and Charles, prospered in the US, becoming pillars of their community in Hartford, Connecticut.

Grandfather David's beautiful first wife Maggie, whom he met during a visit to Harrogate Spa, died shortly after their son, Hugh, was born in 1891; a wet nurse and a succession of nannies followed. Four years later David fell for the forceful Eileen, who, after training at the Rotunda Hospital in Dublin, had been appointed matron of the Derry City Hospital. A photograph records a modestly dressed couple, heads bent in joint study of the Good Book. David was an astute businessman, but respected in the community as a man of probity. His tastes were not extravagant, and I suspect the vulgar tiepins inherited by me were gifts from Eileen; one a seven-diamond horseshoe, the other a shamrock of ruby, sapphire and diamond. His heavy signet ring I wear to this day. The mock-Tudor mansion on the outskirts of Derry had been built for Maggie, of whom Eileen expunged all traces, apart from a pair of mother-of-pearl opera glasses engraved with her initials. The presence of Hugh, however, was a constant reminder of his first marriage, so she manipulated David – in the best interests of the child of course – to send him to boarding school in Cumbria at the age of seven. At what stage Charlotte joined the family is not known, nor how much time passed before she was certified insane. My father's account of a trip to Paris, during which her over-indulgence in wine had resulted in unbecoming behaviour, cannot be without foundation.

David was also responsible for his Uncle John, said to be not the full shilling. Photographs show a fine-featured elderly man with a goatee beard. A bachelor who went on frequent shooting excursions to the Free State, his handicap cannot have been severe. He was still alive, having suffered years of Eileen's brutal regime, when my mother took over management of the house late in 1922 and my grandmother moved to a flat in Crawford Square in the centre of Derry. His last years were, in comparison, tranquil.

What sort of man is my father? He has shown so little interest in me that I fear we may never get to know each other. His interests seem limited to breeding fox terriers, shooting wildfowl and maintaining his image as a generous man-about-town; with a sense of humour arrested at schoolboy level, his cultural interests are apparently nonexistent. Well-read nineteenth-century books in the library bear the names of his father or great-grandfather, who founded the family business in 1820. He was sent to Sedbergh, the same school as Hugh, at the age of thirteen in the hope that he might acquire some polish and lose his regional accent. He absconded to join the army at sixteen, but Eileen exerted influence to ensure he never saw active service. Hugh was killed at Passchendaele in 1917, which is how my father came to inherit Stevenson's Bakery and Restaurant on the death of his father in 1921. Six years later the small empire was in dire straits and a manager, who was to hold 51 per cent of the shares, took over its direction.

Three weeks elapse after my birth, at the end of which my

mother is allowed out of bed. She instantly takes charge by dismissing the nurse and driving to the pharmacy in search of advice on the best brands of infant formula, it having transpired that what was in my bottle was watered cow's milk. Two grandmothers and one grandfather have joined the support group, the most voluble being Eileen, whose repeated enquiry, 'No sign of a little stranger yet?', had exasperated my mother. She is overjoyed by the event, which she predicts will bring her son to his senses. My mother's parents, Stonard and Rosa, are quieter, having learned only recently that the marriage was in deep trouble – and why.

A Protestant cook and Catholic parlour-maid take care of running the house, while the kennels and stables are in the care of a general handyman. There is a full-time gardener and a chauffeur, whose duties involve not only maintaining the Alvis in shiny, roadworthy condition, but accompanying my father to business meetings and liquid lunches in Derry. At the conclusion of these he is expected to deliver his boss home for an evening with the family. Sometimes the car does not return, so it is assumed a whim has taken it into the Free State to some pub in Donegal – Buncrana, Greencastle, Carndonagh, or even as far as Malin. The telephone is unreliable, so the adults pass many evenings dreading the state in which my father will arrive home. A legal separation had been agreed before my conception, so we are in the phasing-out period before the house sale is concluded, and new owners found for the livestock. My mother and I are to join her parents at Greenisland, situated on the coast between Belfast and Carrickfergus in County Antrim, while my father will move to Worthing to live with a woman more sympathetic to his frailties than my mother. They met at the Dublin Horse Show, which makes it unfair that my mother is not divorcing him on grounds of adultery rather than settling for a legal separation. Such social stigma is attached to divorce that only the aristocracy or the royal family get away with it. Already I am cynical.

They put me outside in a smart baby carriage, sprung on high wheels, with a silk canopy to protect my face from the strong spring sunlight. Hours pass while I sleep and swell. I am fed at regular intervals by one grandparent or other, but seldom by my mother, who is busy packing her few belongings with sentimental value to take to Greenisland. Because Eileen left the house fully furnished as a thoughtful gift to the newlyweds, they are few – a grandfather clock, bought at auction in Lifford, a Georgian bureau and bookcase, a Victorian corner cupboard, a George II silver tea-service, some ivory carvings and a green lustre bowl on a Chinese carved base. My father has sold her hunter, Nimrod, to a woman with a notoriously hard hand on the bit, but she still has her Kerry Blue, Michael. Sometimes they bring my pram into the oak-panelled dining room while they eat a light lunch – my father does not appear for these meals, as he will join the young business bloods of Derry for lunch at the club. No doubt he is taking legal advice from his friends on how best to settle on an annuity for his estranged wife. They will stick together, these superior young men, making excuses for my father's irresponsible lifestyle. A minimal pay-out will be deemed sufficient, as 'after all, it's not as if it were a son needing a public school education, but a daughter who need only acquire a modicum of ladylike accomplishments, before going on the marriage market'. So, with those thoughts in mind, a legal separation is arranged, allowing my mother a fixed income derived from a capital sum, considerable in the thirties, but dwindling to borderline poverty by the end of World War II.

I am precocious, always an outsider, observing, listening, judging, wanting to voice my opinion, to influence events. Power is what I would like, but so far it is restricted to infant bawls. I can experiment with the volume and intensity, reach a crescendo, then stop abruptly. This technique guarantees the arrival of an adult fearing I have stopped breathing: an engaging smile ensures being picked up and cuddled.

There are pictures of my first Christmas. I am sitting on the floor beside a decorated tree, surrounded by toys, most prominent of which is an orange velvet cat with long bendy limbs, a flat black fur face, hands, feet and long tail. Known as Black Pussy, he has survived the years, now a bit twisted, fur thin in places, but recognisable. Felix, the cartoon cat, is satin-stitched on a bib with a scalloped blue edging. Felix's tongue is padded and bright red.

My mother and I are soon installed at her parents' house. My Aunt Rosemary attends the Belfast School of Art, and has been evicted from a large first-floor bedroom because of our presence. Her room is now in the attic, next to the maid's room, and she is not best pleased. In time I grow to love my aunt, despite her gift of emitting an aura of displeasure, ensuring all within range keep their distance. An explosion would clear the air, but so repressed are emotions on my mother's side of my family that a wary atmosphere can last for days. I much prefer the less inhibited approach of my Derry relations, whom I would like to think of as pure Irish. Inspection of the family tree indicates the Waterford connection goes back only as far as 1832 when Plymouth Brethren from south-west England settled in Ireland. The Church of Scotland forebears on my paternal side moved to Ulster from Dumfries and Galloway in the late eighteenth century. On my mother's side, Grandfather, otherwise known as Gramp, came from the Barrow-in-Furness peninsula, and Grandmother Rosa from Newcastle upon Tyne, as recently as 1910, when my grandfather was Lloyd's surveyor for the *Titanic* at Harland and Wolff's shipyard in Belfast. They fell in love with Ireland to the extent of spending their first summer holiday at Gweedore in County Donegal.

I have a highchair to the left of my grandfather's carving chair. My mother sits opposite me, my aunt on my left, and Grandmother Rosa, with her back to the bay window, which overlooks Belfast Lough, at the opposite end to my grandfather. My plate has a raised rim; it has a painting of two bears playing golf on the bottom. I also have a silver spoon and pusher. I like the formality of meals and the fact that Gramp often serves me first, even if he does comment on my table manners and the fact that sometimes I am greedy in demanding another slice of meat from the Sunday joint. Meal patterns do not vary from week to week: Monday brings cold cuts from the previous day; Tuesday shepherd's pie; Wednesday, toad-in-the-hole; Thursday, mutton stew; Friday, fish; Saturday, roast chicken. The only things I really do not like are herrings, which have little prickly bones no matter how carefully the grown-ups say they have removed them, and tripe and onion casserole, which Rosa, with her Newcastle background, and my mother encourage the rest of us to try. Gramp and Auntie Rosemary resist, so they are given an alternative. Puddings are sometimes the nice sticky variety with custard, more often tapioca or semolina with a blob of jam or rhubarb, which I hate. Michael, whining piteously, nose to the door, is not allowed in the dining room. Across the hall, opposite the dining room, is the drawing room, where Gramp has a globe of the world and a brass telescope. There is a stuffed Indian alligator, although I do not think any of my ancestors have been to India. When I get a little older, I am told to say that my father works there. This is my favourite room. Gramp reads fables from Aesop, Greek myths adapted for children, *The Water Babies*, many Beatrix Potter stories, my favourites being *Peter Rabbit*, *Two Bad Mice* and *Squirrel Nutkin*. He tries to interest me in stories from the Bible, and my lack of interest disappoints him. With the help of a torch, a ping-pong ball and the globe, he teaches me the rudiments of the solar system. He has a workshop with a lathe – a fine example of his work survives: a doll's cradle too fragile to be played with, and sadly missing a finial, from which the net curtains should drape. We mark the tennis court together, or rather he lets me think I am helping, and we potter around the garden deadheading flowers.

Rosa discourages my presence in the kitchen, but there are many hours, when she has gone shopping with my mother, that I can spend with Annie, our maid. Annie is a devout Methodist; with infinite patience she lets me mess with starch and the blue bag. She also allows me to make butter-balls with two wooden pats; only perfect globes go into a bowl of cold water before being taken to the dining room. Larger portions are forced from a wooden mould with a daisy pattern on the bottom. The laundry room houses an enormous mangle, which can wring blankets, and several vast tubs for various stages of the wash: all this Annie copes with five and a half days each week. On Sundays she goes by bus to visit her married sister who lives in Connswater, on the other side of Belfast, with her husband and two children. I cannot hear too much about Billy and Winnie, who are about the same age as me, but do not meet them for many years – during the war in fact, when they were temporarily homeless after their house had been damaged during the German bombing of Belfast in 1941.

I do not often meet other children. When we go for drives, either in my mother's Austin Seven or in Gramp's huge dark green Singer coupé, I see them playing in the streets of

Whiteabbey, where they have tops which they whip with skill; the boys have rickety-looking home-made carts, and a few have footballs. Some of the girls have corkscrew ringlets, which I envy, and I ask my mother to do my hair that way. She says that I do not have that kind of hair and, anyway, it is a vulgar style. I retort that Shirley Temple has ringlets and the sort of dress I would like in satin, with a tight waist and a bow at the back. My dresses are invariably home-made, in beautiful fabric, often embroidered or smocked, but I long for shop-bought fashion. I get ideas from the drawings and fashion magazines Auntie Rosemary brings home from the art school.

Gramp's life has been blighted in many ways, some of which would have soured a lesser man. An uncle, charged with the administration of his father's estate, had embezzled a capital sum, so that by the time my grandfather was twenty-one little was left, and the early days of his marriage to Rosa had been shadowed by financial insecurity. Their first child, a boy, did not thrive owing to a heart defect, dying before his first birthday. After my mother was born in 1896, there were several miscarriages, ending with the birth of Auntie Rosemary in 1909. Gramp never speaks of the *Titanic* disaster, nor the fact that he was not on the maiden voyage – was he not invited, or did he choose not to go? The breakdown of my mother's marriage must be agonising for them. He and Rosa are so unworldly (or is it naïvety?) that no rumour reached them until the situation reached crisis point not long before my birth.

He is thinking about what the future may hold for his daughters, and has already made plans for a bungalow to be built for my mother at Knock, a considerable distance from Greenisland. Why this choice? Probably the Malone area is already too expensive, Glengormley and Whiteabbey bleak, but Knock is a good centre from which to explore the infinite variety of the County Down coast, its rich farming hinterland, and the spectacular bird life of Strangford Lough, less forbidding than the Antrim coast with its dramatic glens and cliffs. A estimate of £500 is accepted to build a two-bedroom house with large living room, kitchen, bathroom, and attic space, attainable only by ladder; the 'motor-house' is a separate wooden structure. The site is attractive: one of the many tributaries of the Connswater River flows past the bottom of the garden, marking the roadside boundary. Turning right at the front gate, the road rises steeply to Gilnahirk Church and Primary School, then a further mile to Mann's Corner, which is the limit of the bus run from central Belfast. A few prosperous red-brick houses with well-kept lawns and shrubberies stand back from the road, screened from curious eyes. The main interests at Gilnahirk are a duck pond and the shop, which smells strongly of paraffin, as do all such shops throughout Ireland – I like it.

2
Outer Suburbia in Knock

Our new house overlooks open farmland; always put to bed too early, I can hear the persistent call of a corncrake as I lie awake. In late summer neat haystacks pepper the fields, where the outer suburbs melt into countryside. Seventy years on I realise that the six houses – after Gramp's death, my mother and Auntie Rosemary used his legacy to build more houses in the same area – built by my mother were part of the malignant growth of characterless dwellings that now reaches as far as Dundonald and the drumlins of north Down.

We move there in early 1932, but there is no great wrench on parting from Gramp because we drive down to Greenisland every Sunday. It is an interesting journey via Cherryvalley, within walking distance of our house, Sandown Road, Neill's Hill Station, Ballyhackamore, then down the Upper Newtownards Road to the Holywood Arches, past the ropeworks, over the Queen's Bridge, where one can see the red funnels of cross-channel boats and Rank's flour mill, an early skyscraper, in the near distance. Many of the streets in the docks area are cobbled, and stalwart shire horses drag flat-bottomed trailers loaded with sacks of coal up the slope to the bridge. A few women wear black shawls – they look poor. There are hundreds of pigeons and sparrows, and I fear my mother may squash one. Sometimes we go by Mountpottinger and the Albert Bridge, passing the main market and the Law Courts before joining the Queen's Bridge traffic heading for the Shore Road via the Albert Memorial clock-tower. We pass the York Road railway station, and I get bored until we come to Whiteabbey, a mix of poor, back-to-back, terraced housing with a few isolated affluent mansions. The red lantern over the public house means we are getting near Greenisland; we pass huge ornate gilded gates with lamps, which my mother says are the entrance to the lord mayor's residence, and I can see Knockagh Monument on our left; we are nearly there. My mother has contrived some sort of high seat for me, so I always have a good view. Michael sits on his rug on the back seat, resigned and greyly smelly. We turn right, off the road to Carrickfergus, onto the gravel sweep between the house and the tennis court, and we are there. Gussie, the one-legged gull is sitting on the sea wall as usual, and Michael goes on a wild tear around the garden.

It is high summer and the house is bursting with unusual activity. The adults hurry from the kitchen with jugs of lemonade and plates of sandwiches, heading for a long table set in the shade under my favourite tree: the one with the deep dark hole so high I have to be lifted to look inside. The tennis court is perfectly marked and Gramp is checking the height of the net. Rosa is dressed more elegantly than usual in a long coffee-coloured silk dress, with matching wide-brimmed hat and parasol: to my mind she looks too dressed up. Gramp's concession to the occasion is a blazer, which he soon takes off, and a new panama hat, instead of his battered old one with the wispy edge. Auntie Rosemary is dressed for battle in a white knee-length dress with a pleated skirt; she wears a shiny green eye-shade. My mother too is dressed in white and has brought tennis shoes in case she is called upon to make up a four. Auntie Rosemary has an admirer called Johnny, whose two elderly aunts own the house next door. I overhear whispers to the effect that he seems nice enough, being a law student at Trinity College in Dublin, but that he is a Roman Catholic. I gather this is not a point in his favour. She has another admirer – here today – whom I detest because he is always trying to be jolly, asking stupid questions and trying to play games with me – I suppose he thinks this will add to his popularity. He has flaming red hair and a shiny, freckled face, and I can tell he is no good at tennis. I have an articulated snake made in Hong Kong in the pocket of my dress, and am fiddling with it; he spots it and asks if he can have a go. Reluctantly I hand it over. We are standing near the steep, slimy green steps that lead from a gap in the wall down to the water's edge; the rippling tide is full in. Suddenly my snake contorts out of his hand and plummets into the sea. 'Oh dear,' he says, 'I'm so sorry. I'll get you another one.' I am furious and flee crying to my mother for comfort. She says with some asperity that she supposes it was just one of those unfortunate accidents, and he promises again to replace my snake: needless to say he does not. The next time I see a similar one is in Nairobi forty years later.

The move to Knock brought opportunities to expand social contacts, but my mother remained aloof from the only family with a child who lived nearby. Their house was on the corner where Gilnahirk Road was joined by Kensington Road, the houses on which varied from late Georgian to prosperous Victorian and Edwardian, with a sprinkling of architect-designed new houses, generally regarded with disfavour.

My mother advertised for a nanny, whose principal duty would be to take me for walks and look after me while my mother went into Belfast to do shopping and change her books at Anderson & McAuley's library – I did not know why she preferred this to the Linen Hall Library. Occasionally she met friends dating from her days at Richmond Lodge School under the aegis of Miss Violet Nairn, a scholarly woman for whom she had great respect. One friend had married a kindly man, but had TB, still referred to as consumption at that time, and was 'delicate'; they were childless. Another had gone to university and taught in a private school. A third had married a garage proprietor from outside her social circle, although this was not voiced in so many words. I gathered it was deemed an unfortunate choice; the fact that he resembled the film actor Charles Boyer may have something to do with it. Lust, in other words. Another, who lived not far from us, had a son of my age, and several times we visited them for afternoon tea. The golden-haired child later in life became a successful illustrator of children's books, so we might have had something in common, as I had an aptitude for art from an early age; but my mother found the family dreary, so we returned the hospitality once only.

There were contacts to be made within the show-jumping fraternity, and my mother soon found a friend whose family had a large house in Comber. Flo was a fearless horsewoman, and impressed me when she broke her collar bone for the second time. Her father owned a riding school and stables, so horses were always in need of exercise – but what a comedown for my mother from having had horses of her own. She swallowed her pride and they passed many hours hacking companionably around the lanes of north Down. The subsequent failure to turn me into a competent horsewoman was added to her list of disappointments.

Mrs Anderson, the only applicant for the job of nanny, came from a Protestant family from Swords, near Dublin, which moved north soon after the South became independent in 1922. She was married to a nice man called Murray and lived in Ballyhackamore. San, as I soon called her, was beautiful, fair-haired, with large cornflower blue eyes and a skin that turned in summer to golden brown: surely there must have been a Scandinavian ancestor. She took a pragmatic view of life, had a wicked sense of humour, and a devilish talent for imitating pretentious people. Some of her remarks were slanderous, but never malicious. We bonded from the start, and my mother enjoyed her wit, although San's lifelong incomprehension of modern technology, such as vacuum cleaners and gas pokers, tested her patience. 'This auld thing's up to its tricks again.'

One of my earliest memories of an outing with San is the day – 16 November 1932 – we joined the crowd on the Upper Newtownards Road to see the Prince of Wales in an open carriage on his way to open the new Parliament Buildings at Stormont. I waved my small flag although disappointed that he was wearing a naval hat with feathers instead of a jewelled crown. Afterwards we went to the Post Office at Cabin Hill, for a chat with the postmistress, a kind lady of teutonic build: she had thick, corn-coloured hair dressed in coils around each ear.

Rosa, whose physique was sparrow-like, was now in her early sixties with seemingly inexhaustible energy; her mother and grandmother had lived into their nineties. If we met in the hall at her and Gramp's house, she would tell me not to go so fast on my red wooden-seated tricycle. On the rare times she bathed me in the scratchy-bottomed bath with lion's claw feet, I used to pray that she would not try to clean my navel with a probing fingernail, even asking my mother to intercede, but she too had a fixation with cleanliness of that sensitive part, in which only a small ball of fluff was ever found. However, bath-time at my grandparents' house brought the pleasure of Pears transparent soap – at home my mother favoured red Lifebuoy. I remember Rosa warning that a firm line would have to be taken with me, as not only had I a tendency to interrupt, I had been known to contradict – regarded as almost as bad as hitting back when smacked. In January 1932, Rosa dropped dead in the hall. A call from Auntie Rosemary broke the news. Gramp was in shock, and remained so for some days, but I did not cry.

The summer of that year was a sad one, although we always joined Gramp and Auntie Rosemary for Sunday lunch. Rosemary continued her studies at the art school, while Annie, the maid, who was about the same age as my aunt, became a housekeeper. I have no idea if she was remunerated accordingly. How soon after Rosa's death Gramp began his decline to inoperable stomach cancer, I do not know, but I remember clearly the sickly smell that pervaded his bedroom when my mother took me to see him. When I was asked to recite my numbers up to ten, paralytic confusion struck as I neared six and seven. My reading skills, however, were a source of pride to everyone. These visits were short and in his final months a resident nurse hovered in the background to ensure that visitors did not stay too long. I drew pictures of her in full nursing regalia, but my favourite subject was the Loch Ness monster, sightings of which were frequent throughout 1933. In the autumn Gramp died: again a call came from Auntie Rosemary, resulting in one of the few times I saw my mother moved to tears. The others were on the death of her dog Michael the following year, and on hearing Chamberlain's broadcast on 3 September 1939 telling the nation that it was again at war with Germany after an interval of only twenty-one years.

Auntie Rosemary, with the help of Annie, cleared the house at Greenisland, put it on the market and moved to Knock, where, with their father's legacy, she and my mother now owned a total of eight houses. This was done with the aid of the Halifax Building Society, and by the time I was eight or nine, one of the jobs I most dreaded was to be sent to deliver the shiny red, imitation moiré-covered rent books. This became excruciating when I learned that one of the tenants – a widow whose son attended my school – was behind with her payments.

We moved to one of the newly built houses in 1934, with Auntie Rosemary and Annie living next door. This arrangement worked well: Annie worked for both sisters, lived rent-free, and was content to be nearer her own sister in Connswater.

Rosemary had finished art school without having graduated, and was now a civil servant at Stormont. Johnny was in his final year at Trinity College, but remained under the influence of his elderly parents, who owned a large estate in Mullingar in County Westmeath (later purchased by J.P. Donleavy, author of *The Ginger Man*). Rosemary was never invited to visit, as they remained adamant in their belief that she was an unsuitable future wife for their only child. Despite this, for several years, she wore a large aquamarine engagement ring.

My mother was a reluctant chaperone during the thirties. When Johnny coxed a Trinity crew at Henley regatta in 1936, he was determined that his fiancée should be present. Photographs show the weather was benign and both women were elegantly dressed – in no way lumpen lasses from Ireland – which must have gratified the already pompous young man, who insisted on referring to me as The Brat. My mother's photographs show Rosemary in a skiff, languorous hand trailing in the water, with a swan in the background. My mother wore an elegant black and white calf-length chiffon dress with a ruffled skirt. In the mid-thirties women's clothes had all the sophistication associated with the dance routines of Fred Astaire and Ginger Rogers, materials were often cut on the bias, silks, satins, chiffon and fur wraps were in favour.

While they were away, I stayed with San and Murray, who had moved from Ballyhackamore to a new house on the Gilnahirk Road. I had the time of my life – liberty at last! San was tragically childless although not barren – there had been a traumatic miscarriage some years earlier. She also claimed to have only half a stomach and ate frugally. Murray owned a garage in York Street; it never flourished, due to his generous nature, which allowed customers to run up considerable debts, some of which were never paid. A countryman at heart, he kept a pony and trap, in which we went for excursions all over north Down. Pulled by the obedient pony, these excursions were pleasant compared with outings with my mother on a variety of horses, all of which followed their inclination rather than respond to my ineffectual commands.

Murray kept a dinghy at Whiterock, from which we fished for easily caught mackerel. My feelings were mixed; I loved being in the boat and the idea of fishing, but confronted with the reality of a terrified fish flapping helplessly at my feet, I recoiled. Seeing this, Murray dispatched them with a blow to the head, which I did not like either. He kept ferrets and there was always a dog in their house: the earliest I remember was a snuffly Pekinese which San adored, to be followed by a fox terrier called Patsy. I do not think these dogs ever got any formal exercise, although they had the run of a large garden, which was planted with military precision, like an allotment: pretty rows of sweet pea, as well runner beans, garden peas, broad beans, carrots, lettuce and, of course, potatoes. When the time came, there was no need to urge them to dig for victory.

Murray had a sister, the one with 'brains', who was a senior civil servant at Stormont. Their mother, by the time she came to stay with San and Murray, was in an advanced stage of dementia; she had to be incarcerated at Purdysburn asylum after being found lurking behind a door, carving knife in hand. San was thought to be her intended victim. All I remember is a frail little wisp of a woman, who wandered around in an Edwardian high-necked dress, wearing a fixed vacant smile.

San's domineering sister, Molly, lived with her hen-pecked husband in Carrickfergus. She bore no physical resemblance to San; her imposing corseted bosom tapered in a tight 'costume' to slender legs like a pouter pigeon. She seldom removed her hat as she installed herself in an armchair beside the fire, from which she fired intrusive questions at me. Despite the length of her journey, she never lacked energy to conduct an inquisition into all aspects of San's affairs. Thereafter, she would pontificate on how much better the lodgers, the dog, the laundry, San's hair and, not least, Murray could be managed. San just got on with laying the table, lighting the next fag, or arranging a vase of sweet pea. I do not think that Molly expected any response to the diatribe, and she always tucked in with relish to high tea before leaving. One time she arrived regally, driven by her husband in their Rover; tall and thin, with a highly polished pointed dome of a head, he spent most of the visit talking to Murray in a shed at the far end of the garden. Their sanctified only child, an RAF pilot, was shot down off the coast of Sicily in 1941 – missing, presumed dead. Molly never fully recovered her sanity, and there were shaming incidents of shoplifting. San grieved deeply too, but with more restraint.

Female lodgers, for the most part from Lancashire, widened my experience of humanity. One, tall and thin, owned a dance studio in Belfast, while her sister, short and fat, owned a newsagent/confectionery shop near the Holywood Arches. Early in the war extra staff were recruited for the top security establishment, locally known as the Listening Station, near Manns Corner. Some of these lodged with San, and without exception took advantage of her generous nature – she was aware of this, but never seemed to bear any grudge, sometimes excusing inconsiderate behaviour with a sigh, remarking: 'Och, she's just a poor lonely soul, but good at heart.' My mother and I thought several among them blatant spongers. Murray reserved comment.

San was a chain-smoker who had recently abandoned Players, with a bearded sailor on the packet, in favour of Craven A – kinder to your throat – with cork tips in a neat red box. I regretted this, as there were no more cards to collect. She was addicted to the extent of doing the washing-up, fag in mouth, a length of ash trembling over the bowl. I would hop around offering an ashtray, but she always managed to avoid the ash actually falling in with the dishes. Long before twin-tubbed washing machines became commonplace, she coped with an enormous wash and hung it outside to dry; if the weather was wet, it would hang drearily in the garage. A vast pile of ironing was then taken up to the hot loft space, which Murray never got around to fully flooring. They had a seldom used sitting room with a cabinet containing Belleek baskets, china dogs, horses and rabbits, but pride of place went to the bride and groom from the top of their wedding cake. There was always a bottle of fizzy lemonade in her kitchen – a real treat for me, as fizzy drinks along with sherbet and gobstoppers were not allowed at home.

My mother brought gifts back from the regatta week: a cress-growing set, a devilishly difficult maze puzzle in Bakelite with nine small silver balls to be trapped at the centre, and a blue Box Brownie. Later that summer she acquired a trailer for camping equipment and we – my mother, Rosemary, Johnny and I – set off for Dunaff Head in Donegal. The weather was not propitious, so we ended up sleeping in an abandoned Black and Tans barracks on the headland. The following year we went across Ireland to Sligo and Achill Island, where I looked in vain for amethysts. The first pictures taken with the Brownie are landscapes with slightly sloping horizons, and Conrad, our dachshund, makes his first appearance. At Emlagh, near Roonagh Quay where the ferry now sails to Clare Island, we asked permission from Mrs MacHale to park the caravan on her land. She was unsparingly hospitable, allowing us to use her little stone well fed by pure spring water, and giving us a daily supply of warm milk from her one cow. She insisted that I should try my hand at the milking, with dire results; a true suburban child, I hated warm milk, and was none too keen on the proximity of her curious cow. I did my best to co-operate, but it must have been evident that I was not in my element.

I suspect the acquisition of camping paraphernalia and a caravan was an attempt to show my grandmother Eileen how well my mother could manage as a single parent. Grandma Eileen had paid for three summer holidays at Drumaweir Hotel in Greencastle. For me they are treasured memories, but for my mother, enduring the daily company of Grandma can only have been stressful. Her antics, such as emerging dripping from a swim to exhort fellow guests, quietly enjoying the sun in their deck chairs, to join her, as the water was 'really warm', and her claim to have met the ghost of my grandfather, referred to as 'dear Dav', at dusk, in a pink cloud, on her way to the shore, tested the other guests' ability to repress mirth and adopt a sombre expression of sympathy. She was a fast, impetuous driver who used the horn frequently, and her car bore evidence of past impingements; offers to 'take the child for a spin' were difficult to refuse without being downright rude. These visits to Greencastle must have been punitive for my mother who had happy memories of visits dating back as far as 1910.

Gramp and Rosa had brought my mother to Drumaweir when she was fifteen, and Rosemary a toddler; it was a family-run hotel and she had formed a lasting friendship with the owner's daughter. Here she first met the Stevenson family, and she told me that in 1912 Hugh had talked about how, when he was very young, Eileen had played her role as wicked stepmother – 'those rings of hers can cut you know'. They had played croquet and badminton; there had been wild horse-play, and my father, two years younger, had pushed my mother into a clump of pampas grass. She had stayed as a guest of the family, without her parents, in the summer of 1918, grieving for the loss of her fiancé, Jack, who had been killed just before Christmas 1917. But the wound had already begun to heal; in August 1918 her diary records dancing into the small hours in the boathouse with officers from the US navy who were stationed at Culmore. They seem to have had no difficulty in getting hold of assorted vehicles, in which they went joy-riding as far afield as Malin Head.

Gradually contact with Grandma dwindled to visits to Belfast, when she stayed at the Royal Avenue Hotel, and we would be summoned to lunch. It was clear she would have liked to see more of me on my own, and in this respect I fear my mother was insensitive, seldom releasing me; when she did, strict rules were dictated about the hour of return. Once only do I remember Grandma coming to visit us at Knock. She thought, correctly, that I was getting no spiritual guidance, and that a spot of church-going would not go amiss. Attendance, when it did take place, was not calculated to implant any wish for repetition. Grandma sang so loudly as to attract glances, particularly when joining a congregation in which she was unknown. I was acutely embarrassed, not least because I had difficulty in finding the right place in the hymn book, and could not bring myself to join in, despite hissed encouragement. On the way out Grandma would collar the minister to introduce herself and 'me grand-daughter', with a garbled explanation about why we were not seen more frequently.

Despite the eccentric antics, I enjoyed her company to a degree – a fact that had to be disguised from my mother, though some incidents, such as yoo-hooing down a lift-shaft when impatient to descend, and checking that a cubicle in the ladies was occupied by bending down to see the feet, make me cringe today. The worst was when she tried to force entry to a small cinema in Derry: the doors were shut and a queue had formed outside, awaiting the exit from the last performance. She, determined to have a word with the commissionaire, could be seen from the foyer, jumping up and down like a chimpanzee, rattling the doors until he opened them. Then she demanded if he knew who she was, and that she wanted two seats in the dress circle. Admirably he kept both his cool and a straight face, while

9/2185838

informing her that she would just have to take her place 'like any other body'. This was bonus entertainment for the queue, which had in the meantime lengthened, and the end of which I joined, wishing the ground would open. During the screening of the Marx Brothers comedy, which I found unfunny, she commented loudly on the block to her view caused by the entwined couple in front of us, eventually prodding them apart with her umbrella. When the lights came on after 'God Save the King', I expected a counter-attack from the young seaman, but he contented himself with a grimace. She had a fixation about tracking down silk/wool mixture stockings, once putting a still shapely leg on the counter for the blushing young male assistant better to see the style she wanted.

3
Kindergarten with the Misses Fitzgerald

The fact that at seven years old I could read fluently, but had no formal education, had to be faced. My mother enrolled me at a small private kindergarten run by the Misses Fitzgerald. The red-brick three-storey, semi-detached house was a fifteen minute walk from home, and knowing every short-cut in the neighbourhood, I insisted on going alone on the first day, carrying an orange cardboard attaché case. It contained a pencil-box, with a picture of Mount Fuji on the lid, an assortment of Venus pencils – I knew all about their degrees of hardness from Auntie Rosemary – an India rubber, a six-inch ruler, a compass and a box of multicoloured crayons. Books and stationery were to be supplied by the school. Here, at last, was a chance to mix with other children, but I cannot remember anything about them, except that there were about six, all larger than me.

We were introduced to rudimentary French – not verbs, just the genders and words for familiar objects. Each pupil had a Vere Foster copy-book, beginning with elementary pothooks, which I was already skilled at reproducing. I remember taking great care in copying a picture of the Taj Mahal. There was a big map of the world showing many of the countries red, which I knew meant they belonged to the British Empire, of which I was supposed to be proud. However, I had difficulty in distinguishing India from Africa, or in which one my father was supposed to be working. We drew pictures of 'a native outside his hut'. As Christmas approached preparations for a stage production were under way, and my mother was soon in conflict with the Misses Fitzgerald. Crêpe paper in various colours had been suggested for the costumes, but my mother said this would not be adequate, adding that the room designated for the performance was inadequately heated. The Misses Fitzgerald's argument that Chilprufe vests or other warm underclothes would be hidden under the paper was brushed aside. What part had been assigned to me I forget, but I did not appear in the Nativity play.

Both my mother and Auntie Rosemary were cinema addicts, going at least once a week to the Astoria or the Strand, which were within easy reach, or to the Picturedrome in Mountpottinger, despite the latter being known as the Flea Pit. They bought magazines devoted to the movie stars of the time, and I spent much time colouring and otherwise embellishing the pictures of Joan Crawford, Claudette Colbert and a host of others, lengthening already lush eyelashes and outlining pouting lips. Premieres were screened either at the Classic, or the Ritz (with Joseph Stone on his Mighty Organ) in central Belfast. The sisters took lessons in tap-dancing, to which they drove in the Austin Seven, dressed in what I felt were unsuitably short skirts. They also drove to Armagh Observatory to hear Patrick Moore lecturing on astronomy, and my aunt went to classical music recitals in the Ulster Hall.

Experience of live theatre was restricted to Jimmy O'Dea's pantomimes at the Empire Theatre, regarded by many as often 'going too far' and unsuitable for children. The Empire was shaped like a windmill, decorated with multicoloured lights. Modelled on Parisian theatres of the late nineteenth century, it is long gone, as is the marvellous cast-iron gents in the middle of Victoria Square and the narrow graffiti-ridden streets in its vicinity. I never got a satisfactory answer to my question, 'What does "Fuck the Pope" mean?' 'It's hard to explain,' came the reply. 'It's very vulgar, but some people do not like the Pope, who is head of the Roman Catholic Church. He lives in Rome. You must never, ever, use that word.'

I can remember seeing Jean Forbes-Robertson 'flying' on all too visible wires as Peter Pan at the Grand Opera House. I was enchanted by the first Disney *Silly Symphonies*, *The Tortoise and the Hare* and *Three Little Pigs*, and many Laurel and Hardy comedies. Gory drama was provided by Wallace Beery in *Treasure Island*, and *Captain Blood* and *Robin Hood* starring Errol Flynn, whose father was professor of zoology at Queen's University, Belfast. I too had become a cinema addict, known as 'going to the pictures', and by the time I was eleven or twelve, was allowed to go on my own to cinemas to see frightening films such as *The Tower of London*, Boris Karloff as the monster in the *Frankenstein* films, and Charles Laughton and Elsa Lancaster in *The Old Dark House*, based on a story by J.B. Priestly, as well as Bela Lugosi in a variety of repulsive roles. This freedom was riskier than my mother knew: several times I had to move my seat because of explorative hands from the next seat. Needless to say, I never mentioned this at home, or even to San, who helped my mother after Annie left to care for her late sister's children. After much agonising, inhibited by the teaching of her Church, Annie married her brother-in-law. She confided later to San that she had not known marriage was 'like that'. Notwithstanding, the marriage proved solid, and she a perfect stepmother.

My prowess at ballet was on the same level as my equestrian skills. Classes were held at Miss Lena King's Studio of Dance in Belfast, and annual displays were staged at the Empire Theatre to advertise the proficiency of her pupils. The fact that I had never seen a stage production to inspire me may have explained my footlessness, though lack of talent is the more likely cause. My mother often attended lessons – the only parent to do so. During the drive home, my performance was analysed in detail. I was tone-deaf, had no sense of rhythm, which accounted for my movements seldom being in time with the beat, I was not 'turned out' enough, and my hand movements lacked delicacy. Notwithstanding, I had been chosen as one of four cygnets in a parody of *Swan Lake*, and one of four red-jacketed galumphers waving whips and crying 'Tally ho!', to appear in Miss King's annual display at the theatre. Dressed in old net curtains and holding hoops, the class stood as nymphs in a Grecian frieze, waiting for the curtain to rise: a voice hissed from the wings, 'Take your shoes off'. A *Belfast Telegraph* photographer recording the event took a group picture in which I appear with an unbecoming wispy fringe, wearing a too-long tutu. The star performance was Lena King herself dancing *The Dying Swan*. She had danced at Sadler's Wells in her youth, but was now in plump middle age. To my mother, who had seen Pavlova dancing the original version at the Grand Opera House in Belfast, Lena's performance was a sacrilegious travesty: my lessons ceased at the end of the term.

Edward VIII abdicated on 10 December 1936, which threw the press into the sort of frenzy we now take for granted where royal affairs are concerned. I think the adults decided not to discuss it in front of me, lest it should provoke questions about mistresses, divorce and duty. In any case, I was much more interested in Christmas, in the acquisitive rather than the spiritual or moral sense; after the early ones at Greenisland, there were no more decorated trees. Maybe it was economic constraint, but I suspect my mother had some cranky idea about the display of trees in windows being vulgar ostentation. I shall never know, but I made sure my own children never had cause to complain, not even when we lived on the shores of Lake Victoria and the tree bore little resemblance to a Scandinavian conifer. We were a pathetic little group, my mother, aunt and me sitting down to a traditional luncheon. A small turkey was roasted, delicious stuffing made from a recipe of Rosa's, bread sauce, sausage and bacon rolls, and a variety of vegetables cooked healthily in the new pressure cooker which looked like a bomb, and of which I was frightened lest it explode. Rosemary made the pudding and rum butter, also a recipe handed down through several generations. I loved rum butter and the cider that was their celebratory drink. Afterwards, in late afternoon, if anyone could face it, there was a fruit cake with almond icing, crystallised fruits and chocolate bottles filled with liqueur; surprisingly I was allowed one, and I thought it was the most delicious thing I had ever tasted.

4
Strathearn School under Miss Miskelly

I entered the transition class at Strathearn grammar school, the entrance to which was on the back road from Belmont to Parliament Buildings. A regular bus for civil servants, which I took on days when the weather was too bad to cycle, passed my school and the entrance gates to Campbell College, a boys' preparatory and public school, often referred to as an establishment for the cream of Northern Ireland society – 'rich and thick', according to Samuel Beckett who taught there in the late twenties. Strangely enough I do not associate entry to the new school with any particular trauma. The transitional, co-educational class led to Forms 1 and 2, above which the school was for girls only. Miss Miskelly, the headmistress, was a formidable woman built on the same pouter-pigeon lines as San's sister. Small in stature, and firmly corseted, she favoured dresses with a lacy corsage, worn with high-heeled beige kid shoes. She presided over morning assembly, the roll call, and the singing of two hymns, before we went to our respective classrooms. She and my mother had a guarded relationship about which I can only conjecture: I suspect my mother had been forced to reveal her straitened circumstances, and negotiated the fees. Her own record at Richmond Lodge School, which had an excellent reputation, will have been used to some effect. The assembly hall also served as a gymnasium under the direction of a gym mistress, who also took us for rounders, tennis and hockey. Not truly sadistic, she nevertheless had unrealistic aspirations, and could not accept that not every spine was flexible enough to bend backwards till the head touched the floor. The vaulting horse was my greatest enemy, particularly when the pummels were removed and we were told to attack it short end on and somersault off the far end: to this day orthopaedic surgeons mutter about old injuries I suffered during PE. Among us were a few naturally gifted gymnasts, flexible, courageous and never breathless; they were in their element demonstrating skipping and floor exercises at the end-of-term display. The rest of us just muddled through, hoping not to attract attention. Mary, a country girl large for her age, had won a scholarship to the school: when the rest of us stripped to vests and knickers, it was revealed that she was wearing a boned corset. On being told that she could not possibly do exercises wearing such a garment, she became stubborn, pleading: 'Me mammy says I'm not to take it off.' The matter was referred to the headmistress, and Me Mammy won: Mary was excused gymnastic lessons.

Almost instantly I formed a crush on a wiry little boy called Cecil Heron, the son of a schools inspector; this was not noticed by anyone, least of all the object of my passion, and after my first term we never met again. The other boys were two studious sons of a local doctor, and the son of a well-known landscape artist, rough, loud, grubby and untidy, who constantly tested the teacher's patience. He was not a bully, but I was afraid of him. Among the girls there was a tyrant who imitated my speech, stole some crayons, and, having identified a number of vulnerable spots, teased me ruthlessly. I never developed any effective defences. She was big, verging on fat, with fuzzy fair hair and, I now see, of limited intelligence.

The class included several girls three years older than me. One, daughter of a colonel, would today be called 'an army brat'. She came from India where she had been educated by governesses; though bright, she had a lot of catching up to do. Another, also bright, was struggling with left-handedness and probably dyslexia. Then Celia, who was to become one of my best friends, was bone idle, but fancied a career in theatre and took elocution lessons – an expensive extra. Annie, a scrawny girl with a prominent nose, was the adored only child of elderly parents who lived near the school. San was quick to point out her oddities: 'That's a quare freak you've picked up.' Poor Annie developed anorexia; sometimes, after we had been playing, her parents would ask me to join them at the evening meal. These were protracted affairs, punctuated by parental exhortations of 'Will you not take a little bit more, wee sweetheart?' I, who did not need any urging, was acutely embarrassed. Annie often fled the table and disappeared upstairs, probably to be sick. I went with Celia, now a burgeoning young woman of thirteen, to visit her in a mental hospital, where, weighing just over five stone, she was being force-fed. She used to stroke her lower abdomen, from which the hip bones stuck out like a starving animal's, and say: 'Look how fat I'm getting.'

Not long before my tenth birthday, Conrad, now almost blind as a result of the distemper he had developed the previous year, escaped from the garden and walked straight into the path of a bus. The driver, who was very upset, had come carrying the corpse, to explain that he had not been able to brake in time. I was at school, and my mother, after burying Conrad in our Pets' Cemetery, beside defunct tortoises, budgies and goldfish, came by car to collect me and break the news. Grieving as much as I, she arranged a trip to Dublin in an effort to take my mind off the loss. The Austin Seven had been replaced by a Morris Eight: I thought the design beautiful, in particular the red jewel in a silver mount on the door of the boot. I was bursting with pride as we drove in FZ 5440, what was then regarded a long distance, to Dublin. My mother had booked a room at the Ivanhoe Hotel in Harcourt Street; the next time I stayed there was on honeymoon, just after Christmas in 1950.

This was my first visit to that beautiful city; quite ignorant of architectural epochs, it struck me as much superior to Belfast. There is a photograph of me standing at the top of Nelson's Pillar in O'Connell Street, sadly to be blown up in March 1966, to mark the fiftieth anniversary of the Easter Rising. We visited the crypt of St Michan's Church, where the guide encouraged me to touch the crusty belly-flap of one of the mummified corpses. Why on earth did my mother think this a suitable place to take a grieving child? Then we visited the zoo. I have hated zoos since my first visit to the sunless Zoological Gardens under Cave Hill in Belfast, but did not have the guts to say so. All the grown-ups assumed that children liked both zoos and circuses. I had my fill of the latter too after being terrified by a clown at Duffy's travelling circus near Killyleagh, County Down. I did not like the elephant, either – much too close for comfort. Nor did I like the spectacle of lions and tigers performing tricks in response to the prods and cracking whip of the ringmaster.

Six white horses, ridden by a plump woman in a red spangled suit, were nice, and the sea lions were OK, apparently enjoying themselves. I was not sure about the chimpanzees, feeling then, as now, that our relationship is uncomfortably close. My mother must have retained pleasant memories from visiting the zoo in the early twenties; her albums from those years contain pictures of big cats behind bars and an adult elephant. I know that, like white hunters who turn to conservation, she would ultimately have changed her views on the incarceration of wildlife. As a final 'treat' I was given a ride on a bristly, warmly smelly baby elephant. But when I was taken to follow and witness the end of a stag hunt, I finally voiced my disgust as the terrified animal jumped the sea wall near Groomsport, and launched itself in the direction of the Copeland Islands.

Race meetings at Downpatrick, on the other hand, were thrilling: the jockeys' multicoloured satin blouses, the jostling crowd, and the fact that both my mother and aunt coyly placed miniscule bets on some of the horses. We had a seat-stick, too, but I was not tall enough to use it properly. The atmosphere was far removed from anything I had ever experienced. If it rained, we retired to the car, which steamed up, to eat sandwiches and hard-boiled eggs.

We were a household of animal lovers and pets of all kinds found a home with us. The shelf under the north-facing kitchen window was devoted to an aquarium of coldwater fish deemed too delicate for the pond; multicoloured fantails and Othello, a black specimen with protuberant eyes, lived in harmony with a burgeoning snail population. A mature *Dytiscus marginalis* beetle, its larval form, and several snail species inhabited a tangle of weed in an old battery container; the beetle was a deliberate internee, but the larva had come with weed taken from a pond near Manns Corner. The beetle used its formidable pincers, with slow deliberation, to ingest large worms until only a pallid, pasta-like string remained before it fell to the foul bottom; only then was a new sacrifice offered. It was my job to dig for worms and select the daintier specimens for the newts who lived in a designer vivarium in the living room. My mother had modelled something on the lines of a miniature stage set for *King Kong*, complete with cave where the newts slept; wriggling bait was offered at the mouth of the cave, held by a pair of long-handled tweezers. The inhabitants – sexes unknown – numbered four – Napoleon, almost black, Josephine, yellow, and two nameless, light brown; they were fussy eaters, but my mother told me not to be so squeamish and chop worms, rejected as being too large, into bite-sized pieces with her pearl-handled penknife. A display tank with overhead lighting, containing small goldfish and shubunkins took pride of place in the sitting room, next to the wireless, on a shelf above the *Encyclopaedia Britannica*. Any fish suspected of having a fungal infection, or with a depressed dorsal fin, was given a bath of potassium permanganate, then subjected to running water treatment in a milk can in the kitchen sink: sickly fish seldom survived. My mother's ventures into the world of pisciculture came to an end after she installed a heated tank with an aerated oxygen supply to house a pair of angel fish and several neon tetras: there were power cuts with inevitable results, the only survivors being the snails and weed.

On many Sundays my mother did not emerge from her room fully dressed until after eleven, so when Conrad was alive, I rose early to let him out into the soft light, before the sun burned the dewdrops off the spiders' webs. I would inspect the pond that my mother had built unaided: it was circular concrete, with vertical sides, and had no sloping points for easy access by amphibians. It was over-stocked with several conventional goldfish, four spotty shubunkins, a pair of golden orfe, and a catfish. The orfe grew quite large and sometimes jumped out to flap helplessly on the stone surround, to be put back if lucky. Two freshwater mussels burrowed in the bottom sludge, and there was a healthy snail population. I would do a head count of fish, and try to calculate how much my favourite – a large orange carp called Augustus – had grown. Carefully selected waterweeds grew in abundance, and a water lily produced several white flowers each summer. I would check the blackbird's nest, and the dense column of snails I hoped Mr Boyd, who helped my mother with the garden, would not discover. He did, and they ended their days a brown foamy mess overflowing a seldom-emptied stone jar next to the water butt. One day I found a black cat sitting where the blackbird's nest had been.

When Conrad and I went back indoors, I would grub around the kitchen for the rudiments of breakfast, and return to bed with a bowl of raisins and nuts for another reading session. I was in love with Bulldog Drummond, and detested Phyllis when she came on the scene. Lord Peter Wimsey was also the object of some affection, although I felt inferior to the formidable Harriet. I ploughed my way through almost all of the Sherlock Holmes stories, and the more popular Dickens novels. *Three Men in a Boat, The Diary of a Nobody, Ruthless Rhymes for Heartless Homes,* and Belloc's *Cautionary Tales for Children* were favourites. Later I fell, as did Jane, for the glowering Mr Rochester, and Jo's Professor Baer. My bizarre choice of first husband, Rudolf Beer, may well have been coloured in some weird Freudian way by *Little Women.* H.G. Wells I found difficult. Some of the historical romances by Sir Philip Lindsay, favoured by my mother, gave clues about the lustful aspects of romantic love. Words such as 'libidinous', 'lascivious' and 'carnal' had to be looked up in the dictionary, and there were references to 'pert erect nipples'. I do not recall any bulges in groins, but despite their historic accuracy, there was a Mills & Boon element. Unfortunately his books were often returned to the library before I had finished my sneaky dips into them. The stories of E. Nesbit, the *Just William* series, *Treasure Island, Robinson Crusoe, Huckleberry Finn* were all devoured, although I fear not retained in detail. Bad habits were formed during those years, and speed reading probably achieved at the cost of limited retention.

Listening to the BBC was universal, so I became familiar with much classical music, as the wireless was on almost continuously at home. Despite our near breadline existence, we had a recent model in a walnut cabinet with an art deco fretwork sunburst design on the front. Although dubbed tone-deaf, I soon had favourite pieces of music: Grieg's *Peer Gynt* suite, Liszt's Hungarian Rhapsodies, Bizet's *Carmen*, Tchaikovsky, Borodin, Ravel, Sibelius, Dvořák, Mendelssohn. My mother, while an accomplished pianist, did not like Bach: it was therefore many years before I discovered the delights of the Brandenburg Concertos or heard a harpsichord recital. She loved Gilbert & Sullivan, and was familiar with all the scores, but music was not essential to her, and she played infrequently. I, on the other hand, used to spend hours trying to work out the notes and get both hands together, but pleas for lessons were dismissed as a waste of money. Most of my contemporaries said I was lucky as they hated having to practise. I listened regularly to *Children's*

Hour with Uncle Mac, never missing an episode of *Toytown* with Larry the Lamb, Mr Growser and Dennis the Dachshund. San's taste ran to Gracie Fields, George Formby, Harry Hemsley the ventriloquist, with his puppet Horace, Paul Robeson and Count John McCormack, but the Irish folk songs she adored were seldom broadcast in unionist Ulster. Albert Sandler and his Palm Court Orchestra was another favourite, as was Henry Hall. She sang 'Old Faithful, We'll Roam the Range Together', 'Tiptoe through the Tulips', and 'There's a Hole in the Bucket, dear Liza', as well as painful interpretations of tunes made popular by Nelson Eddy and Jeanette MacDonald.

During the early years of the war, we all became fans of Tommy Handley, Arthur Askey, and the Kenneth Horne–Richard Murdoch duo. Sitting around the too-small open fire in our living room, knitting companionably and listening to the wireless, the blackout curtains tightly drawn over taped windowpanes, brought us as close as we were ever to be. During the next decade Johnny volunteered for army service and was sent to Ceylon; Auntie Rosemary broke off the engagement and joined the Women's Auxiliary Air Force; I became a restless rebel against I knew not what; and my mother used a variety of talents, ranging from dressmaking to modelling miniature rock gardens, in an effort to swell our coffers. She got a contract with Valentine's postcard firm to photograph views all over the province, one assignment taking her to the Isle of Man. That job boosted her ego, and travelling expenses were paid, but in truth I do not think she made much profit.

The war brought curtailment of all frivolous pursuits: the aviary was abandoned and riding excursions, to my relief, ceased, as did visits to the stables at Comber because of petrol rationing. Flo, whose looks epitomised an elegant hunt follower, in tight jodhpurs, hard hat and skinny, knee-high boots, had, like Auntie Rosemary, joined the WAAF.

When a letter came in 1940 with the news that my father had died, no tears were shed either by my mother or me. He died in Worthing at the home of the devoted woman to whom he left the residue of his estate, 'in gratitude for her care during my many illnesses'. No record exists of any issue, but a friend, somewhat unhelpfully, suggested the possibility of a half-brother or sister.

5

Victoria College under Mrs Faris

The outbreak of World War II coincided with the beginning of my first term in the lower-fifth class at Strathearn: after passing the Junior Certificate two years later I moved to the senior school, Victoria College, on the opposite side of Belfast near the university. With commendable speed, new regulations were announced and gas masks were issued with instructions on how to put on and remove them. Their presence, added to the pile of books that accompanied us from one classroom to another, was an annoyance; they were also an encumbrance when riding a bike. We soon learned that trumpeting noises could be produced by applying the snout to the cardboard box in which they were kept, but were sharply told that the threat of a gas attack was a serious matter and not to be so infantile.

For pupils whose parents wished to evacuate them, the school had a base at Portballintrae, on the north Antrim coast, and our relatives in Connecticut telephoned to offer me a home for the duration of hostilities. My mother never seriously considered the offer, and it was graciously declined. Although I was not consulted, my feelings were mixed: I would have loved to visit the US, but had misgivings about whether or not I would have got on with my distant cousin, Jane, with whom I was encouraged to have a pen-friend relationship. We had been born in the same year, but the letters she sent were written in an unformed hand, describing a way of life that bore no resemblance to my own. She enthused about summer camps, attendance at baseball matches, and school grades. I was remiss about replying, resorting to the excuse that some letters must have been lost in the post.

My experience of the great outdoors was limited to camping with the Girl Guides, which I had joined because I liked the pack leader, Miss Knox, who was also our maths teacher.

She took us through some of C.S. Lewis's childhood haunts, into the Holywood hills. I remember feeling chilly, making ineffectual attempts to light a fire, the all-pervasive smoke, pits of ash with a small red core where dark grey scabby spuds stayed an interminable time, before it was decided they just might be ready to eat. They were always hard in the middle, and I did not like potatoes much in any case, so I confined myself to lukewarm baked beans and cocoa. The only practical thing I learned with the Guides was how to turn hospital corners when bed-making.

It was to Miss Knox that I went when I found my knickers bloodstained: she was reassuring, and probably accustomed to such emergencies, because she gave me the necessary elastic belt equipped with a hook at each end, plus a bulky pad. Thanks to my older best friends, I knew more about menstruation than either Miss K or my mother suspected. Surprised at its early onset, my mother apologised, saying she had intended to give me a book titled *Growing Up*, printed by the Lilia firm of sanitary pad manufacturers. During furtive forays into my mother's chest of drawers, I had already read it, as well as leaflets about what looked like a much more practical method of dealing with the flow – Tampax. It was explained that this was unsuitable for young girls, but after some months of those pads, which had a way of shifting out of place, thus making a revealing lump either fore or aft, I persevered and boasted success to my slightly shocked mother and aunt.

My mother, like journalist John Simpson's father (*Days from a Different World: A Memoir of Childhood*), warned about 'herd mentality' and encouraged me to question authority. Her counsel was superfluous, as I had entered the world a 'defiant individual', though this was diagnosed only many years later, under life-threatening circumstances.

Maths was not my strong subject. After infant failure to impress Gramp, the next stage had been in primary school, when told to head the left-hand column T and the right-hand one U: nobody explained that these letters stood for 'tens' and 'units'. Then there were LCMs and HCFs, which I eventually learned stood for 'Least Common Multiple' and 'Highest Common Factor' – although to this day I have not grasped their purpose. Our primary teacher had been Miss McMaster, thin, gaunt, bow-legged, flat-chested, with hair worn in a tight little knob on the nape of her neck. She must have been at least seventy in 1939, and her mission was to teach us scripture and arithmetic. I muddled through until the homework consisted of a sheet of long-division problems. I must have missed a critical lesson, because all I knew was how a worked-out sum should look. Accordingly I produced a neat sheet of arbitrary figures, with the Xs in the right places to indicate that a unit had been borrowed from the line above, and handed it in for correction. I was summoned to Miss McMaster's desk, where she glared at me witheringly, took a purple crayon to score right through the work-sheet, shut the book, and hit me smartly on both sides of the head with it, before firing it to the back of the classroom, from where I retrieved it against a background of subdued sniggers. We did a lot of parrot memorising of tables, not only numbers but rods, poles, perches; pecks, minims, pints, quarts, gallons. Height and distance involved inches, feet, yards, furlongs and miles; then there was weight, which began with fractions of an ounce, of which it took sixteen to make a pound, otherwise written as '1lb'; fourteen of these made one stone, and eight stone made one hundredweight, and twenty hundredweight made a ton. When it was thought we had a fair grasp of this lot, it was time to acquaint ourselves with The Decimal System. Star pupils apart, most of us were faced with yet another torture, although we were assured it was really simple. Millimetres, centimetres, kilometres, milligrams, centigrams, kilograms, leading, if I remember rightly, to a metric tonne. It did not work for me, and I still think of my height in feet and inches, my weight in stones and ounces, and distance in terms of miles rather than kilometres. Grams versus ounces in the delicatessen are easier, but I prefer rooms measured in square feet rather than square metres.

Any latent appreciation of Shakespeare's works and the classic poets was extinguished by the uninspired teaching of a succession of Protestant spinsters, allied to the fact that the plays we studied were *The Merchant of Venice, Julius Caesar,* and in my final year *The Tempest.* The first time I had any awareness of the bard's stature was at a sixth form production of *King Lear,* staged at the Royal Belfast Academical Institution (or Inst., as it was commonly known), the boys' school where my friend Celia's mother and my maths coach taught. Cramming for examinations, we were encouraged to commit long passages to memory, and to learn narrative poems by heart. All that remains are thunderous parts of Macaulay's 'Armada', much of Tennyson's 'The Lady of Shallot', bits of Christina Rosetti's 'Goblin Market', and Yeats's 'Lake Isle of Innisfree'. Nothing was taught about Yeats's politics and lifelong association with Lady Gregory – uncomfortable stuff for the Protestant ladies, and tainted by the whiff of republicanism.

My lifelong love of maps is probably inherited from my mother, who introduced me to Bartholomew's series of the British Isles, and Ireland in particular. I learned about contour lines, and how to draw mountain profiles. I spent many hours poring over my Grandma Eileen's copies of the *National Geographic* magazine and the 1933 edition of the *Encyclopaedia Britannica*, which had fine colour plates of marine life. In an avid search for information about male anatomy and human reproduction, I consulted *Harmsworth's Home Doctor*. Some of the books on art were helpful in this respect, although the Victorian fig leaf was still all too prevalent. Gradually I became aware of artists such as Laura Knight, Russell Flint, John Lavery, the pre-Raphaelites, Whistler, Landseer, and Winterhalter's paintings of Queen Victoria, Prince Albert and their brood. Despite my aunt's years at art school, she took no active interest in the international art scene, so names of late nineteenth- and early twentieth-century artists were unfamiliar; the exception being Picasso, whose work was abhorred, although there was grudging admission that some of his Blue Period paintings were talented. I misguidedly bought Sir William Orpen's book *The Outline of Art*; a heavy tome, printed in black and white, it was not 'child friendly'. Reading an article in *Lilliput* magazine, which Rosemary sometimes brought home, introduced me to Salvador Dalí and Max Ernst.

My own artistic potential was considerable, and I came first or equal first, in school examinations; but again teaching had been uninspired, consisting of designing 'all-over' patterns, making potato-prints, and drawing still life. I remember a pair of fur-lined boots, an open book, and a gas mask. On complaining about the dreariness of the subject, I was told to move to a more challenging angle. It was anticipated that I would get a top award in Northern Ireland, but on the day of the examination I sat staring blankly at sheet after sheet of paper, tearing up several, bereft of inspiration. I got an ordinary pass.

There was no careers guidance at Victoria College; the headmistress at that time was Mrs Faris, widow of a clergyman, to whose office I was called when I was reprimanded for not 'respecting' the kitchen staff. The incident involved my discovery of a snail in some lettuce surrounding our lunch-time (twice weekly) slice of Spam. I had popped a derisory note into the suggestion box mentioning that protein in the form of *Mollusca* was not appreciated. Only girls of outstanding academic potential went to university; a few who, due to financial constraints, would be forced to work, were sent to a secretarial college; and the rest were expected to marry not long after leaving school. I suspect Mrs Faris regarded my mother's single parent status with distaste, so any aspirations I may have expressed were brushed aside as being unrealistic. She patently had little interest in what the future might bring, and said goodbye with no more than a formal handshake in 1944.

The battle with mathematics had continued through geometric progressions, logarithms, trigonometry, geometry, algebra, and eventually rudimentary calculus, for which coaching was needed to matriculate, which I did in 1945 – in the second division. Through the decades, with the exception of areas, weights and basic monetary calculations, none of the aforementioned has been of the slightest use. I did, however, enjoy geometry, the Pythagoras theorem, and calculating the content of cylinders and cones with the aid of the magic π. Maybe some part of the brain was late to develop, because by the time I was seventeen and had completed a year studying physics and chemistry in a class of first year engineering students, I could cope with simple mental arithmetic with relative ease. It was a year wasted, though I learned the chemical symbols and some understanding of bridge construction. The majority of the students were male, and one in particular, to whom I was not attracted despite his flashy good looks, too-long fair hair, and natty brown double-breasted suit, pursued me relentlessly, slipping an empty Durex packet into my handbag.

During the war years, my mother and San volunteered for first-aid classes held at the Lower Braniel Primary School under the aegis of Mr Magee, the principal. A long, low, white, rough-cast building dating from the mid-nineteenth century, with two rows of outside lavatories, one for the boys, one for the girls, the school was at the junction of the Lower Braniel and Gilnahirk Roads. Mr Magee, Murray, and most of the adult males I knew, were air-raid wardens, and we all became expert stickers of criss-cross tape on windows to lessen danger from flying glass. Reality struck at night no fewer than three times in April and May 1941. To begin with, we heard an unfamiliar throb of aircraft overhead and the searchlights of Belfast were swinging wildly in all directions; then when a few flashes at ground level were followed within seconds by a loud *wump*, my mother decided it was time to hide under the stairs. Unfortunately the underground shelter she and my aunt had dug in heavy clay had slowly filled up to knee height with water. I remember being frightened only when some landmines were dropped in the Castlereagh hills. I also recall feeling sorry for whatever Nazi bomber crew were caught by searchlights, thinking they were so far from home and were, after all, only doing what they considered their duty. I was at the time hopelessly enamoured of an RAF bomber pilot whose family lived nearby.

Ration books were issued, and soon the weekly food ration was in operation. Northern Ireland, in the rural areas at least, suffered less than Britain, almost everyone having a contact within the farming community. Rationing presented my mother with a new challenge. Hitherto unknown dishes would appear: crumbed sweetbreads, stuffed lamb's heart, eel, and even, I regret to say, whale. The sweetbreads were quite palatable; the hearts – which strangely I did not connect with frisking lambs – tended to be rubbery even after long baking, but I liked the stuffing. I shall never forget the writhing of chopped eel in the frying pan – although dead, the bits appeared to be in death agonies and I refused to try them. Whale, I gave a try, but even the grown-ups decided that once was enough. Marmalade was concocted from a gelatinous, artificial lemon-flavoured mix, in which fine ribbons of carrot simulated Seville orange peel. Butter and margarine were whipped up with milk to increase the volume. It shames me now to remember how little thought my peer group gave to the war that was raging in Europe, or the dangers the merchant navy encountered in order to keep the civilian population from starvation.

6
Work, Recreation and Liaisons

By the time I was fourteen the three-year disparity in age between me and my best friends was more apparent. Annie, temporarily in remission from anorexia, had been accepted by the WAAF. Celia, now a succulent young woman, had joined the Women's Royal Naval Service based on HMS *Caroline* at Sydenham, under the command of the Earl of Kilmorey, whom she worshipped. We kept in touch by meeting for coffee either in Robinson and Cleaver's restaurant, or Campbell's Coffee Shop opposite Belfast City Hall. The latter was furnished with art deco scarlet upholstered chairs with tubular steel frames, grouped around low red metal-topped tables; the walls had been decorated by Rowel Friers, with cartoons of local characters. The coffee, served in mugs, was deplorable by today's standards, but Campbell's rolls, liberally filled with a mixture of bacon and mushrooms, chopped hard-boiled egg, sardines, or grated cheese and chutney, were deservedly popular and, at three pence, very good value. There was also a variety of sticky, fruit-spotted buns topped with a swirl of white icing. The first floor was favoured by artists, architects, playwrights, and the embryonic Reverend Ian Paisley, who even then, had a loyal circle of acolytes. The ground floor was where teachers from Inst and other grammar schools, my own included, socialised after school. Among them, Celia's mother, who had, to universal astonishment, a science degree, and had been recruited to fill a gap caused by loss of staff to the forces. Memorably, on spotting one of the few African students at Queen's, she was heard to say: 'It's funny them being black and us being white.' By this time she was a widow. Celia's father, an imposing figure, always dressed in a fine tweed suit, was a Great War survivor, probably suffering from depression, though this was never mentioned. He drank heavily, about which his wife spoke in confidence to my mother, who otherwise seldom had much in common with my friends' parents. On one of his regular coastal walks, he fell to his death from the path onto rocks near Helen's Bay. There was a lot of gossip about whether it was suicide, or whether he had been drunk, and lost his footing. Celia had loved him very much, and I too had been fond of him.

Celia's plumply packed WRNS's costume gave her the edge over me in my navy blue and maroon sixth-form school uniform, although, after removing the elastic chin-strap, it was possible to adjust the brim of the maroon felt winter hat to a becoming angle, and in spring the beret, also carefully angled, could look almost Parisian. Such modifications, combined with copious amounts of lipstick, did not escape notice and one of my teachers, who must have spotted me in Campbell's Coffee Shop in central Belfast, reported them to our head. I was carpeted for degrading the image of the school, of which I should be a proud ambassadress, should be ashamed of myself, show some respect for tradition, and so on.

A group of international bridge players met regularly in Campbell's: these predators made a determined effort to tempt us with offers of lessons to take place in the evenings at a venue in Duncairn Avenue. We were not interested in learning this social accomplishment, although Celia was tempted by the fact that one of the pair had influence within the Group Theatre. I wonder, had they been more attractive, whether we might have succumbed. Most persistent were a portly, balding man in his late forties and his bridge-playing partner, who liked to be addressed as 'Major'. The latter was sinister, with cold reptilian eyes and tinted glasses – a Bond film character. Our evasive tactics became transparent to the point that they finally got the message, blanking us thereafter.

Many factors led to Celia and me drifting apart: I had developed vague leftist tendencies and, in the absence of a Communist candidate, my first vote went to a Labour candidate at Sydenham. My mother must have been hurt by this break with Conservatism, which had been taken for granted in her family. Free love was in, Empire and the royal family were out, and I despised those dark-suited, bowler-hatted Orangemen with their Lambeg drums, twirling batons and banners of King Billy on his white horse. Celia was deeply wary of Roman Catholics, and habitually referred to working-class people in lofty tones: 'What else can you expect from these people?' Obsessed by fear of 'ending up on the shelf', her ambition was to marry early and bear many children. Having already seen off a number of ardent suitors, she regaled me with details of how far they had gone without actually 'doing it'. She was determined to reach the altar a virgin. I had other plans.

Celia had not long to wait. The directors and trainee managers of Ewart's linen mills were habitués at Campbell's, and one of these, an ex-RAF officer, was not long divorced from the wife he had married in a whirlwind wartime romance. Tall, personable, socially well-connected, and an Oxford graduate, he was thirty-eight by the time he met Celia. She told me how much more secure she felt in the company of a mature man, compared with the callow youths she had gone out with in the past. Their engagement was announced, despite the social ostracism that still lingered where divorced persons were concerned. Celia's mother was none too pleased, nor was the prospective groom's ambitious American mother, who felt her son had learned little from his earlier experience. His father, on the contrary, was indulgent, having also fallen under the spell of Celia's pneumatic charms.

Meanwhile, in September 1945 I drifted into an apprenticeship with a commercial photographic firm in Belfast owned by the husband of a woman my mother had befriended at the group which met to knit balaclavas, scarves, socks, mittens and gloves for the forces. My mother paid £500 for the apprenticeship, which was to last three years: I was to be paid thirty shillings a week during the first year, £3 the second, and £5 in the final year. He got a good deal – an efficient slave for three years. The premises were Dickensian: a long, narrow slice of property fronted Howard Street; the gated porch, which it was my job to sweep, gathered litter and stray cats, and was sometimes used as a urinal – thankfully syringes and condoms were not yet commonplace. There was a display window, the dressing of which was also my responsibility; behind that, a reception area and waiting room, leading to the finishing room/general office, and then a warren of darkrooms, containing enlargers, sinks, cascade washers and flat-bed driers. A corridor shelved with negatives, both glass and celluloid, led to a recess for a mirror and hooks for outdoor clothing. At the end was the lavatory: lit only by a tiny cobwebbed skylight, it, like the rest of the premises, had neither handbasin nor ventilation. The pan was brownish yellow with age and worse; I do not recall there being a brush or tin of Harpic, but a charwoman sometimes appeared accompanied by the owner's wife.

I negotiated a higher salary, eventually screwing seven guineas a week out of him by the time, in 1951, I decided there must be more to life than spending much of it in a darkroom. I enrolled for a seven-month course in shorthand and typing; book-keeping was part of it, but after a week it was agreed this was a waste of everyone's time, so I concentrated on keyboard skills instead. This was probably the wisest decision of my life: I have used a keyboard, in one form or another, on an almost daily basis, ever since.

The tennis club, where I spent most evenings in summer, was in south Belfast, so I would go straight from work by tram to the Stranmillis terminus and walk along the Lagan towpath to the clubhouse. From September through to April many hours were spent at the ice rink at Balmoral – even more distant from home. At work I met colourful people, many of whom had escaped from Nazi Germany just before the war, and a few survivors of concentration camps. The Jewish community worked untiringly on their behalf, and many were talented musicians and artists. Heinz and Alice Hammerschlag were violinists belonging to the Music Society, but Alice was also a gifted artist who painted abstract designs in the early days of acrylic paints under her maiden name (Berger). I have one of her paintings and some hang in the Ulster Museum. Some, such as Zoltan Frankl, the art collector who established a knitting factory in Newtownards, were active in any local artistic enterprise: I was always on the fringe, having nothing to contribute, everything to learn, and despite good school French, being virtually monolingual.

Many of the girls at the club fitted Betjeman's description of Joan Hunter Dunn – wholesome, hearty, outdoor types and probably good breeding material. Though not unpopular, I did not fit the image. Derek, one of the male friends I made, was five years older, sang in a light-opera group, was interested in ballet and played a fair game of tennis; additional attractions were that his office was near my workplace and he drove an

MG sports car. It made sense therefore to hitch a lift, rather than take the slow, clanking tram to Stranmillis. We went to many ballet performances at the Grand Opera House during the years 1945–47. Only when an indiscreet friend told me that Derek had confided that he did not seem to feel the same way as the rest of the men about women did I begin to understand why our relationship remained platonic. Twenty years were to pass before homosexual acts between consenting adults became legal.

On my miserable salary I maintained a fashionable image, devoting far too much thought and time thereto. The New Look arrived to lift female spirits after years of utility clothing. But evening dresses posed a problem, in that they now used yards of fabric, which was costly, and required clothing coupons. My mother really enjoyed making ball gowns, and was unstinting with her time and sewing skills: I wish I had expressed appreciation more than I did, but she had to be discouraged from adding 'little touches' to otherwise plain styles. Sometimes she won: my first formal dress was pale blue taffeta, after Gainsborough's *Blue Lady* – at the final fitting an intricate panel of appliquéd silk flowers appeared at mid-calf level on the lower skirt. Economy still reigned in 1948, when I wore a black silk taffeta skirt inherited from Grandma Eileen who had died the previous year. Evening shoes were almost impossible to buy, and I remember painting, with limited success, a brown suede pair belonging to my mother with silver paint. Finally persistence was rewarded when I tracked down some gold brocade shoes with a high wedge heel and peep toes – they cost a crippling three guineas.

With various escorts I always enjoyed a visit to the Grand Opera House. A celebration of late Victorian exuberance, complete with gilded elephants, red velvet curtains and seating, during the immediate post-war years it hosted many ballet companies. Ballet Jooss proved too avant-garde, but Mona Inglesby's International Ballet, although not top grade, introduced a thirsty public to the great classics of the nineteenth and early twentieth centuries: *Swan Lake, Les Sylphides, Sleeping Beauty, Coppélia, The Nutcracker, Don Quixote*, even *Scheherazade*. Dame Marie Rambert brought her own company with the young John Gilpin fresh from Sadler's Wells, when it was already clear that

45

he would go far. I shall always remember his Albrecht in *Giselle*. Kenneth MacMillan had a commanding stage presence by the age of nineteen when he came to Northern Ireland with Sadler's Wells, which staged a brilliant performance of Bizet's newly discovered *Symphony in C*, and Kodály's *Dances of Galánta*.

I became friendly with a Royal Navy lieutenant who had seen active service but now had a shore job. He looked like James Mason, played reasonable tennis and, in addition, was a fair skater. He was musical and had his own violin, which he insisted on bringing to our house to give a recital. This did not go down well with Auntie Rosemary, who had ambitions of her own in that field, nor did the fact that he was thirty-eight, the same age as she. We went to cinemas and dances, and he taught me marksmanship at the Customs House rifle range. After dances, in the back seat of the car, he would cradle me in his arms, and maunder on about his working-class childhood in north-east England, how he had worked his way up from doing paper deliveries, through grammar school, ultimately becoming a lieutenant in the navy. He was fond of me to the extent of addressing notes to 'Dearest Bluebell', and was generous with gifts. Transferred back to England, he disappeared from my life.

There were other men to whom I did not get so close. Then there was Douglas, also ex-Royal Navy, who had come to Belfast as an apprentice mill-manager at Ewart's. He too was twice my age, and lived in digs in Eglantine Avenue, where he would take me after skating, for which he made an acceptable dance partner. His orientation was not in doubt, as, given the opportunity, he would fling himself on me without preliminaries and thrust his tongue down my gagging throat, only detaching himself after a sharp knee jab in the groin. He was a pompous public school product, and parsimonious – using a tray purse when we went to the cinema – so I gave him the push.

Now, without a skating partner, I began to cast my net again. It was not long before another victim presented: this one had the advantage of playing tennis as well. The Canadian aircraft carrier *Magnificent* was undergoing trials at Sydenham Docks, and many of its officers lodged in the Malone or Stranmillis districts of the city. Harry, the chief engineer, joined my tennis club in the summer of 1947 when I was nineteen; he too was thirty-eight, and a dead-ringer for John Mills.

Soon he asked me to dinner at the Grosvenor Rooms – where the Europa Hotel now stands – then considered the most fashionable place to eat. At last I was catching up with Celia's sophisticated lifestyle, having too long envied her accounts of dinners eaten and drinks drunk – Pimm's was her favourite – at this restaurant. I do not remember much about the meals, apart from Harry asking for French fries, and the waiter not understanding what was required. He was not a culture vulture, so most of our outings were to cinemas. I brought him home to meet my mother and aunt. Rosemary was by now working for a radiologist in private practice; the fact that she was the same age as my swain was again not a plus point, although I chose to ignore it. His Irish ancestors had emigrated from Ennistymon not far from the Cliffs of Moher in County Clare; his childhood was spent in London, Ontario, before he went to university to study engineering, prior to joining the Royal Canadian Navy. None of us enquired, nor were we told much, about his extended family; his mother and sister sent parcels of fruit cake and other delicacies unobtainable or scarce in Northern Ireland, and he sometimes went to Donegal in the Republic on shopping expeditions, bringing back nylon stockings – this was before the life-transforming advent of tights – and lengths of Donegal tweed, destined for Canada, where it was regarded as very fashionable.

Thus began a hectic social life involving many drinks parties both at the captain's flat and in the ward room of the *Magnificent*. Captain Balfour, of Scots descent, was a towering figure with what can best be described as a rough-hewn countenance, rather like the Easter Island statues. Renowned for a fiery temper, and unpredictable outbursts of venom, I was warned that being female was no barrier to becoming a target. His wife, of the same craggy build, wore little make-up, and in contrast to the other officers' wives, dressed informally, preferring tweeds and jerseys to more feminine styles. When she came under fire, rather than engaging in fruitless defence or argument, she ignored him, knowing he would soon turn on another victim. Having no experience of the dramatic changes in personality and behaviour excessive drinking can provoke, I did not recognise the mood swings were due to a prodigious intake of alcohol. The officers under his command were in no doubt, but accepted his abrasive personality without apparent censure – heavy drinking, after all, was the norm in all naval circles.

For the first drinks party I attended I wore the blue taffeta Gainsborough dress, sensible that it emphasised my youth and compared unfavourably with the more svelte styles worn by the wives of other officers. A few of the junior officers were unaccompanied, and Harry was the only senior one to bring a local girl – me. Rum and Coke was a favourite tipple, and at one point I remember being asked: 'Just how much does it take to get you drunk?' I despised those women who became giggly and unsteady on their feet, or worse, would disappear in haste to the ablutions, emerging looking pale and sweaty. My mother, despite the fact that alcohol had been the root cause of her failed marriage, had little experience of social drinking, but had warned me that drink affected one's judgement and lowered female resistance to opportunistic advances: she did not mention its effect when the advances were welcome. I suspect most of the advice was based on hearsay, as apart from the cider at Christmas, she never drank, explaining that even a glass of sherry made her feel out of control and slightly dizzy.

My deflowering took place early on New Year's Day in a jeep parked in the Castlereagh hills: the temperature hovered around freezing, and the stars were brilliant. The vehicle was a pioneer jeep with canvas seats stretched tightly on metal frames, the sides open to the elements. It was an urgent and uncomfortable experience, during which I climaxed while precautions were being put in place: such was my innocence I did not realise it was an orgasm. By the time we got home sobriety was setting in, along with guilt when I saw the light in my mother's bedroom. After some difficulty getting the key into the back door lock, I slunk to my chilly bed, dreading having to appear at work by nine thirty on the first day of January, which in Northern Ireland was not a general holiday. For the first time I had a hangover, and a face reddened by what was popularly known as 'stubble trouble'. There was, however, a distinct feeling of achievement, and from then on I thought of myself as being a fully fledged woman – not to mention one up on Celia.

During the next couple of weeks, I agonised about the efficacy of the condom, and the awful possibility of being pregnant. In those days the dread was ever present, and continued so until the Pill came into general use. In fact, sex, both illicit and within marriage, continued to hold an element of apprehension for many years – particularly for those who abhorred condoms and relied on the 'safe' period or sundry unreliable sponges, gels and foams.

The likelihood that Harry might be married had, of course, occurred to almost everyone but me: his fellow officers all knew, and had been waiting for the denouement. One of them, kindly, middle-aged and patently uneasy, turned up at the ice rink to convey the message that Harry had left that morning to attend the funeral of his mother-in-law in Portsmouth, but would get in touch with me very soon. Memory possibly deceives me, but I like to think I did not give any hint of the shock inflicted: I just thanked him, suppressed tears, and with a pounding heart went to remove my skates and leave the session early. During the journey home by tram and bus, I tried to analyse what I felt – not angry, just numb, and conscious for the first time of my naïvety. I dreaded his return, uncertain what attitude to adopt. I do not remember any profound apology for the deceit, but he spun a pathetic story about his wife preferring to remain in England with her mother and two children – already in their teens – and her refusal to join him in Belfast. The marriage had been dead for some time, and he spoke of divorce. I planned to join the WRNS as soon as his tour of duty finished with the commissioning of the aircraft carrier in May 1948. He wrote frequently and at length, while the ship was on trials off Newfoundland, and I believe he was in love, or thought he was, with me. There were glimmerings of dissent, however. His politics were fascist, even racist – I remember remarks about having had to share lodgings with 'coloured' sailors while he was in Vancouver, and how 'they' had a special smell. When I voiced my intention to continue working after marriage, the stuffy response was: 'Naval officers' wives do not work.' When we met six years later, after I had, in his words, 'thrown myself away' in marriage, we were awkward with each other, finding little in common, although he insisted on making a visit to pay his respects to my mother.

Ego led me to think of myself as the lead in a romantic drama on the lines of many films of that era. I remained an avid cinema-goer, adoring Trevor Howard, James Mason, Eric Portman, Rex

Harrison and George Sanders, and had a penchant for the elusive bounders they played. I chose to ignore it, but my liaison had caused much adverse comment within the conformist tennis-playing fraternity. A degree of ostracism could be detected, and invitations to dances, cinema and theatre were few during the summer of my laments. To my mother's relief I did not join the WRNS, but continued my photographic apprenticeship.

Meanwhile, preparations for Celia's Big Day reached a peak. A mutual friend, not long returned from a 'finishing' establishment in Scotland, and I had been chosen as bridesmaids. The social polish her parents sought remained elusive, and the unfortunate girl was for the most part mute and uncomfortable during the selection of suitable material, patterns and seamstress. I was equally miserable, if for different reasons, but vocal when it came to suppressing some of Celia's more grandiose ideas. My mother was outraged that the bridesmaids were expected to pay for their dresses, furious at the choice of silk chiffon to be tortured into complicated draped bodices, and, in particular, the choice of a dressmaker affiliated to one of Belfast's leading stores. The wedding took place at one of the few parish churches whose minister agreed to marry divorced persons. Celia was radiant in oyster silk, Douglas my ex-would-be ravisher, was an usher, the best man, also an ex-RN officer, was the suave commodore of the yacht club. After a reception at the country club, the bride appeared, elegant in a dove grey New Look ensemble trimmed with black velvet. A crowd of us saw them off at the station, where the long journey to a luxury hotel in County Cork began. In the evening a dance was held, at which copious amounts of alcohol were downed. I must have been dreary company, hoping that I exuded a sophisticated aura of mystery. One of the ushers saw fit to advise me to 'beware of those Canadian wolves'. Too late – the *Magnificent* had already sailed down Belfast Lough for the last time.

After her marriage, Celia and I drifted further apart, although I was asked to be godmother to their first child, a compliment I should have refused, but did not know how to decline. They lived in one of the first 'executive style' red-brick houses to be built in prosperous north Down during the early fifties. Their life revolved around bridge and dinner parties, regattas and involvement in fund-raising for local charities. Celia's mother, now retired from teaching, occupied a granny flat, from which, though a convenient baby-sitter, she emerged more often than was good for marital harmony. She voiced open criticism of their drinking habits, while Celia bleated: 'What's the matter with a wee drink, if it makes the party go?' A lot, as it turned out.

A period of reappraisal followed when I began to face the fact that there was now no environment in which I felt at ease. Memories returned of the headmistress who had dubbed me a bad mixer – she may have had a point. Tennis continued, but I now had a 'reputation' and this brought me to reflect on my mother's admonitions about 'shop-soiled goods', and not 'flying in the face of convention'. Maybe she too had a point. When the skating season began in September, I continued to practise figure skating after work before the now lonely public sessions began.

I 'trifled with the affections' of a self-taught artist a mere six years older than me. He was tall, reasonably personable, but afflicted by contorted diction, hampered further by the pipe that seldom left his mouth. He had a natural talent for drawing buildings, and had toured Ireland sketching ancient monuments. He liked classical music and ballet, although due to his perpetual penury, we seldom went to the theatre. He was not in the least athletic – so tennis and skating were out. He lived with his parents and sister in a council house on the opposite side of town. His father, a retired riveter in the shipyard, had a large library and was a devotee of Dickens and Galsworthy. His mother and sister regarded me with suspicion when, during my visits, we disappeared for long periods to the front room, which was the 'artist's studio' and strictly private. The relationship went no further than protracted snogging on the hard floor. Shortly after his declaration of profound feelings, I felt it was time to put an end to his misery: so, while conceding his natural talent for drawing buildings, I urged him to take lessons in life drawing, as it was clear he knew little about ballet positions, and less of human anatomy. Spoiled at home by uncritical adulation, he was hurt by my cruelty and withdrew to lick his wounds.

Rudolf had been a third-year student of botany when his Jewish father, a leftist political writer, fled Berlin in 1933 to settle in London with his Catholic wife and five children. The patriarch got a job at the London School of Economics, two older sons, already graduates, found employment, their elder daughter joined a kibbutz in Israel and the younger, a talented violinist, went to Singapore and married, much to Rudolf's disgust, a Chinese pianist. Rudolf joined the Berlitz school of languages, which sent him to Belfast. Too proud to accept the offer of the Jewish community to support continued university studies, he opened his own school near my workplace. We met when he brought films to be developed and printed; he was a finicky customer, with an inflated opinion of his photographic skills.

What motive I had in pursuing him eludes me even now. Born in 1909, he resembled a young Bertrand Russell, wore glasses and had, as both my mother and aunt were quick to point out, a Prussian-shaped skull. He was dogmatic, self-satisfied, and patronising, but his manners were irreproachable. He was musical to the extent of writing an article for the *Music Review*, in which he challenged the views of Hans Keller on the function of ornaments in mediaeval English music. He was interested in painting and sculpture, good food – for what that was worth in 1950 – and the Great Outdoors, Donegal in particular. He had also been through a catalogue of women – the most recent, who had just ditched him, was a member of the Savoy Players. The whiff of bohemianism may have been part of the attraction. Anyway, I began to study German as a means of getting to know him better, and soon we were what is now known as 'an item'. At lunch time we joined a table of middle-aged people at Anderson & McAuley's top floor restaurant. The acknowledged head of our group was the writer Denis Ireland, a senator in the Irish parliament; his partner was Mary Hawthorne. Others were Thea Morrow, who lived in a threesome relationship with another woman, and George Morrow, son of the cartoonist, who held court at his house in the Holywood hills where writers and artists gathered at weekends. I tagged along, out of my depth, more conscious than ever of my limitations: ill-concealed amusement at Rudolf's latest appendage did not escape me. Drink mostly flowed, but he was abstemious, almost puritanical in his attitude to alcohol, so I did not dare resort to that. We went for brisk walks over hills last visited with the

Guides, and I was shocked by his nonchalant farts as he spring-heeled along rocky paths, goat-skin rucksack, a relic of the Great War, bouncing on his back: he claimed to average 1,000 feet in half an hour. We attended meetings of the Gramophone Society, string quartets, and lieder recitals.

Rudolf's teaching schedule meant that he did not return home until almost ten during the week, so any socialising took place at weekends. Soon a ritual was established: I cycled to his flat near my old school about midday, and back home in the late evening. If the weather was good, we put our cycles on the train to Bangor, from where we would go by the lovely coastal route as far as Groomsport and Donaghadee, often finding a sheltered spot near Portavoe for a picnic and quick swim in the icy water. Excursions further afield to Whitepark Bay on the north coast, or, at Easter, to Dunfanaghy in Donegal, involved my mother and her car to put a stamp of respectability on the relationship. Amazingly, Rudolf accepted this intrusion, and they formed an odd relationship; once, much to her annoyance, he described her as 'a thoroughly good woman'. After our engagement, marked by the purchase of an Edwardian sapphire and diamond ring costing £18, an unescorted holiday was sanctioned in the summer of 1950. The ring, however, did not ensure lack of curiosity at our hotel in Glencolumbkille, where a small boy greeted my appearance for pre-dinner drinks, in front of a blazing fire in the lounge, with 'Hello, fancy lady'.

A date for the nuptials was set for 28 December 1950. Celia thought Rudolf a comical choice; San and my mother kept their counsel; but Auntie Rosemary's dislike was such that she ostracised us. He viewed her with faint amusement, mocking her mud-coloured Fiat 27, and nicknaming her 'Juml' after the number plate JML. Hers was an extreme reaction, adding to my mother's worries for years. I was hurt, as she had been more like an older sister, teaching me how to knit, sew, look after my nails and, with Annie's help, rudimentary cooking and cake making. Only after we separated, Rudolf having got work in Scotland, and Rosemary was engaged to marry in 1956, did she extend an olive branch to ensure I would attend her marriage to a really nice man, Uncle Arthur, who survives to this day. My mother's comment: 'He'll need to be a saint.'

7
Marriage, Separation and a Radical Decision

There was a surreal element to the solemnising of our union. One of Rudolf's pupils, a Presbyterian minister, was approached. Palpably uneasy, he met us in the hope that we would demonstrate sincerity, and promise to raise any fruits of the union in the faith. We did not confess that children were not envisaged. Never having wanted a fairytale wedding, suitable clothes for the event were hard to find. Eventually I settled for a blue-grey crêpe silk dress under a three-quarter-length moleskin coat, an unforgiving black hat, and peep-toed black suede shoes with platform soles. After stubborn resistance, Rudolf agreed to buy a suit for the ceremony and chose brown. In the absence of a close male relative, my boss's father-in-law was pressed into service to give me away. Celia, as matron of honour, wore her New Look going away suit. Her husband, and several other men, declined the invitation, pleading pressure of work. Nevill, an artist with whom Rudolf had shared a house before the war, was best man and I suppressed the fact that he was physically more attractive to me than the groom. He remained distant and, in any case, had a French wife and two children. His marriage did not endure.

Less than a month later, when Rudolf announced that he expected his Aertex underwear to be boiled *twice* in a huge galvanised tub, deep misgivings set in, and I told him to do it himself. My mother had been urging us to move to a house nearer her own, and set about 'managing' the change. An early Victorian semi was bought for less than £1,000: it had damp rising almost to ceiling height, dry rot, a flat-roofed kitchen extension, the ceiling of which amassed large drops of condensation, and a windowless dining room. Much time and money was spent by the three of us to make it habitable. Rudolf, to his credit, laboured hard, and my mother was in her element doing DIY jobs. I had finished my apprenticeship, finished the course in shorthand and typing, and was working for a firm of architects, typing bills of quantities and specifications in the mornings and working on the drawing-board in the afternoons, fired by the dream that in ten years' time I might have a Royal Institute of British Architects qualification. Fat chance.

Rudolf heard from the librarian at Queen's University that they were urgently looking for someone to take over the Department of Photography. Instead of hard-selling myself, I was engaged as a lowly technician, but was expected to knock the department into shape. Its reputation was so dire that orders were few, so with time to spare, I typed catalogue cards and acted as secretary to the librarian while the incumbent was on her annual month's holiday.

On a glorious summer day in 1955 I walked past the ancient laburnum tree that was a feature of the quad, to the basement of the Anatomy Department, which housed such basic equipment as the photographic unit possessed. I was met by Professor Pritchard, who was clearly ashamed of the dungeon that was to be my base until alterations to a house owned by the university in Camden Street had been finished.

By this time Rudolf and I were already leading separate lives under the same roof. Mutual indifference best describes the relationship. He had accepted a job as librarian at the Shell refinery on the Firth of Forth in Scotland, and my refusal to join him would later provide grounds for desertion.

Meanwhile, in the late summer I went alone from Edinburgh by rail and ferry to the Outer Hebrides, spending ten days on Barra, walking, bird-watching and reviewing my prospects. They were not good: now twenty-seven, the biological clock was ticking, although I do not recall much being written about the subject then. I was not an attractive prospect on the dating scene: separated but not to be free for at least three years – assuming that no hint of 'collusion' impeded the granting of a decree nisi – the queue was not long in pursuit of my company. I played tennis only occasionally and had given up ice skating. Some men were discomfited, avoiding me; others were interested but tentative. There was a scattering of married men, potentially even more dangerous company than me. It was not a healthy scene, but belied Philip Larkin's claim that 'sexual intercourse began in 1963'.

I joined a Workers' Educational Association field trip to the north Antrim coast, hoping to meet more university staff as well as students interested in archaeology, ornithology, botany and geology. The weather was wonderful and I learned a lot about the biological sciences and human nature. Evenings spent in a smoky pub in Ballycastle were lively, fuelled by live music and steady consumption of the national drink, Guinness, or, for the monied few, Bushmills whiskey. Carousing continued after hours at the field centre, where figures flitted stealthily between the segregated huts well into the small hours. On a walk from Murlough Bay to the top of Fair Head I saw for the first, and only, time a corncrake at close quarters. We ate our sandwiches looking down at a seal colony seven hundred feet below.

It must surely have been fate that brought Fergus into my life at precisely that time. He had returned to Northern Ireland to write a PhD thesis on field studies conducted for the Ministry of Health in the Gold Coast during the years just before it became independent Ghana. He had many rolls of negative film to be printed, so his mentor in the Department of Zoology suggested a visit to the photographic unit, which, it was rumoured, had been taken over by 'a right looking bit'. Contrary to family prejudice, I had always been attracted by beards, and also liked suede shoes. Fergus ticked all the boxes. He was three years older than I, shy and largely unaware of how attractive he was to women, although he had a reputation for being elusive. Discreet enquiries revealed that he was unmarried, and had been allocated a small room over the main entrance to the university for the duration of his stay. Observation established where and when he parked his car, and at what time he was likely to appear in the Great Hall to queue for lunch. He, too, had been making enquiries, deciding to ignore gossip and follow his intuition: It was a *coup de foudre* and soon we met daily. At the newly established Arts Theatre we saw *Waiting for Godot* and *Look Back in Anger*, revealing that we shared more than physical attraction. Our reading tastes were similar. This friendship was going somewhere serious, but the path would be long and tortuous.

Having returned from watching a tennis match in the summer of 1956, we were finishing a meal when Rudolf appeared unexpectedly after a day's walking in the Mournes. Giving his customary short, stiff bow, he showed no surprise at the introduction. All three sensed a watershed, although the situation was not thrashed out formally until divorce proceedings were finalised. My solicitor was emphatic that any hint of collusion during the three-year separation period required prior to a decree absolute would jeopardise the outcome.

Fergus and I both had 'baggage' to be cleared. One of his colleagues was an American woman with whom he shared many interests apart from their research. He was not in love with her and set about extricating himself the relationship. This drama was going on concurrently with several platonic work-related friendships – on my side at least – in Ireland. One was with an eminent scientist whose talented wife shared his interest in painting and the contemporary art world. They hosted lively parties at which much alcohol was consumed, but he was a background figure, while his lively, beautiful wife sparkled at the centre of animated groups. Two children made a brief appearance early in the evening before formality gave way to less inhibited behaviour. In all honesty I do not think it entered my mind how uneasy the wives of these men, whose company I found stimulating, may have felt. My self-esteem was low at the time – although fifty years ago that expression had not become a cliché.

Then there was the Pharmacist: he had been an acquaintance of Rudolf, who disliked him, an antipathy based, I suspect, on jealousy of someone better looking and better read. The sound of scrunching gravel, followed by a tap on the window, would announce his arrival at dusk for a chat about literature, cinema, arts in general. He was never in any way creepy – he had a devoted wife and, other than his house, was uninterested in material things, apart from a collection of old books unearthed during regular visits to Smithfield market. He formed a pen-friendship with Ezra Pound, even flying to Italy to meet the great man. After qualifying as a pharmacist, his entire professional life was spent behind the counter of a chemist's shop; the interior was darkly panelled, with white china apothecary's jars on display, and two giant red and green bottles with pointed cut-glass stoppers in the window. He travelled to work on a temperamental Vespa scooter, or when the weather was vile, by bus. His appearance was eccentric: dark-skinned, he had a large head and abundant, springy, iron-grey hair, his ties were always loosely knotted, knitted silk, worn with a plain-coloured shirt, and he had a collection of three-quarter-length coats, ranging from reverse sheepskin to leather. His footwear never varied from styles of the Beatles/Teddy Boy era with heavy rubber soles; a stubby compressed umbrella completed the outfit.

We never exchanged more than a hug and chaste peck on the cheek, despite our corresponding for over forty years. When I returned on leave from Africa, we always met for drinks or a meal. No epicure, he would settle for fish and chips, finishing with coffee and a green chartreuse. On parting he would say: 'Consider yourself kissed.' His handwriting was beautiful – thick black Italic – covering wide sheets of parchment-like paper, which he had liberated from Horatio's Pharmacy. Gradually, letters came at wider intervals and the writing became more difficult to decipher; telephone chats were less spontaneous while arteries hardened and recall became less sharp. Now history – the letters, which cover the years when the Troubles were at their height in Northern Ireland, rest among my papers, and another friend was gone for ever.

During the early days of my marriage to Rudolf, I met Fintan, a devout Roman Catholic, married with numerous children, while I was working in the typing pool of a local authority. His opening greeting was: 'What the hell are *you* doing here?' He was tubby, pinkly balding with pebbly glasses and an impish sense of humour – he was a compulsive teller of jokes, the point of which often eluded me, delivered as they were in a conspiratorial hush against background noise in bars and coffee shops. We met regularly, but it was a very long time before he introduced me to his wife or children.

It was the Pharmacist who introduced me to the Poet, and we 'clicked' instantaneously. A small neat figure in his late thirties, over whom I towered, he tried to cover advancing baldness with thin wisps of hair brushed laterally over the dome; his countenance, faintly mediaeval, reminded me of a portrait of Henry VII. A Jaguar only emphasised his diminutive stature, and I suspect his purchase of a Morris Mini as a second car was not unconnected. When we first met, I was living alone, finding it hard to make ends meet, even considering taking in lodgers. He lived with his wife and their brood of children. He was drifting, drinking too much, writing poetry, buying tranches of derelict property in insalubrious parts of Belfast – I accused him of profiteering. He socialised with writers, poets and journalists, as well as vintage car enthusiasts.

I hesitate to call these two misfits, but in many ways they were. Both admirers of Joyce, they used puns and bizarre names for people and places probably as a defence from any unpleasant repercussions that might result from their behaviour. I was complicit in the game-playing, and in retrospect ashamed: a strong element of *Liaisons Dangereuses* pervaded our activities.

By the autumn of 1956 Fergus had accepted a two-year World Health Organization consultantship with a Health and Nutrition Scheme in Northern Rhodesia (now Zambia). He spent some time in Lusaka, but was based at Fort Rosebery near Lake Bangweulu. He had yet to become the conscientious correspondent of later years, and there were often weeks between letters, sometimes just a postcard from a field trip. During his first local leave, he went with colleagues to the Ruwenzori range – known as the Mountains of the Moon – where he was an early visitor to gorillas in their natural habitat.

Home for leave in 1957, Fergus took me to Donegal for the Easter break; daringly we booked into the hotel as a married couple, risking our cover being blown, and divorce jeopardised. I flew to join him in Geneva late in 1959 – my first time outside the UK – for a skiing holiday, which we spent at the then modest resort of Verbier. Then Fergus returned to a new WHO project in Ghana, and I to Ireland. We had agreed I should resign my job at the university and sail to West Africa in May the following year on a six-month visitor's permit, hoping this would prove the strength of our relationship. Fergus was pessimistic about the effect Africa had on many women, having witnessed 'Happy Valley'-style activities in Ghana, as well as during his stay at Fort Rosebery. Foolhardy, courageous, intrepid, whatever it was, there was no escaping the fact that I would be on approval.

My mother took the news with apparent equanimity, though she must have had many misgivings. She now faced the prospect of having to explain my departure to relatives and friends. There was a possible opening for me at Legon University in Accra, but the project for which Fergus had been recruited was based more than a hundred miles north of the capital, so this would be too remote. I told her to say that my 'friend' would steer me through the corridors of officialdom, and it would be, after all, for six months only. To her credit, she made no effort to dissuade me. The Poet and the Pharmacist predicted disaster, Rosemary, now happily married, thought Fergus a distinct improvement on Rudolf, and Fintan, whose father knew Ghana and the West African coast from service in the merchant navy, blessed the enterprise and wished us well.

8
Weighing Anchor – Liverpool to Takoradi

The Elder Dempster liner MV *Apapa*, one of two ships that plied alternate routes to Ghana, one via the Canary Islands, the other via the Gambia and Sierra Leone, was at the quayside in Liverpool when I disembarked early in the morning from the Belfast boat. Already it was warm, promising one of those glorious early spring days that Northern Ireland, the west of Scotland and Lancashire enjoy before an unpredictable summer sets in. Details have faded, but I negotiated the transfer of three suitcases to my cabin without actually boarding the ship. A steward, uniformed in white, topped with a red fez, had been assigned to take care of my baggage. Instantly likeable, he assured me it would be safe until late in the afternoon, when passengers would be allowed aboard, and told me there was a bunch of red roses waiting for me in my cabin. I asked him to try to keep the roses alive.

Aimless hours in this city, at first sight no more appealing than Belfast, allowed time for some self-examination. In the back of my mind lurked tales of young Ulster women who had disappeared without trace after boarding the Liverpool boat: rumours of white slavery were rife at the time, but I had loftily dismissed them as baseless scaremongering. Now I began to look at some of the solitary characters leaning against walls, or sitting alone in the numerous small cafés, as possibly loitering with intent. Too timid to go to the centre of the town, where I would have found more salubrious cafés and better shops, it was not only fear of the sinister that deterred me. My right leg was hurting: crêpe-bandaged on the advice of a doctor who had failed to diagnose deep-vein thrombosis after treatment for bronchial pneumonia, I knew that by the end of a hot day both legs would be swollen. I picked at dreary sandwiches, and drank cups of viscous coffee – some tasted of chicory, reviving memories of wartime Camp, but by this time espresso bars had begun to flourish in Belfast, so I knew what coffee should taste like.

I rang my mother, but had little to say that had not already been said, apart from telling her that my cases were in good hands. I did not mention the roses. Telegrams were sent instead of e-mails in that era, and while in theory it was possible to telephone Ghana, Fergus had discouraged me from trying, saying that to do so would reduce me to a frustrated, gibbering mess while expensive minutes ticked away. Air letters were the best option, although slow, and in the early days of Ghana's independence, mail, particularly that of international aid workers, was liable to be opened. An incident from early childhood came to mind. It must have been Student Rag Day, when a very tall black man had rattled a collection box in my face and I had burst into tears; both he and San had been embarrassed. Afterwards San told me that he was a prince from the Gold Coast, and could jump longer and higher than any other student at the university. Apart from that encounter, the few Africans I had met had been studying medicine, dentistry or engineering at Queen's.

Towards the end of the afternoon I joined the queue of passengers waiting to go on board. The deck swarmed with stewards chattering in a variety of tribal dialects. Cheerful, and willing to a man, I found them difficult to understand – this was my first exposure to West African pidgin, and six months were to pass before I became familiar with its manifold bizarre interpretations of the Queen's English. There is no parallel: in East Africa Swahili is widely spoken, while in the ex-French or ex-Belgian colonies, French is the lingua franca. Ali, the steward, led me down to my cabin, which, although second class, had a porthole, shower, basin and WC. Compact would best describe it, and already I knew I had brought too many things.

Loud bangs and the chuntering of heavy chains, against a background of shouts from the crew, were soon joined by a throb from the engine room. It was tempting to lie down and rest, but I went up on deck to watch as the distance between boat and quayside widened, and screaming gulls swooped to catch midair scraps jettisoned from the galley. The dark, rainbow-oiled, gently undulating water, its surface thick with bits of stick, plastic bottles and paper cups, tangles of coloured nylon rope and a few floating black plastic bags, the contents of which did not bear contemplation, held no resemblance to the sea I loved. The breeze freshened and chilled as the liner slid into the open waters of the Irish Sea. Only a few fellow passengers were on deck, and I realised the others were probably resting prior to dressing for dinner. Most were seasoned travellers on the West African route, returning for yet another tour.

It was a challenge to present myself at the entrance to the dining room, where it was obvious that the arrival of a single woman, neither nun nor missionary, aroused curiosity. Being a class B passenger eliminated any risk of being seated at the captain's table, and I was shown to one at which two married couples with strong north-country accents were seated; also an insignificant man, balding, with a small moustache, who spoke with a southern English accent. The couples, stationed at Jos in northern Nigeria, knew each other and exchanged gossip of mind-numbing banality: 'You remember Gordon and his wife, Gwen? They 'ad a little son last January, John they called 'im, aye John, that's right.' Polite attempts were made to include me in conversation, so demanding an edited version of my background. On learning I was Irish they remarked that I did not have what they called a brogue. The unvoiced question – Protestant or Catholic – was always present and conclusions drawn according to prejudice. My standard answer was intended to discomfit: born in Derry, raised in County Down – ultimate dream a united Ireland. The other man at our table confessed that he always spent home leaves with Mummy, a widow in poor health, who lived alone in a large house that cost a fortune in upkeep. He worked in a bank, at what level was not revealed.

Short of pointing, the Yorkshire women gave me the background of several diners. The only other lone female was the daughter of the harbour master at Takoradi: they suspected that she and that nice-looking engineer with the hyphenated name, who worked on Nigerian railways, were an item, having been on the same ship three months earlier. 'That corpulent man, you wouldn't believe it, is only forty-four, looks ten years older – let himself go to seed, it's the drink you know, but very clever, heads a giant engineering project based at Lagos.' The vast man with a black beard like Captain Haddock in *Tintin* was the ship's doctor. I knew I would soon have to visit him to discuss my leg – not a plus point on the glamour scale, and I worried it would get worse as the temperature and humidity rose.

Talk turned to the menu, which looked exciting, but I was warned off all that muck – much better stick to good old English grub – none of the native stuff, all that chilli pepper, palm oil and coconut, 'and you couldn't trust *them* not to put goat in the stews'. As for okra, aubergine and peppers – steer clear of all that. You were safe enough with blancmange, ice cream, whipped jellies – invariably pink – and trifles. I did not follow their advice, and after consommé soup, I ordered 'Fish curry – traditional West African dish', which was delicious; for pudding I had my first taste of pawpaw, a large slice served with fresh lime. This fruit became a staple part of my diet: a fruit-bearing tree can be grown from seed sown the previous year, and flourishes all over West Africa; the miserable specimens that appear on supermarket shelves in Europe bear little resemblance to freshly picked fruit from one's own plot. The same goes for mangoes, although the West African mango – stringy and tasting slightly of turpentine – is a poor substitute for the East African variety, but I did not learn that until seven years later. My fellow diners watched with morbid interest, predicting I would come to my senses after a dose of 'belly palaver'. I fear the north-country people thought me stuck up, and heading for a comeuppance. No wedding ring, listed as 'Mrs' on the passenger list, evasive not only about her past, about who was going to meet her at Takoradi – very odd.

Next morning was cool and overcast when we sailed down the Pembrokeshire coast to the Bristol Channel and the Scilly Isles. Breakfast was served in two sittings, the first for children with their attendant mothers. Once fed, swarms of calorie-fuelled brats thronged the corridors and ladders, thundering about in search of entertainment. Deck games would be organised later, but there was universal disappointment that the swimming pool would not be open during this voyage. The mothers then joined the second sitting for their own breakfast. The 'full British' was the most popular choice, though some passengers were cautious, in dread of the Bay of Biscay, and retreated to their cabins at the first hint of a swell.

By mid-morning I had found a deck chair in a sheltered

corner, and began to assess the occupants of neighbouring chairs, from behind my book. The sun had still not burned off the low cloud, so I had to fetch a sweater from my cabin, treating metal stairs, at which I was far from nimble, and steps, which were trip hazards, with care. Back on deck, I found the chairs arranged in little groups, one of which I was asked to join. It would have been rude to demur, and thankfully this lot were more animated than my companions of the previous night. At 11 a.m. the first round of drinks was ordered, but still replete from breakfast, I settled for fruit juice, while the others ordered beer, a few gins and tonic, and new to me, gin and Dubonnet, or Campari soda, which later became my favourite drink. The passing of the sister ship MV *Accra*, heading for Liverpool on its homeward voyage via Grand Canary, brought nearly all the passengers to their feet, waving like children. Other highlights were the sighting of a school of dolphins, the arrival of a solitary bumble bee, and a house martin sheltering in one of the lifeboats.

I reflected on Grandma's addiction to cruises lasting months, and wondered how she had endured the monotonous routine: regular meals, for which it was impossible to work up a healthy appetite, and unremitting trivial exchanges of social banter. She will have been avoided by many, but her entertainment value as a garrulous Irish woman probably filled a need, and by her own account she often dined at the captain's table. She was a formidable bridge player, which will have helped to pass the time, but several cruises in the late twenties and early thirties, including two to New Zealand, made serious inroads on her estate. She is on record as boasting, tongue I now suspect loosened by alcohol, that I would be 'one of the richest young heiresses in the province'. After her death in 1947, when her will was read, there was not enough capital to honour her many bequests to 'dear friends'.

The first port of call was Bathurst in the Gambia. I was shocked by the attitude of most of the passengers when the question of going ashore was broached. 'There's nothing to see, it's not worth the bother,' they said. From where we were anchored there was indeed little to be seen. A solitary pied kingfisher perched, almost within reach, on one of many rotting timbers; a red dust track led towards what was at that time little more than a straggly settlement of corrugated-iron-roofed shops. There were a few two- and three-storey villas, which had known better days, their balconies supported by damaged pillars or insubstantial timbers, the bright pink, blue and peppermint-green façades defaced by dribbles of black fungus.

Down the middle of every alley ran an open drain, explored by children, goats and ribby, short-coated dogs with white-tipped tails and a diamond on the forehead. Several children came shyly to touch my pallid skin, but only one tried the give-me-penny ploy; in truth, they did not expect much from visitors. A few tall, dignified Wolof women sold both fresh and dried fish from a variety of containers: but even then, baskets and clay pots were less common than enamelled basins of European or Asian origin. What had survived were elaborately structured headcloths and large, pure gold coiled earrings, symbol of success as a 'market mammy'. I had a camera, but was careful not to direct it at anyone without consent – many were delighted to pose, but a few clung to the belief that their soul would be stolen, and turned away. Pied crows, glossy starlings and vultures abounded, the last hopping sideways along the roof ridges, before plonking heavily to the ground, where they would bounce to inspect the latest gobbet of refuse chucked in the direction of the drain. Walt Disney got them just right in his version of *The Jungle Book*. The courthouse was the only substantial building not in terminal decay. The sky remained overcast, and the air, heavy with smoke, smelled uniquely of Africa: a mixture of charcoal burning, roasting plantain, cooking oils, dried fish, body odour, rotting fruit and vegetables, and open drain. For a 'not a lot to see' place, I had enjoyed my first footing on red laterite soil.

Back on board, plans were being hatched for a fancy-dress evening to take place before the next stop at Sierra Leone. By this time the heat had reached such a peak that I had stopped trying to apply make-up, as it slithered off my red face. Showers brought short-lived relief, and any exertion, such as patting oneself dry, provoked more beads of sweat. It was the peak of the rainy season, and I suffered so severely I thought a serious error of judgement had been made and I would expire if it got any hotter. However, I was never again to suffer as badly. I made an appointment to see the medical officer, who greeted me warmly, saying he had noticed my bandage and anticipated a visit. After making some perfunctory notes, he said: 'Well you had better strip off – I'd like you to walk to the end of the room and back so that I can assess your balance.' Too startled to question the necessity of this, I complied. He prescribed a new bandage, and when I recounted the story, it was greeted with hoots of laughter. He had form.

We glided into Freetown so early in the morning that horizontal wisps of cloud partially obscured the heavily forested hills, which formed a backcloth to the town. An ethereal scene, it reminded me of mornings on the west coast of Scotland; but as we got closer the similarity faded as brilliant flame trees and other flowering bushes came into focus, canoes came out to welcome the ship, and small boys dived for coins as we neared the jetty, where I saw my first sea snake. Steerage passengers of both sexes who had boarded at Bathurst, in the hope of finding work in Sierra Leone, jostled around the gangplank, each with a huge cloth-wrapped bundle. Security was top priority, and Ali warned me on no account to leave the cabin door unlocked or the porthole unscreened as 'They outside, they come and take them shoes with long stick'. Despite these precautions, one of the A deck passengers had awoken to find a shadowy figure in the act of removing some of his property: a well-aimed kick in the crotch ensured the figure fled to its own part of the ship.

There was a subtle change in the women's clothing; many wore a tight bodice with a little valance just above the waist, below which was a narrow, ankle-length skirt – I was told it was a style introduced by early missionaries to conceal pregnancy. Many cloths were beautiful, in particular the blue and white vegetable-dyed ones from northern Nigeria and Ghana. Cruder cloths were chemical-dyed prints from Holland, which sometimes displayed a giant portrait of Queen Elizabeth or the Ghanaian leader, Kwame Nkrumah, on the wearer's rump. The kente cloth for which Ghana is famous is a superb example of craftsmanship, although its garish colours do not appeal to me. It is mostly worn on ceremonial occasions.

One of my group was pounced on by an old school friend. Sowerbutts was a slender, towering man of about fifty, with a Clark Gable moustache, black Brylcreemed hair, white shorts, knee socks, and the then ubiquitous suede desert boots. The white socks were impractical in the laterite environment, but old colonial habits, like changing for dinner, die hard. He would take no refusal of an offer to accompany a chosen few of us ashore: an additional car – with driver – was waiting, so soon we were sweeping in convoy up a steep hill, with many hairpin bends, to a sprawling bungalow with a panoramic view over the town, sea and mountains. The gardens, designed early in the century, had matured into a fine collection of bougainvillea, jacaranda, and giant mimosa, with hedges of hibiscus. Tiny iridescent birds flitted about, and the air was full of giant butterflies – pinned specimens of which were displayed in the cabinet our host showed us as soon as drinks were in hand. Several of us were hungover from the previous night, and in need of rehydration, but little notice was taken of pleas for pure fruit juice without gin: Sowerbutts was by this time into his third brandy and soda. An elderly factotum was commanded to prepare lunch-time snacks and sandwiches, before Sowerbutts instructed his drivers to take us to the beach for the afternoon, during which he had important 'business' to conduct in the town, but would join us on board for drinks before dinner. There had been a wife who had left and gone home; now he lived alone, surrounded by books on geology, local topography, wildlife and butterflies, looked after by the old servant who remained loyal, despite the demanding nature of this benevolent tyrant. Many perks went with the job.

Apart from our group, the beach was almost deserted, and an insulated bag of assorted drinks – mostly alcoholic – had been provided. We were even able to go for a swim, rugs and towels having been brought by the drivers, who parked at a discreet distance in the shade. It gets dark very quickly near the equator, so the drivers warned us when it was time to pack up and return to the *Apapa*. True to his word, our host was waiting, now swaying slightly, and speech slurred; he sat down for a last drink before all visitors were ordered ashore. The men were slapped on the back and promised future hospitality; the women subjected to an uncertainly aimed kiss.

The corpulent engineer proved on acquaintance to be a soulmate but he was a pathetic example of the ravages a dissipated lifestyle can inflict. His torso sagged beyond its forty-four years, blackened teeth cried out for attention, and his ankles were swollen – the next drink was always within reach.

But only in the small hours did he show signs of inebriation as we stood together gazing at the Milky Way, the Pole Star and myriad others, about which he was exceptionally well informed. Sensing my ignorance, he sought to teach me how to identify individual stars and galaxies, before lapsing into soliloquy on what he now saw had been a wasted life. A public school education had been followed by a first at Cambridge, and an early childless marriage that had failed. I do not know if he blamed his drinking and broken marriage on the colonial lifestyle, or saw them as inevitable consequences of his behaviour. I wish I had been a more effective sounding board, able to offer more solace than I did, but I had yet to gather knowledge about alcoholism, the disease from which he was now in the terminal stages, so offered little more than sympathetic noises. He kissed me sadly, and we returned to the fancy-dress dance: he, dressed as a porter, wheeling a trolley, on which I, in an animal-print bathing costume, was the 'baggage'. I wish I knew the end of his story, but after I went ashore at Takoradi, we never met again.

It was a company rule that nobody was allowed off or on the boat before nine in the morning, and I was surrounded by the chaos of last minute packing when Fergus appeared at the cabin door on the stroke of eight. Behind him, at a respectful distance, hovered the two Ghanaians who had 'facilitated' him. This was not the Bergman/Bogart reunion I had been looking forward to; I was told to get a move on as a Land Rover, driver, two field assistants, and laboratory equipment, were waiting on the dockside. After the hastiest of goodbyes to such of my companions as were on deck, we drove off through an agglomeration of fuel storage tanks, warehouses and vast stacks of timber, to the guesthouse where we were to stay the night.

Adda and I were introduced, both aware how critical our compatibility would be. He was wary, having known situations where a loyal servant had survived a few weeks only after the importation of a memsahib. For the time being, I resolved to behave as befitted any well-mannered visitor to a strange country, and keep negative comments to myself. After leaving my luggage in his care, Fergus drove me in his own car – a Ford Zephyr with red plastic seats and no air-conditioning – to the centre of Accra for a last minute visit to his bank and the only big stores, Kingsway and UTC (United Trading Company).

He had asked me to list everything I thought indispensable for basic needs at a field station some 150 miles north of Kumasi – adding, superfluously, that stocks of European foodstuff were low and that in the Ashanti region the situation was likely to be worse. My mind, then as now, went almost blank when asked to make a list at short notice, but I did make a plea for a large stock of Kleenex, Tampax, mosquito repellent, lavatory paper, a good tin-opener, kitchen towels, and Wettex cloths.

The shelves of Kingsway and UTC were, as predicted, sparsely stocked, but we found some delicacies, such as tinned frankfurters from Czechoslovakia, crab from Russia, *marrons glacés* and tinned artichoke hearts from France. We bought a sack of coffee beans, large cans of vegetable oil, and many tins of dried milk powder. Staples like tea, sugar, tinned margarine, sardines, tomato paste, Oxo cubes, Bisto, and jelly crystals – the last three an indictment of British colonial wives – could be found in wayside stores as far north as Navrongo, near the border with the Volta region. Not until we visited Mexico, on the shores of the Gulf of California, thirty years later, did we see such almost bare shelves in what called itself a supermarket; rusting, often bulging, cans with indecipherable labels, mildewed packets of pulses, poor quality tea-sets, enamel bowls, and Pisa-like towers of pots and pans, almost all from the People's Republic of China.

We lunched at the Accra Club – an old colonial haunt recently opened to all races. After parking in the shade of an ancient mango tree, we ate an excellent meal, served with all the courtesy and competence of a first-class UK restaurant. The heat and humidity, on top of exhausting shopping, were having their effect, so I welcomed the afternoon siesta from two to four. Fergus played a long-arranged tennis singles match, after which he and his opponent were literally streaming with sweat. He took me to dine at the Ambassador Hotel, where, at that time, there was a well-kept aviary of South American macaws, as well as various parrots from Africa. We dined on lobster thermidor, and I remember being warned to make the most of it, as it would probably be six months before I ate anything comparable.

From sublime to ridiculous, next morning began with a typical guesthouse breakfast: limp cornflakes swimming in reconstituted dried milk, lumps of egg scrambled in Blue Band margarine, incinerated white toast. In redemption, there was a huge slice of pawpaw with half a lime. Tea was strong and stewed, coffee indescribably awful. Water, which had to be boiled and filtered, was tepid. The driver arrived late with the Land Rover: his excuse, according to a wrathful Fergus, transparently untrue. It delayed our start on the four- to five-hour drive to Kumasi. Thus began life in Africa.

9
Induction

The tarred road out of Accra stopped abruptly not long after we passed the gates to the university campus on the left, the airport on the right, and the recently erected Black Star arch, one of many extravagant symbols of Ghana's independence: the surface thereafter was rutted laterite with a deep ditch on each side. These ditches were the graveyard of so many lorries that soon I was counting them. The number was unsurprising, taking account of the speed at which most were driven. A few slow specimens progressed in a curious crab-like way, their axels twisted beyond repair. I was fascinated by the slogans that adorned these 'mammy lorries', as they are called in Ghana: 'Snakes and Women', 'Only Jesus', 'All Africans are Brothers', 'Trust in God', 'Fear No Devils', and, ironically, 'Travel Safely'. All were overloaded with exuberant passengers, cheering and waving any time Fergus thought it prudent to pass – a manoeuvre requiring sangfroid and fierce acceleration to penetrate the dust and establish there was no oncoming traffic

We climbed the escarpment that overlooks the Accra plains, a site favoured by government ministers for their luxury residences. Wayside villages offered the hazard of unfettered goats, chickens, and sometimes children, as well as deeper ditches with sharper sides. Suddenly we entered the forest zone, where giant cotton trees with massive buttresses at the base supporting smooth silvery trunks soaring to gaps in the distant sky lined the route. From time to time, a clearance in the roadside vegetation marked the entrance track to some hidden village. Often a small group of children would gesticulate furiously that they had something to sell. I would have liked to stop, but Fergus was adamant that we would lose valuable time in protracted negotiations, only to buy something we could get at half the price in the next market. There was an added risk of emotional blackmail if offered a deliberately orphaned or injured animal: he spoke from painful experience, blaming sentimental Europeans for encouraging the practice. I came into this category, and newly imported women were notoriously vulnerable. Later I became victim of the persuasive powers of Muslim traders in wood carvings, woven blankets and crocodile skins. I have always loathed the concept of bartering, but Fergus said it was a tradition to be enjoyed by both parties. So I tried hard, once pointing disparagingly to a hole in the skin of a small crocodile – embarrassed giggles ensued and Fergus intervened, hissing at me: 'It's the anus, you dimwit.' He and the trader, who knew him from bachelor days, then embarked on a session of good-natured banter, before concluding a deal satisfactory to both.

Shortly after we left Kumasi, school geography lessons describing rain forest giving way to savannah grassland came to mind as the overhead canopy and giant cotton trees phased out, and open country dotted with assorted bushes and trees, and massive sculptural ant hills came into view. Fergus, who had a set of *Bannerman's Guide to West African Birds*, was able to name the unfamiliar exotic birds: flocks of common bee-eaters, guinea fowl, various shrikes, a stunning long-tailed drongo, bulbuls, and the occasional ground hornbill. A few small rodents skittered across the road, but as Fergus sadly remarked, little game was left because anything that moved was regarded as 'chop' designated for the pot if it could be shot, trapped, or caught by any means. We did, however, see a troop of baboons, some vervet monkeys, and the flattened corpse of a large snake, before reaching the escarpment on which the research station and housing for senior staff had been built. The site for the headquarters of the Medical Field Units (MFUs) had been chosen when British colonial influence in the Gold Coast was at its height by Chief Medical Officer B.B. Waddy. The current director, David Scott, was Fergus's 'national counterpart'. David was a relic of the old colonial system, known and respected by both Africans and Europeans, but nevertheless a despot, and ill at ease to find himself lumbered with a UN counterpart – albeit a parasitologist rather than a medical officer – for whom he was expected to provide transport, laboratory facilities, field and laboratory assistants, and a house.

We drove up an incline, past the laboratory block, to a

compound where twelve modern bungalows were scattered among ancient mango trees. Some were surrounded by flowerbeds, an indication that the occupants were European, others stood much as they had been left by the builders, but with a dirt yard populated by children and chickens. Each dwelling had a group of pawpaw trees, frangipani and oleander bushes and the ubiquitous bougainvillea; many had beds of strident canna lilies, and masses of blue morning glory climbing the walls. First impressions were good, although on inspection it was clear the houses were badly finished. Shortly after our arrival, I traced the cause of the cascade from the roof above our bedroom – loose guttering jointed with dried-out putty. A mosquito-proofed porch led directly into the central living area, to the left of which was a large kitchen with a big wood-burning range, a double Belfast sink, rudimentary shelving and several deeply scarred wooden tables encrusted with grime. Everything was smoke blackened. Outside were a woodpile and area where clothes washing took place, and callers were entertained to mugs of strong sugary tea. Enquiry about washing methods revealed that buckets and enamel basins were preferred to the sinks in the kitchen, where cold water was on tap. After being wrung into a tight rope, washing was hung to dry on a line – Fergus having discouraged the use of bushes. Improved methods would have to be tactfully introduced. Ironing, with a collection of different-sized heavy charcoal irons, was also done in this area, and any iron considered too hot plunged hissing into a bucket of cold water. Here too neighbours, aspirant garden boys and casual traders would congregate to chat with Adda while he worked – I had a lot to learn.

Painters from the Public Works Department were instructed to paint the kitchen: they arrived promptly at seven thirty but did not start work until nine, having taken time off for morning chop. No attempt was made to prepare the walls before the first thin coat was applied to the walls; the result was dirty grey streaked in places with white. Two hours later the workforce was comfortably lolling on a variety of seats outside the back door. I stirred the lumpy mixture used and understood the streaks, but not why it was taking such a long time to dry. The head painter then said this was all they had, but notwithstanding they would return the next day. It was my first experience of a master obstructionist, and I remembered Albert Schweitzer's advice: 'Never get into an argument with your garden boy, he will always win.' I pointed out that in the absence of paint there was little point in their returning, and told him and his team to make themselves scarce. I got the impression that Adda was enjoying the impasse, and had, in his role of translator, deliberately fuelled the flames. At this point Fergus appeared, quickly assessed the situation, and reinforced my order that they were not to return until a supply of Snowcem was in hand. Crestfallen, they dispersed.

The opposite wing contained two bedrooms and a bathroom at the end of a dark corridor. Inside the mosquito netting were glass-slatted louvres adjusted by metal levers. In theory the mosquitoes were kept out, but a great variety of insects got trapped, only to batter themselves to death between netting and glass, from where they were difficult to remove. Vacuum cleaners did not then come with the variety of nozzles we now expect, although I had brought a spherical Constellation – now a design classic. Prior to that, cleaning had been done by dustpan and brush. Electricity, from a generator situated near the laboratory block, went off at ten in the evening. Hot water for the bath came from an ill-disposed bottled gas geyser, supplemented by the contents of a giant black kettle, which sat permanently on the warm kitchen range.

After much conflicting advice from friends in Ireland and Accra, Fergus had installed a hi-fi record player, complete with stereo amplifiers, and we had a collection of long playing records, some of which survive to this day. There were no curtains, but I had bought a Singer hand-powered sewing machine in Accra, as well as some material, and set to work, wishing I had taken more notice of my mother's expertise – she could cope, not only with curtains, but loose covers, jodhpurs and riding habits. I do not imagine she was ever called upon to turn a shirt collar, something I had to tackle after we moved to the far north two years later. At night, after the generator shut down, we depended on kerosene lamps, of which I was afraid, seeing them as a fire hazard. I never mastered their idiosyncrasies, any more than I conquered the rusty tank and burner that fuelled the refrigerator. Both of us spent frustrating hours, kneeling on concrete, among spiders' webs, sugar ants and cockroaches, trying to coax our own specimen into action, as well as those at rest-houses if the caretaker had given up hope. Keeping refrigerators working was a nightmare of wick-trimming, recalcitrant burners, glass chimneys and mantles, which cracked and broke, with spares, when available, hundreds of miles away.

Wherever one travelled in Africa, the dream of ice cubes and cold water at the end of a long journey was seldom realised. A caretaker, if he could be found, would only recently have filled the water-filter, and the refrigerator would, with luck, begin to chill before night fell. The ice-cube container was often missing, so we learned to bring our own, as well as a tin-opener, egg whisk and at least one saucepan, not to mention tea towels and wipe-cloths. Most caretakers used a bunch of twigs to sweep the floors, and the arrival of visitors was often a surprise, despite the reservation having been made well in advance through the district office.

I soon adjusted to rising at dawn, early breakfast, and the departure of Fergus for a working day which ran from seven in the morning to two in the afternoon. Adda had, as is the custom, recruited one of his extended family as a 'small boy': which meant he got a cut from the youth's miserable monthly wage, and Adda's own workload was lessened. I was not happy about the arrangement, as it meant even more loss of privacy, and many of the 'services' offered were a source of irritation: cushions would be plumped, tables, on which one had reading matter, taken outside when the floor was cleaned in preparation for yet another coating of Cardinal polish, or 'Calindar' polish, as Adda wrote it on his shopping lists (his fair English and good handwriting a tribute to the White Fathers), while feeble efforts were made with a feather duster to remove dead insects from the screening.

There was an Edwardian element to the situation: I had the key to a storeroom in which we kept bulk supplies and our duty-free liquor allowance, and Adda had to ask for release of bar soap and cleaning materials. It was accepted practice that a blind eye be turned on servants' consumption of sugar and tea, and the amount of soap used not questioned, even if it was suspected that some might have been sold; all other commodities were sacrosanct. Tins of Hero Black Cherry jam, of which we ate little, were a frequent request, and the amount of Blue Band margarine asked for did not tally with what we were using. For baking, I had bought tins of Spry, luckily not so popular. Fergus voiced his suspicions about the boy to Adda, who conducted his own inquiry. Apparently stores in the servants' quarters had also been filched, so the 'small boy' was sent back to his village in the north.

The director's house was an imposing two-storey edifice; built at the highest point of the compound by the founder of the MFUs, it had a panoramic view over a vastness of savannah scrub, where guinea fowl were abundant, and it was rumoured a few lions had survived decades of indiscriminate hunting. Shortly after my arrival we were invited for dinner. David was of the old school in which protocol is strict and conventions observed, yet his counterpart had blatantly installed, not a wife, but a 'kept', apparently married, woman, in one of the official houses. It must have been a testing situation for him, and I look back on my initial performance with some chagrin: he was discomfited on his own patch and I made little allowance for that. I was impossible to pigeonhole, and he had probably never been faced with a similar situation, although one of his medical officers, a Tamil, had recently brought a very pale-skinned, sari-wearing bride from England.

We got on surprisingly well and enjoyed one of his formal dinners, which varied little over the years. Simba, his servant of long standing, served consommé with freshly baked rolls, roast guinea fowl stuffed with Paxo, accompanied by rice and a mixture of small aubergines and sweet red peppers; the pudding was a pink foam concocted from jelly cubes and Carnation condensed milk. After the meal, we sat on the terrace, companionably sipping coffee and liqueurs under a starlit sky, against a background of croaking frogs, while geckos gorged themselves on moths.

David read *Blackwood's Magazine*, and we read the *Guardian* and the *Listener*, although we soon changed to the *Sunday Times* and the *Observer*, always at least three weeks late, and costing five shillings. The BBC World Service was an invaluable link with the rest of the world, but reception was poor and, like the refrigerator and lamps, a cause of many obscene outbursts from Fergus as he repositioned the set in various positions, using a variety of aerials.

David had a pedigree female Siamese cat on which he doted, a collection of fine Persian carpets, some family silver, and several foxed engravings of the Northumberland coast. He grew Jerusalem artichokes, and any other vegetable tolerant of the unforgiving climate. For recreation there was a murky swimming pool and one cement tennis court with greenery sprouting from its many cracks. Fergus soon had the court made playable, and found several enthusiasts among the field assistants and the doctors. This was dangerous territory, as David, while captain of Kintampo Tennis Club, seldom made an appearance on court, and, to put it mildly, was not athletic. The club was almost defunct, but with our arrival interest in the game revived. We had to tread carefully, and matters were not improved when our common black cat impregnated David's Siamese; he made no effort to conceal his annoyance, and relations were distant for weeks after a splodgy litter was delivered. We were not told their fate.

Months later a tennis match was arranged against a team from Lawra, a village in the north bordering the Ivory Coast. The ball boys, a few of whom turned up naked from time to time, were told that shorts were to be worn for this event. Plans escalated to durbar level, and David, now president of the club, welcomed the visiting team, accompanied by two tribal chiefs, in full regalia, who thundered into the compound mounted on short-reined, snorting stallions. This was exceptional because horses, notoriously, did not thrive as far south as the Ashanti region. Placated by his eminent position, David fulfilled the role of gracious host and presented the prizes, most of which went to our own team, apart from one singles player from a remote village near the Black Volta, so naturally gifted he would, if transferred to the UK, have been a county player. In the words of Francis Kofi, a senior field assistant: 'We beat them into the ground.' It was almost midday when Fergus and I gave way to pressure and played an 'exhibit' match against Karel Sin, a Czechoslovakian surgeon, and his wife, Marta. I was by this time better acclimatised, but found the experience, despite the applause, utterly draining. At the end of play the ball boys got pocket money and ice cubes to suck – a great treat. The adults downed Tusker beer, Pepsi-Cola and Fanta, before the visitors went to spend the night dispersed around the compound, leaving at dawn the following day on their the long drive back to Lawra.

My horizons were being widened on a daily basis: our immediate neighbours were Dr von Haller, his wife and two daughters, who came during school holidays. Von H. displayed many characteristics I had found intolerable in Rudolf, but Frau von H. was a pleasant, animated woman who claimed to be an artist of some standing; this was hard to swallow judged by the efforts displayed in their house. She was intrigued by the dominance of laterite in the local scene, painting it a raw terracotta, conflicting with pillar-box red flame-trees, purple bougainvillea – canna lilies, zinnias and orange Cape marigolds thrown in for good measure. Their girls were charming, deferring always to Pappi, and coming to me for advice on how to deal with a cat that belonged to the children of the Ghanaian accountant, but which repeatedly came to them, quivering with fright, for succour. Conscientiously they took it back, but it always returned. Despite Fergus's embargo on pets, when the girls went back to Germany the cat adopted us.

Luciano Rosei, another of the resident medical officers, came from Rome with his wife, Maria, ancient mother and two young children. He was pleasant and spoke English with enthusiasm; Maria, painfully shy, spoke haltingly. The children knew only Italian, as did their deaf grandmother who lived in a world of her own, munching and nodding her way through memorable meals prepared by her daughter-in-law. They often invited us, and it was our first experience of authentic Italian food. I learned how to make pasta with the aid of a machine bought at the UTC store in Accra; how to prepare beef, chicken liver and tomato sauce for tagliatelle, and to assemble lasagne. What came as a shock was the number of courses served: antipasta, little artichokes, a pasta dish, followed by steak and frites, fruit, cheese and biscuits, finishing with ice cream and coffee. Conversation was exhausting and topics limited because of Maria's poor comprehension; the unfortunate Luciano had to bawl a translation to Grandma, whose nutcracker face remained expressionless throughout her munching. The children ate small portions early in the meal before being dispatched to bed. A sullen-looking steward in a fez, assisted nervously by Maria, served the meal. Reciprocal entertainments were poor in comparison, although I remember producing a delicious toad-in-the-hole and classic English trifle, which was always a hit with the French, Germans, Poles and Italians. Pride disallowed my use of Bird's famous powder, but I could have saved myself much futile egg-breaking had I done so. Of eggs bought by Adda at the Kintampo market, roughly half were past their 'sell by' date, so one learned always to break them singly. The steady supply we anticipated from our own chickens never materialised, as they were picked off one by one by a literal snake in the grass.

To compensate for the inadequacy of our 'table', we provided translation services for all the medical officers who were required to send a quarterly report of their activities to David. This was often tantamount to writing the report, based either on a verbal account or a draft copy from the author scrawled in longhand or, worse, typed in single spacing without punctuation. At that time my typewriter was an Olivetti portable. The Imperial and Royal machines in the office block being for the exclusive use of the typists who dealt with the director's correspondence, Fergus had to rely on David's goodwill – and that of the typists – for secretarial services. I cannot recall how it came about, but soon I was dealing with all correspondence to WHO headquarters in Geneva and the regional office in Brazzaville in the Congo Republic, as well as editing and producing monthly reports to the WHO representative in Accra. At field level things were better: Fergus could rely on Francis Kofi, three junior assistants, a driver and a Land Rover. One of the juniors, Daniel Kofi, Francis's younger brother, proved to be a gifted draughtsman, capable of drawing maps, diagrams and tables related to the field studies. To reproduce these for quarterly reports, as I had no official position on the project, it was necessary to be circumspect about use of the darkroom, so as not to antagonise any of the 'technicians'. Unfortunately it proved far from light-proof and I had to resort to fumbling about in our bathroom late at night. Photocopiers were in their infancy, multiple carbon copies of letters commonplace, telephone services erratic, and mail generally slow.

Fergus and his team were conducting snail surveys at bilharziasis transmission sites throughout Ghana – the Volta River project was in its infancy, and Lake Volta did not exist. The collection of snail species was vital, being the intermediate hosts of both the intestinal and urinary forms of bilharziasis (the common name for schistosomiasis). One site we surveyed was a large dam on the outskirts of Kumasi, where I first saw a lily-trotter, a beautiful purplish-brown bird with long legs, its wide feet adapted for doing precisely what the name implies. It was oppressively hot, the grass was long, and I was grateful that Fergus had insisted on my wearing rubber boots when a six-foot black cobra slithered from the undergrowth to cross my path.

We went to the far northern region, where native, bare-breasted women carried huge hand-coiled clay pots on their heads; some wore only a bunch of leaves fore and aft. Colonies of wood ibis nested in the baobab trees, and of the numerous small dams most had an area at one end where the women washed clothes and children bathed; at the opposite end sacred crocodiles basked on the sandy shore. Sinister incidents involving these creatures were infrequent, but larger specimens found in the Black Volta, which forms the border with the Ivory Coast, were much feared. David's empire extended to Gambaga in the north-east and Wa in the north-west of the country, and we visited both the MFU doctors, who came to Kintampo only if summoned by David. At Gambaga a young Frenchman, who was to marry within the year, lived a solitary existence; his only companion, apart from a manservant, was an importunate vervet monkey, which leapt around the house and ate from his master's plate without constraint. That they escaped incineration, as the result of a lamp being knocked over, astounds me: the animal was deported to the bush shortly after Philippe's bride, a Parisian ex-ballet dancer, took up residence.

The Polish doctor in charge of the clinic at Wa, Dr Korabiewicz, was an uniquely built giant, well over six feet tall, with a disproportionately short torso. In his mid-fifties he had, in addition to a medical degree, worked in a Warsaw museum on anthropological studies, and was an obsessive collector of native carvings. His personality was overpowering, but his second wife was far from subservient; the first had perished during a canoe trip down the Volga to the Black Sea. On our first visit he greeted us dressed only in a towel around his waist; a friend later commented: 'You were lucky, mostly he's naked.' 'Come in, come in,' he said. 'You must join us for lunch, my wife is crying, the fridge is broken, but you are most welcome.'

He seized me, kissing my arm from hand to elbow, before thrusting us into standard, kapok-cushioned, PWD chairs, and offering the first of a succession of drinks. Weather-beaten, with a pleasant, Slavic face, his now dry-eyed wife emerged from the kitchen to give us an equally warm welcome, seemingly unfazed by having to provide food for two unexpected guests. What the meal consisted of, I do not recall, but I shall never forget his insistence that we lower a glass of schnapps in one go before starting to eat. This was the start of a long friendship, though at the time we had no inkling that within two years we also would be stationed at Wa, helping to assemble his quarterly reports, the improvement in which David appreciated, while suspecting their authorship.

Back in Kintampo, there would regularly be an incident or dispute involving Adda's extended family, who lived north of Bolgatanga in Navrongo near the border with Upper Volta, which Adda needed advice from us in order to resolve. I had already learned much from Fergus, so was not quite the easy touch he took me to be, but in truth the skills of the old colonial district officer were missed by the autochthonous people.

Snakes, scorpions, toads, mud-wasps, giant centipedes, swarming termites, soldier ants, praying mantes, a variety of exotic butterflies, an orphan civet cat, and a royal antelope became familiar during the six months before Fergus managed to amass the documents required to formalise our union, which was to take place late in November at the Municipal Council offices in Kumasi. In the meantime I offered to help any of the laboratory staff who wished to improve their English or learn keyboard skills. Initial response was enthusiastic, but when it became clear a lot of 'homework' would be expected, the class dwindled to the Kofi brothers. Both improved their standard of written English, and Daniel became an accurate typist.

Fergus, on his return for lunch one day called, 'Come and look at this', opening the boot of the car to produce five feet of writhing, brilliant, iridescent green snake. Going to see the cause of hue and cry outside his office, he had found that the team of compound cutters armed with machetes had so horribly injured it that he intervened to finish it off. Never having seen an example of muscular contraction after death, I found it hard to believe it really was dead; examination of the head revealed no front fangs, but some snakes have poison glands at the back, and David, no stranger to snakes, was convinced that this was one of them.

A young pangolin, found clinging to its mother after she was killed for chop, was brought to Fergus with a five shilling price tag. Curled up in a scaly ball, it stayed like that until dusk fell, when it uncurled to reveal a soft pink belly, beady little black eyes and a strong tail. Thumbing through wildlife books made depressing reading – there were no records of success in rearing. I mixed up dried baby formula, but was unsure what strength to offer, and using a glass pipette, dropped milk around the creature's avid mouth. A lot got spilled, but enough went down to provide energy, and within days it was lumping around the house, climbing door frames and curtains, always returning to me, even, unless confined to its box, climbing into bed with us. I knew its only chance of survival lay in weaning, and teaching it how to find and break into ants' nests, so I took it outside at night and released it at the bottom of a hollow tree, apprehensive it might not return. Suddenly the silence was broken by something unidentifiable making a hasty exit, followed by the pangolin. During the days I broke into ant hills, hating the panic it caused in the ordered community. All to no avail – Pangloss, as we called him, resolutely returned to climb my trousers without showing the slightest interest in the swarming feast on offer. From time to time I gave him a warm bath to get rid of the smell of sour milk lodged between his scales, but gradually signs that all was not well began. He became listless and uninterested in milk, his little belly was clammy, and his gait wobbly. The vet thought the symptoms were due to malnutrition and vitamin deficiency, so it was unanimously decided the kindest solution would be to put him to sleep in his box with chloroform-saturated bedding. This task fell to Fergus and we both shed tears. Later I learned from the zoologist George Cansdale that a diet of finely chopped meat mixed with egg white might have worked. This was the first of many emotional involvements with orphaned animals.

August brought a wire from Rudolf announcing that our divorce had been finalised. I was surprised to learn – not from him – that he had married, almost immediately, a Scottish woman he had met at a Highland dancing group. She was still of childbearing age, and within a year Rudolf, in his mid-fifties, who had never shown the remotest interest in children, was the proud father of a girl, to be followed by a boy two years later.

It was now a matter of urgency to arrange our own marriage before my already extended residence permit elapsed. So we set off for Accra, where Fergus, as well as routine meetings with Ministry of Health and WHO officials, had several lectures to give. A ring had to be bought for the forthcoming ceremony, but while there were countless goldsmiths in Accra who worked with pure gold, it was thought wiser to buy one of European origin. At the UTC there were only three to choose from, but my mind was preoccupied with the whereabouts of the nearest lavatory: in the throes of my first attack of belly palaver, I fled to the staff facilities, saying, 'Oh that one will do' and leaving Fergus to settle the bill. Made in Switzerland, it is a thin band of eighteen carat gold, engraved with a floral design now worn smooth.

A tennis-playing friend of Fergus, Leslie, and his Australian wife were to be witnesses, and had planned a celebratory feast to follow the ceremony. There had, however, been a major domestic upheaval, precipitated by the dismissal of their servant Kwaku, who had been with Leslie during his bachelor days. Kwaku's attitude was analogous to that of the painter at Kintampo – obstruction, feigned deafness, deliberate misunderstanding, and ill-disguised resentment at the presence of a woman in the kitchen. There had been insolence, too, but not in Leslie's presence until the week before our marriage when Kwaku had rashly asked if they wished to lose his valuable services. Stunned by the affirmative reply, he had turned nasty, cursing and threatening violent retribution, including intent to set fire to the house: the police had come to evict him. A succession of trial servants ensued, staying on average for two days; possibly 'memsahib' did have unrealistically high expectations.

For the wedding, I wore the tight-waisted black-and-white cotton dress my mother had made for Auntie Rosemary's marriage two years before; crippling, kitten-heeled winkle-pickers and a shocking pink clutch bag completed the ensemble. Fergus wore the usual shorts, white knee socks, desert boots, crisp short-sleeved shirt and a tie. Litter-strewn cement stairs led to the noisy council offices, where we hung around for a while before anyone noticed us. Then a clerk, whose job it was to fill in the marriage certificate, escorted us to a large boardroom, where many junior clerks were scribbling and sorting forms. He began, with the deliberation of an Irish country policeman, to fill in the necessary information. 'Parasitologist' appears on two lines as 'Parasito-Logist', but he coped better with 'Photographer'. After he had breathed heavily his way through two copies, we were herded into the Clerk's office. He was an English-educated Ghanaian who had been good enough to dress smartly in a black suit and bow tie, and was very pleasant – apart from a tendency to indulge in banter on the lines of 'You've had it now', addressed to Fergus. The passage he chose to read from a fat, red legal tome concentrated on dire warnings about understanding that if either of us contracted a bigamous marriage during the life of the other, he or she would be open to punishment by the judiciary irrespective of where he or she was residing – not a word about loving and cherishing, though wifely subservience was emphasised. Then Fergus handed me the ring and I hissed, 'Put it on' – he claimed he was getting around to it – and that was that. Afterwards we went for drinks at the club, where Fergus and Leslie played two sweaty sets of tennis before we sat down to the best dinner the club could provide.

The following day we drove down a rough, precipitous track, in which heavy rain had carved deep fissures, to the crater lake of Bosumptwi. From where the track narrowed to a footpath, it was a steep walk to the shoreline settlement, carrying field glasses, camera, and a container for snails. We did not take the usual long-handled metal sieve – a tribal tradition dating back many centuries prohibited metal objects in the lake – but we saw many buckets and enamel bowls among the rickety chairs and tables outside a line of poorly maintained palm-thatched huts, the inhabitants of which, verging on hostile, were the surliest we were ever to encounter in Ghana. Despite the fact that visitors were a rarity, the children were persistent in their demands – 'Massa, you give me penny.' There was none of the light-hearted chatter associated with most village communities, the shoreline of the crater was hazy, and only a few primitive hollowed-out log boats, propelled by hand alone, were to be seen. Fergus found no interesting snails, and it took half an hour to climb out of the crater in the oppressive heat of early afternoon. Neither of us had worn a hat, and I thought of what I had read on the need to wear a solar topee at all times in the *Guide Book for Young Colonial Officers, c.* 1920. No ill effects ensued, and it was gratifying that neither of us was breathless. Only seven months had passed since my arrival – I was getting acclimatised.

At Kintampo, plans for celebration of the extended holiday over the Christmas and New Year period were already under way. Most of the senior staff, having had their fill of travel during the year, would remain on campus. A few enthusiasts said we should make a trip to a game reserve not far from Ouagadougou, where small populations of giraffe, lion, leopard and elephant had survived. It was not possible to book accommodation, and the risk of travelling hundreds of miles, staying at the most basic of rest-houses, only to see not much more than could, with luck, still be seen in northern Ghana, was high. While Kintampo remained fairly green, further north the dry season had already begun, leaves had curled brown, scrub fires were widespread, and the harmattan wind blew for the first time on the day the French let off their A-Bomb, so we probably got our share of fallout. The woodwork in the house started to crack like a pistol shot, and our noses felt in need of picking – mine often bled.

Three weeks in advance of the feast Adda suggested we might like to buy a turkey from a friend of his, and that it should stay with us, pending execution, to benefit from better feeding. I cannot recall the exact sum paid, but it struck me as no great bargain, even allowing for Adda's 'cut'. A rangy bird was duly tethered on a long rope to the ancient mango tree near Adda's quarters. As one who disliked the process of selecting a fish from the tank in restaurants, I hated its reproachful presence. All this was prompted by horror stories circulating in European circles of vultures having been substituted. When the day of slaughter arrived, Adda waited until Fergus had left before asking if he might have some brandy to anaesthetise the bird. Aware that I was being taken for the fool I was, I handed over the best part of a bottle of brandy. What amount, if any, went down the turkey is unknown, but Adda was paralytic that night, sending a message by a small child to the effect that he had belly palaver. Fergus was furious, as our quarterly duty-free liquor allowance was running low, and the entertainment season imminent:

Rosa Kendall, my maternal grandmother, c. 1930

Stonard Kendall, my maternal grandfather, c. 1890

My paternal grandparents, David and Eileen Stevenson, on their wedding day, 1897

My grandmother Eileen with my father David at the Collon House, c. 1906

My maternal grandmother's family, the Youngs: (back row, L–R) Uncle Fred, Rosa, Stonard, Auntie Gertie; (front row, L–R) Auntie Josephine, Grandmother Young, my mother, Grandfather Young

Auntie Josephine (left) and my grandmother Rosa

My parents on their wedding day, 4 October 1922

My mother, my grandmother Rosa and Rosemary in the grounds of Drumaweir Hotel, Greencastle, County Donegal, *c.*1915

My mother and Rosemary at Port Bradden, County Antrim *c.*1923

Tea party at Carndonagh Rectory, County Donegal, 1932: (L-R) me, my grandmother Eileen in the hammock, Mrs Duncan (the Rector's wife) and two other guests

Michael and me

Mrs McHale at the door of her cottage at Emlagh, County Mayo

Croagh Patrick, County Mayo

Me, Rosemary and my mother, with Conrad in her arms, on Achill Island, 1936

On the beach at Culdaff

On an elephant at Phoenix Park Zoo, 1938

MV *Apapa* docking at Freetown, Sierra Leone, May 1960

Vultures at Axim, Ghana

Fergus and the Uganda kob

Katharine and Dewey, the pied kingfisher

Pangloss, the pangolin

this would include a visit over the New Year from friends in Accra, who were curious to experience the primitive lifestyle in the north, in contrast to the air-conditioned opulence of the capital.

Christmas Day, on which Adda had chosen to work in lieu of later leave to be spent with his family in Navrongo, began with the arrival of two small girls at the back door 'to wish you a Merry Christmas', who were paid off at three pence per head. Although we had already been visited several times by carol singers, another group arrived to render their version of 'Good King Wenceslaus' – I am sorry to say I laughed when it got to looking out on the snow 'deep and crisp and even'. Fergus set up his easel and paints near the entrance doors to the central room, but found the presence of curious children, noses flattened on the mosquito netting, too distracting to continue and retreated to the bedroom and drew the curtains. The kitchen, now slightly less depressing and more hygienic, was mine until Adda came on duty at four thirty, and we fled to the tennis court.

On Boxing Day a fire came close to the house, and all hands were needed to beat the flames back, while cattle egrets sat on the fringe of the fire picking off fugitive insects. David, who had entertained us the previous evening, came to dinner, at which the predictably chewy bird appeared, stuffed traditionally (no Paxo), along with bread sauce, tinned cranberry sauce, such vegetables as I could muster, and rice in lieu of potatoes. Nobody said so, but two of David's guinea fowl would have been preferable. I could not compete with Simba's pink mousse, but managed a pie made from tinned apples mixed with mangoes, served with Carnation cream. I never attempted to make a traditional Christmas pudding or mince pies, as the mixture would have been a magnet for armies of sugar ants. The legs of every table stood in tins of water, but despite this, one would sometimes find tiny bodies in the pasta mix. Frank Wickramasingh, a Sri Lankan medical officer, and his English wife were also moved to entertain us: conversation, despite the wine, was not stimulating, though we did our best to introduce new topics, which were almost invariably cold-blanketed. Frau von Haller and the two girls returned to Germany to resume school, while Pappi completed his contract in Kintampo. There were few

Germans in Ghana at that time, but rumours persisted that an ex-Nazi doctor ran a health centre at a small settlement in the south-east near the border with Togo: his lampshades made of human skin. Said to be an excellent doctor, in an area riddled with witch doctors, where voodoo and ritual sacrifice were rife, the lampshades might not have attracted much outrage.

We put on as good a show of hospitality as we could for the visiting party from Accra. Gilbert and Grace (who had made a pass at Fergus before I came on the scene) and their thirteen-year-old daughter, Charity, arrived irritable, coated with dust and complaining bitterly about the appalling state of the roads. All they wanted was a hot shower and lots of cold drinks. Fergus knew that the rest-house facilities ran to no more than a cracked handbasin and a stained bath, but hoped the caretaker would at least have warmed some water which could be brought by bucket to the bathroom. On his inspection, he had noted holes, not only in the mosquito proofing, but in the nets around the beds; but the lumpy kapok-filled mattresses would at least be dry at that time of year. Aware how much importance Gilbert attached to the chill of his drinks, Fergus had told the caretaker to be sure ice cubes were ready for the visitors, only to hear that the refrigerator 'somehow he spoil', but a replacement had been ordered. Attempting to lighten the atmosphere, we plied them with strong, iced drinks before breaking the news about the deficiencies of the rest-house. They had thermos flasks, which I could fill with cold water or tea, and as the water-filter was working, they would have a supply of tepid drinking water. They brought contributions of spirits and a case of Tusker, but nothing useful such as tinned cheese or frankfurters from Czechoslovakia.

Academically brilliant and studying Russian with plans to become an interpreter, Charity was petulant and as fussy about her food as her dyspeptic father. A plethora of pills was laid out before each place-setting every morning. Satisfying their fads and preferences, and the fact that our stores were running low, made my task as gracious hostess a nightmare. 'No pepper for me ... I'd like *mine* without pawpaw or banana ... no mustard in the sandwiches, please ... I can't take fat ... Oh, no salad dressing for me.' Knowing that Fergus had a short fuse with pernickety feeders, I wondered how long it would be before he voiced his impatience. We organised a trip to the White Volta at Kadelso, fifty miles to the north, where the MFU kept a boat; normally game was scarce, but we had a very rich day. En route we saw a duiker, a family of mongooses, a rare vulture and large flocks of both common and rosy bee-eaters. The Public Works Department (PWD) mechanic in charge of the boat and its two-stroke engine, and two locals said to be familiar with the river and its channels met us and we all packed into a sturdy-looking flat-bottomed boat. One of the locals kept a token hand on the rudder and clearly did not know right from left, giggling every time we shot past large rocks just below the surface, unperturbed when we hit them. Gilbert, who had a boat of his own in Accra, quickly took over the steering and tried to get the mechanic to slow down when everyone shouted, 'Slow, rocks!' We had no idea if the propeller was protected or not, and were afraid of holing the boat. Fergus had noticed there was only one paddle on board – the other was later found in the rest-house. At one point we were rotating slowly on a rock pinnacle from which only a massive shove with the paddle dislodged us. Excitement was heightened by the fact that a magnificent fifteen-foot crocodile was basking on the shore nearby. The party was uncharacteristically silent as, after two incidents of engine failure, we got safely ashore. The second local, it was divulged, had come along just for the ride. The following morning the visitors left, claiming to have had such an enjoyable holiday. I was thankful that Fergus had refrained from acerbic comment – after all, *we* might find ourselves in need of a bed in Accra sometime in the future.

The costs of implementing the Bilharzia Research Project were to be shared between the Ghana government and WHO, but the latter agency was feeling the financial pinch because certain large countries – the US among them – were behind with their contributions. It began to look probable that the scheme, unique in Africa, might be shelved in favour of more urgent public health problems, and would never get beyond the planning stage. Fergus was overdue for home leave and feeling end-of-tourish, but neither the regional office in Brazzaville nor headquarters in Geneva was acknowledging repeated demands for a decision on dates and itineraries for travel to Europe. An application for a month's study leave at Danmarks Akvarium

(Denmark's aquarium at Charlottenlund) with the eminent malacologist Dr Mandahl-Barth had been ignored. It must be admitted, however, that due to continuing unrest and violence in the Congo, the director of the regional office will have had more important things on his mind than travel authorisation for a relatively junior staff member.

Our evenings were spent, Campari or gins and Dubonnet in hand, with thoughts of returning to Europe by car. We would pore over maps of the route to Kano and thence north across the Sahara Hoggar route; the alternative was to head west to Dakar and the Atlas Mountain range to Tangier. Ultimately the time involved, the fact that the Ford Zephyr was showing its age and what went on under the bonnet was largely a puzzle to Fergus, combined with the knowledge that the French authorities demanded a large deposit to cover costs if they had to go on a rescue mission, led to rejection of the plan – much to my mother's relief.

In the meantime, we went on a trip to the south-west, accompanied by several field assistants in the Land Rover, to conduct a survey of transmission sites: the MFU offices and laboratories were at Ho, and the medical officer in charge was another young Italian, Erminio Onori, whose wife had not long given birth to their first child. Inspecting the baby in its cot under a frilly white canopy, I experienced, for the first time, a flutter of broodiness – it might not be such a bad idea after all. Like the Roseis at Kintampo, the Onoris ate well: two generous meals per day were already reflected by Erminio's portly bulk. They were generous hosts, pressing us to stay with them rather than at the MFU guesthouse, and there was much bawdy mirth one morning when we had to confess that our bed had collapsed. Tragedy later struck the family; the baby girl whom we had admired in the cot was killed in a riding accident, and Erminio had a fatal heart attack before he was fifty.

The rains came late in the spring of 1961 and with morning temperatures of 85 degrees Fahrenheit in the house, rising to over 105 during the afternoon, humidity was high. There was no fan in Fergus's office, now twenty-two months into his tour, and he knew his powers of concentration were poor. It was around this time that his resolve that we should not acquire any more orphaned animals was broken when a tiny royal antelope, its umbilical cord still dangling, was presented with a price tag of six shillings: one of the smallest antelope in the world, no longer common, and reputedly very hard to rear. An American game warden infuriated me by repeating while I was in the process of feeding it: 'You sure got a rare little animal there, yeah, you sure got a rare little animal. Very delicate though, very hard to rear, even a loud noise may be enough to kill them.' The last was nonsense, as it travelled many miles with us in the Land Rover, experiencing jolts, banging doors and lurches into potholes. It appeared to be doing well, taking plenty of milk and eating greenery, and its droppings were normal, but it remained shy and did not recognise me outside its pen. When it began to weaken and refused milk, I discovered its tongue was ulcerated and I force-fed it. After two days, it was stronger and I gave it – as recommended by Cansdale for duikers – some chopped hibiscus and cassava leaves. It died in my lap shortly after. Maybe it was not the cassava leaves that were to blame, but the forced-feeding, which is never recommended – I shall never know. My admiration for the Durrells and Attenboroughs of this world, who sacrifice hours of sleep preparing warm, sterile feeds in often unsuccessful attempts to save orphaned animals, remains boundless to this day.

It is true what they say – the smell of the rain precedes, sometimes for days, the first drops; the sky changes and huge white clouds appear against a dark blue backcloth. Faint flutters of wind disturb the air, a pall of hush descends, broken only by squawks from birds skulking in the scrub – the proverbial lull before a storm. The rains came in late March, washing the red dust from leaves and freshening the air, and the tiny green shoots that had appeared soon after the fires ceased rapidly developed into mature plants. Adda returned with his two children and his senior wife, who had a bulge showing under the little missionary-inspired frill of her cloth, so gatherings near the back door were enlivened.

One of the regular callers was an old man who lived in an isolated house hidden in the bush nearby. He was paranoid about his relatives, to the extent that he would accept no help, in the belief that they intended to poison him for his savings, said to be hidden in his hovel. He was illiterate, and advice to put his money into a bank savings account was dismissed as folly – 'All they give you is a small book, and how do you know you will ever see it again?' (Writing, as I am, after the global financial crash and the demise of a few large banks, this viewpoint seems the epitome of wisdom.) He was painfully thin, but always brought some small offering, a pawpaw, some aubergines or a corn-cob, in gratitude for the buckets of water and mugs of sweet tea that Adda dispensed. One day we heard that he was ill, so we went to visit and were shocked to see how frugally he lived. There was a pallet of cassava drying outside the hut, one rickety chair, an orange box, an enamel dish with a hole in the bottom, a bucket and a calabash. A scraggy white kitten scuttled for cover in the palm roof as we arrived with Adda, who disapproved of the mission, as translator. His afflictions were many, ranging from general aches and pains, to lassitude and a shiny swollen foot. He flatly refused Adda's advice to go to the health centre, saying he would die for sure, so we were surprised when he capitulated to an order from Fergus.

I drove him to the clinic, where Dr Wickramasingh, who was on duty, said it was a clear case of blood-poisoning, and he would have to open the foot. This was done in my presence without anaesthetic: I had never seen anything so unpleasant, nor heard such screams as a stream of pus spurted and then flowed steadily into a dish while the doctor continued probing the incision to clear away as much as possible. I feared the old man might turn violent and hold me responsible for the agony, but instead he was touchingly grateful, getting obediently into the car for follow-up trips to have his wound dressed. I sent food while he was too weak to make his own meals, and found one cause of his malnutrition: relatives in the village had brought food while he was sick, but so firmly convinced was he that they were trying to poison him, it had been thrown away.

One morning we awoke to the chatter of a PWD workforce in the compound; wielding scythes, they had started to flatten the area that was ablaze with the annual display of pinkish-orange Ashanti lilies. Some had fallen by the time we got out, screaming 'STOP', but most were saved; we never heard who had issued the order, but it certainly was not David. Another incident involved the wife of a neighbour. Sounds of a high-pitched female tirade drifted over the grass, and I could see the woman, arms akimbo, haranguing one member of a work team disposed in the shade of a large tree, enjoying one of its chop breaks. His responses were strident, and I feared fisticuffs, but when his co-workers loudly voiced their support, they all stomped off towards the office block. The woman had lent money at an extortionate rate, and the man was behind in his payments. David was called in to arbitrate, and told the husband to ensure his wife ceased money-lending, if not entirely, at least to any MFU employee.

My own relationship with David had improved now that I wore a thin gold band of respectability, but sometimes an evil spirit prompted me to strike a wrong note, such as expressing anti-monarchist sentiments and referring scathingly to 'Our Dear Queen' in a tone he must have found offensive. Fergus pointed out such behaviour was more suited to a teenager, and I was contrite afterwards, but used similar ploys at excruciating dinner parties in Accra, where talk inevitably turned to general disillusionment with the post-independence regime, the unreliability of servants, the insanitary state of the hospitals. I found it difficult not to doze off during the interminable after-dinner discussions, often shaming Fergus with feeble attempts to remain alert. He said I looked like an octogenarian, head dropping slowly to chest level, only to jerk up with glazed eyes and a slack smile, pretending that I had not missed a word. I attributed such behaviour to the climate, consumption of too much food and alcohol, plus overwhelming boredom.

I suffered my first attack of malaria – probably contracted at Wa where drug-resistant strains had been identified – and a bout of suspected amoebic dysentery, the latter reminiscent of the food poisoning blamed on cold chicken at Stevenson's Restaurant in Derry. While I was still limp from the experience, we planned another exploratory trip to Wa, increasingly likely to be our next posting, having been chosen as the preferred base for a bilharzia research and control project, should it get the green light. WHO offered Fergus a further two-year contract until the end of 1963, but refused his request to study at Danmarks Akvarium, writing: 'The invitation was sent to you personally, so we do not feel obliged to contribute in any way towards travel costs', with the rider that any time spent there would be deducted from home leave. This was rich at a time when many staff members were flitting off to the US for six months' study leave on full pay *and* per diem expenses covered.

Thus began my list of grievances against the hierarchy at both the regional office in Brazzaville and headquarters in Geneva.

When eventually we went on leave, plans to visit the Canary Islands were scrapped in favour of Greece, where we stayed in Athens, at that time relatively free of pollution. We visited all the tourist sites, then undertook a perilous drive along the cliff-side road to Piraeus, from where we boarded a ferry overloaded with passengers, miserable poultry tied by their feet, and numerous loudly protesting goats, to Cephalonia. The first Xenia hotel had yet to be completed and the Captain Corelli effect yet to strike. We stayed on the west side, in a small hotel perched above an almost too perfect crescent of sand fringed by dwarf conifers; the water was emerald green shading to deep lapis lazuli. It took some days to accustom ourselves to the leisurely pace of life and the siesta, which seemed to last from early afternoon through to nine at night, when signs of activity were heard from the kitchen. Food was not haute cuisine; in fact, the choice was limited to three stews: one based on goat, one on chicken and a fish mixture faintly resembling bouillabaisse, as well as a ratatouille. The pasta, which was served with everything, was glutinous.

We explored the countryside on foot, and were often invited into houses, where a member of the family, home from the mainland, spoke fair English – our Greek was nonexistent. The war, German occupation, the disastrous earthquake and current affairs were favoured topics, and there were often references to the US. There was almost total ignorance about the location of Ireland and its place in the British Isles. The islanders were steeped in Greek Orthodoxy but seemed tolerant of other faiths. They knew little about Africa, apart from Egypt being at the top, and showed no more than polite interest when told about Ghana. We swam in a little bay thinking we were the only people around, but when I went to get the rucksack I had left near a large rock, it had disappeared: so not all the locals were friendly. Luckily I had a spare swimsuit and hideous white floral rubber bathing cap such as seen in early James Bond films. We ate one delicious meal prepared by an enterprising young chef on another beach. The atmosphere was like a family barbecue with fresh shellfish, a giant platter resembling paella and a fish stew much superior to the one at the hotel. Of the other guests

I remember only a French couple with three children: the wife wore a bikini – daring in 1961 – and, despite the children, had a figure to match. The older children were allowed watered wine at mealtimes, but the three-year-old protested rather too vehemently, 'Je n'ai pas bu, Maman.'

After Greece, we spent a few days in Geneva, during which we were invited to a soiree by Dr Ansari, then head of the tropical diseases division, and Fergus's mentor. Urbane, and oozing charm, he was a close relative of the Shah of Iran; his wife and ballet-dancer daughter were discreetly elegant. Not wanting to be totally eclipsed, I bought an outrageously expensive pair of Swiss Bally shoes, and a black and blue checked jersey suit with a very tight skirt. Worn with the handbag made in London from Tamale crocodile skin, a Jacqmar silk scarf and the string of grey pearls Fergus had bought for me in Mayfair's Burlington Arcade, I felt the crawled-out-of-the-bush image was temporarily erased. (But when I got off the plane in Belfast, wearing this outfit, my mother was shocked by my weight loss – a mere eight stone twelve ounces, a low never achieved since.) A benign autumn passed all too quickly, followed by a skiing holiday in Verbier, which, like Cephalonia, had yet to capitulate to the forces of mass tourism. I hope something has been done in the intervening half-century about the pervasive smell of drains.

While in Europe, we took the opportunity to spend a week in Copenhagen, before Fergus left for two months at the regional office in Brazzaville, at the end of which it was hoped the Ghana government would have signed the plan of operations for the project at Wa. We saw the Danish Royal Ballet performing the young Kenneth MacMillan's *Danses Concertantes*, *The Burrow*, and *Solitaire*. The weather was overcast, cold and wet for most of our stay, but Sunday was brilliant and Bengt Friis-Hansen, with whom Fergus had worked in Northern Rhodesia, took us to his cottage in the country. After a long walk through the forest, we returned to a blazing fire and lunch of rye bread with a variety of pickled fish, including eels. During the days, Fergus paid informal visits to the Akvarium in Charlottenlund to assess the place and meet the staff, not least the formidable Mandahl-Barth. I strolled around the shops, in which the prices were almost as intimidating as those in Geneva; I bought my first piece of Jensen jewellery – a smooth silver brooch with a nautilus centre – a lovely silk scarf and an emerald green Robin Hood style hat for good measure. We parted at Amsterdam: Fergus flew to Brazzaville and I back to Ireland: the first of many such separations.

10
Total Immersion

March 1962 saw us reunited in Rome, where icicles were hanging from the fountains. Fergus had prudently bought some fur-lined boots, but for our visit to the Villa d'Este on the outskirts of the city I wore the gunmetal winkle-pickers I had added to the black and blue jersey suit ensemble – now topped by a three-quarter-length black moleskin coat – and suffered accordingly. It was impossible to travel with clothing suited to all climatic zones, and WHO now limited cabin class travel for staff members to long-haul flights, so our baggage allowance was tourist class.

The next stop was Cairo, where we stayed at the historic Mena House Hotel. I do not know how the hotel looks today, but at that time it stood on the fringe of the desert looking directly towards the Pyramids of Giza. The fertile green strip that extended from the banks of the Nile ended abruptly here – on one side of the road, palm trees and luxuriant vegetation, on the opposite side an infinity of Sahara sand. Slow, fat flies were everywhere, persistent in their attempts to settle on one's face. Furious traffic, scuttling pedestrians, honking horns, malnourished donkeys and mules, blind people and persistent touts were, like the flies, widespread. Fergus had won his battle for funding to attend a conference on all aspects of bilharziasis, as he was scheduled to read not only his own paper, but that of a colleague who had suffered a stroke a few weeks earlier.

As 'distinguished' visitors, we were taken everywhere by minibus or saloon car. On the opening day of the conference a luncheon, hosted by the minister of health, took place in the banqueting hall of one of the ex-royal palaces, a gilded room lit by three enormous chandeliers. The menu started with shrimp soufflé, then roast goat and, in deference to Western taste, potatoes. Already feeling replete, we were startled by the arrival of two huge turkeys surrounded by piles of saffron-flavoured rice mixed with pine kernels. That was followed by slices of pink glazed gateau topped by whipped cream and marzipan strawberries, and finally fresh fruit and viscous coffee. The feast over, a tour of Prince Mohammed Ali's palaces began. The palaces were built in the late Victorian era and now housed a museum. Every object was a triumph of intricate craftsmanship, beautiful inlaid work in mother-of-pearl, ivory and wood, some with delicate silver inlay, and ceramic tiles covered entire walls. The ceilings were made of gold-encrusted carved beams with red, blue and green paint detail, interspersed with udder-like protuberances in the same colours. In the vast family room intricately carved wooden chairs lined each wall, throne-like and uninviting; however, comfort was offered by several gigantic red leather studded sofas, set among a plethora of side tables, which displayed signed photographs of most of the British royal family in art nouveau silver frames. Silk Persian rugs in fiddly floral designs almost obscured the marble floor. The next day all the delegates were taken for a private visit to the Cairo Museum to see much of the contents of Tutankhamen's tomb. The masks and animal carvings were timelessly beautiful, but the collection had a neglected aura, making us feel that many artefacts the wicked old colonials had made off with were better preserved for future generations in London and other cultural centres. That evening we were guests at a 'traditional style' dinner in one of the best restaurants in the city. The decor represented the interior of a Bedouin tent, and the air was heavy with smoke and cooking fumes. Again there was an endless procession of dishes, most of which tasted of burned fat, and all meats, by our standards, were tough. The *pièce de résistance* was a pigeon with the head on.

We visited Memphis, where little remained but giant columns, a small sphinx and an immense statue of Rameses II: our guide, a cultured Egyptian woman with some French ancestry, took us to Sakkara where we trudged hotly through the desert from one tomb to another – rather dull to inexpert eyes. But then we were taken into the heart of one of the Pyramids to see hieroglyphics so perfect they might have been recently cut. Outside hordes of shouting men with camels, ponies and mules fought furiously for our patronage, beating not only each other, but their rivals' animals. A timid member of our group was in danger of being torn apart as he got out of the bus, bleating pitifully, 'Is there some trouble?' Fergus, being tall and well built, navigated the crowd, wearing a lofty expression like one of the camels or General de Gaulle.

I attended the meeting at which, on the final day, Fergus presented the two papers to a packed hall. Most of the other papers were beyond my comprehension, so I spent a lot of time in the peaceful gardens of the hotel, reading or writing in the warm winter sunshine. One day I became aware of a small figure dodging furtively between the bougainvillea and hibiscus bushes: it was male, about twelve years old, and his opening gambit was on the lines of '*Pssst*, I take you in the town and you see my brother and sister', for what purpose was not specified. Terrified of being spotted by hotel staff, he departed quickly when I made it clear I had no intention of accepting his invitation.

The Egyptians were just as accomplished as the Russians or Chinese in evading questions: they even managed to prevent us from visiting a local village, despite it being on the official list, to inspect its irrigation system, and see an active transmission site on the outskirts of Cairo. One of the doctors, on learning it took seven years for a medical student to qualify in Britain, told me proudly that in Egypt the time taken was a mere four. We sensed that Egypt was just as great a dictatorship as other better-known ones. Some of the people we met were outspoken in private, telling us that citizens were not normally allowed to leave the country, but that if they decided to emigrate they might do so, taking out only the equivalent of £500, thus sacrificing their wealth as well as their nationality, and risking repercussions on any remaining family members. Parents were not permitted to send children overseas for schooling.

Scheduled to fly to Accra via Timbuktu by United Arab Airlines – known as Misrair – we checked in at ten in the morning. It was already very hot, and the airport flies were of a larger and more persistent type than average. I had a cold at the feverish raging sore throat stage, and both of us were tired after the frenzied activities of the week. Hours passed during which a periodic announcement would be made that our flight would be boarding soon; more time would elapse, then a further delay with the promise of a meal, for which vouchers were distributed. After another long interval the vouchers were taken away and we heard that we would be boarding after all, and food would be served on board the aircraft. My main preoccupation was a desire for early oblivion; the thought of food was repugnant but a cold drink would have been welcome. By late afternoon Fergus's efforts to get me one produced a lukewarm Fanta, and he was toying with a plate of pasta of the Cephalonia variety.

On take-off we held hands tightly as always, while I counted more seconds than usual before we were airborne, allowing time to reflect on what percentage of accidents occur either at take-off or on landing. UAA and its pilots had an unenviable reputation, and we had met pilots from other airlines whose views were unprintable. On a list of notoriously dangerous runways, Cairo featured, as did Athens and one in the Canaries, at which there was a subsequent disaster. But soon we were cruising and the skyline softened through shades of orange, through turquoise to indigo, and I thought of the distances between oases, the bizarre rocks in the Hoggar region, the nomadic Tuareg people about whom we had read, and the vastness so many brave travellers had managed to cross. As we neared Timbuktu the pilot told passengers to resume their seats and fasten seat belts, and some obediently did so, but a number continued to stroll around chatting to their friends, ignored by cabin stewards. On landing, once the doors were opened, even though it was the middle of the night, the temperature was hotter than any we had experienced in Cairo. Many got off and were replaced by women carrying unwieldy cloth-bound bundles too large for the overhead lockers, and a noisy, inebriated football team returning to Lagos after victory in Mali came on board.

At Accra we were met by the Austrian representative for WHO; well used to the exhausted, embittered state in which many of his colleagues reported back on duty, he took us straight to the government guesthouse to recover. The next day Fergus dashed around retrieving the car, getting it taxed, insured and re-licensed before we took the road back to Kintampo again.

We stayed two nights only in the guesthouse, where Gilbert, Grace and Charity had spent the New Year. A new fridge had been installed, there was a clean checked tablecloth, and the mosquito nets had been replaced. David Scott, by then on his penultimate tour in Ghana, had been replaced by Dr Grant and his wife, both Ghanaian, who now occupied the director's house, and were hospitable in every way. We shared the guesthouse with a newly recruited Polish doctor: he was not shy in talking about the state of his own country, but undiplomatic in his criticism of Ghana and its inhabitants: 'These people are so fucking lazy and unreliable.'

Our cat, now in rude health and with a few more battle scars, had settled with Luciano's family and tolerated child company well; his relationship with their cook, however, was guarded. They gave a dinner party to mark our imminent departure to Wa, which was regarded by many as being too remote for a family. Much time was taken up by old acquaintances coming to 'greet' us, including the old hermit who brought me two dozen eggs – a very generous gift. The Kofi brothers were already installed at Wa and Adda, who had been on paid leave during our absence, was soon to join us there.

All advantage gained from our pre-dawn start was lost when we reached Yeji and joined an impatient crowd of foot passengers, lorries and cars waiting for the broken-down ferry, which was stuck on the opposite side of the river. Sucking oranges rather than depleting our supply of drinking water, we stayed there all morning, while the noise, dust, heat and smells escalated. When all hope of reviving the engine had been abandoned, a hand-hauled winch system went into action and the ferry reached our side of the river. Doubts about the safety of the winch were loudly voiced – particularly where heavy vehicles were involved – but eventually foot passengers and cars were allowed on board. We were relieved to land on the north bank after the short, jerky crossing. The rest of the journey to Wa was uneventful, apart from a burst tyre, which, had it not been for Fergus's inspired driving, would have landed us in a dried-out river bed: this left us with no spare tyre.

It was almost dark when we reached the Water Supplies rest-house, where we were met by a disagreeable young German who grudgingly agreed that our reservation was valid. Later we learned that his detestation of the British was notorious. The caretaker, when he shuffled on duty, was more amiable: he lit the lamp immediately, produced some discoloured ice cubes, covered the table with an ancient chequered cloth, and set two places with bent cutlery. I produced some bread, margarine, sardines and two bottles of warm Tusker beer; with fresh pawpaw and lime to finish, it was quite a balanced meal. We lay in a huge tepid bath and scraped the hardened red dust from the interstices of our skin before collapsing on the usual lumpy mattress under a stained, much-mended mosquito net.

Next morning we went to inspect the house that had been allocated to us. The setting was delightful in a large overgrown garden, which owed its design to some long-departed European. The bungalow, built to German design early in the century, had a large central living room, two huge bedrooms and a bathroom. The kitchen was joined to the house by a walkway roofed with rusting sheets of corrugated iron. On the floor of the main room, below holes in the ceiling, were stalagmites of bat droppings, the broken shutters were caked with the nests of mud-wasps, and the mosquito netting was torn in many places. The lavatory pan was encrusted, its seat broken; the chain that dangled from a rusted cistern had lost its handle. The bath and handbasin were also coated in grime. Fergus, prompted by a pervasive smell, made an outside inspection, which revealed that the soil pipe led to a septic tank beside which was a damp area with a meringue-like frothy topping.

I sat down on one of the hard PWD chairs and cried; Fergus was grimly silent. As we were to be stationed there for at least three years, it was important neither to offend local sensibilities, nor adopt an attitude that might be interpreted as colonial; at the same time it was essential to make clear to the appropriate authorities that the house was unacceptable, and failure to provide suitable housing was a breach of contract. The appropriate authority was the district commissioner, who was sympathetic, admitting that Karel and Marta Sin – against whom we had played the tennis match at Kintampo – had also rejected the house and now lived in the only acceptable alternative. Goodwill was expressed, and he promised that repair work would start immediately; in the meantime, the only solution he could offer was for us to stay in the weekend retreat house that the founder of the MFUs had built in the 1920s at Dorimon, a small settlement near the Black Volta, roughly thirteen miles from Wa.

At Wa there was a branch of the UTC, the Love All Canteen Bar and Restaurant, and a scattering of Lebanese stores where – in addition to candles, sugar, tins of tomato paste, Blue Band margarine, sardines, pilchards, matches, needles and coarse thread – brilliant cotton cloths, mostly printed in Holland, and a choice of top quality English woollen suiting was sold. A large market was held once a week, when a pig would be slaughtered for the benefit of the small non-Muslim population – this market would be the main source of our household supplies, so we stocked up before we left for Dorimon.

The Black Volta forms the border between Ghana and Burkina Faso, known before independence as the Gold Coast and Volta respectively. Dorimon, in addition to its scattering of dwellings, had a mud-built mosque and a marketplace. The population was small, with only about thirty adult males, some of whom were from the Lobi tribe, which had its roots in the Ivory Coast, and were not very advanced. The retreat house was sited on a slight hill overlooking the dam just outside the village; it was a traditional thatched round-house with separate quarters for the resident caretaker and visiting servants. A relic from the days of Empire, unlike the bungalow, it had not been allowed to deteriorate, having been kept scrupulously clean by the willing, if somewhat dim-witted, Da, who had been blinded in one eye by a spitting cobra.

Simbu, who lived in the village, was supposed to keep the vegetation surrounding the hut complex short and snake free. Da and he, as salaried government employees, were therefore figures of substance in the community. The caretaker should have commanded more deference than a mere grass-cutter, but nobody had much respect for Da, as he belonged to the Lobi tribe, many of whose customs and taboos were widely despised. They filed their front teeth, were reputed to eat dogs and snakes, did not allow women to eat chicken or eggs; their artefacts were crudely made and personal hygiene was not a priority. Da had a pregnant wife and a two-year-old son; all three looked malnourished – indeed, the child exhibited the classic signs of kwashiorkor: reddish hair and a distended belly. He clung to his mother, from time to time grabbing a razor strap breast for comfort.

It was clear that, as a woman who was going to spend a lot of time on my own while Fergus was at the laboratory, I would have to establish myself as second in the pecking order. Adda had not yet returned, so in the meantime a daily routine would need to be set down. The local pidgin was even more basic than what I had learned, and the regional dialects so numerous that even Adda was to have problems. Now resigned to being 'Mama', I winced when Fergus was addressed as 'Massa'; we encouraged the use of 'Doctor' in preference, but with limited success. I counted the days until Adda's return, confident that he would establish order, and that his dominance, as an 'educant' who had attended a mission school and could read and write, over Da and Simbu would be accepted without protest.

The three bridges on the tortuous thirteen-mile track back to Wa were liable to inundation, and could be washed away during flash floods, so it was imperative that work on the bungalow should be finished before the next rains. The good news circulated that Fergus was a soft touch for a lift, so each morning a hopeful group waited beside the vehicle – mostly the project Land Rover, but sometimes the Peugeot 504 shooting brake, which had replaced our Zephyr: it might have been a Bentley considering the awe it inspired. He learned to inspect the contents of large bundles before allowing them on board; if they contained dried fish or monkey flesh, the owners were encouraged to walk or wait for one of the open trucks that visited the village on market days, but these cost two shillings, well beyond the means of most. Patients for the health centre who displayed open sores, gigantic umbilical hernias or other obvious afflictions were never refused; nor were the very old, even if their excuse for a visit was unconvincing. Pregnant women with bowls of eggs or writhing red and yellow hairy caterpillars to sell at the market were also hard to refuse. The arrival of long-stay occupants of the rest-house was a major event: this couple displayed none of the autocratic ways of some previous visitors, and seemed genuinely interested in the well-being of the people, so goodwill must be maintained to ensure a continued taxi service. Gifts began to arrive within days of our taking up residence: mainly fruit and vegetables, but sometimes a bowl of guinea-fowl eggs, only a quarter of which would be fit for consumption.

The plan of the house was based on two circles: the larger

living area was open to a veranda, from which a path led down to the dam; the smaller was a bedroom with an en suite recess for a handbasin, shelves and a shower, from which a trickle of murky water full of wrigglers flowed. The kitchen was a flat-roofed afterthought leading off the living room. Our priority, as usual, was to get the refrigerator working, as the only other means of storing food was in a wood and wire-mesh meat safe, the legs of which stood in tins of kerosene to deter ants and cockroaches. Not even a long-handled brush, dustpan or mop was to be seen. Da's sweeping technique involved bending double, with a loosely tied bundle of dried grasses; for dusting chairs, shelves and tabletops he used an ancient feather duster. Almost all the letters I wrote to my mother asked for supplies of Wettex cloths, the lives of which were short because my instructions that they should be squeezed rather than wrung dry were ignored. My pleas for the correct use of clothes pegs were also ignored; I pointed out the circular gap that was meant to grip the line, but they were thrust to the hilt, putting maximum stress on the spring. The wooden sort were useless, as they just disappeared. Washing was a back-breaking job carried out between a stone sink and two battered zinc buckets; notwithstanding this and the need to conserve water, clothes always emerged looking bright and clean. This phenomenon exists throughout Africa: on their day off, immaculately dressed men in crisp white shirts emerge from primitive abodes. Compared with the current situation, life at Kintampo had been one of pampered luxury.

I found ample material for missionary zeal in an effort to improve the dietary habits of Da's family: the child ate no fruit, eggs, meat or vegetables, and it was clear that his mother's milk supply was inadequate. To my ultimate regret I encouraged supplementary use of USAID (United States Agency for International Development) dried milk powder: this worked well enough when I was around to supervise, but in my absence milk would be left uncovered or in feeding bottles lying around on the ground, a magnet for flies. Advice was listened to politely, but while the parents were concerned by the child's failure to thrive, no serious effort was made to introduce a more varied diet. Future prospects for the survival of this toddler were grim after the birth of the next child.

Simbu, accompanied by two lively puppies, reported for duty

every day. Smart in appearance, wearing clean cream shorts with matching top and turban, cutlass in hand, he was the antithesis of Da; his life, however, was not without its problems, details of which were later revealed to Adda. His first wife, though nominally a good Muslim, had drunk beer and smoked hash; the second just sat around all day and refused to cook. Clearly disenchanted by lack of success in the marriage market, Simbu said: 'I finish, they be all the same.' It was suspected that his second wife had been pregnant at the time of purchase, so she had been returned to her family, with which there was an ongoing dispute over the price originally demanded, some of which was still, according to her father, outstanding.

Simbu made an eight-hour onslaught on the shrivelled vegetation surrounding the compound, stopping only for a short break at midday to consume a dish of boiled cassava seasoned with chilli pepper and palm oil sauce. The resulting cull was eleven snakes ceremoniously laid out for Massa's inspection when he returned from Wa in the late afternoon: some were pronounced harmless, others were vipers, but there was one black spitting cobra of the type that had blinded Da. The heads, one of which had been in the act of swallowing a toad, were then buried to ensure that nobody would extract the poison to use for tipping arrows.

Late at night, after the day of compound cutting, I was sitting in the lavatory hut, enjoying the beauty of the moonlit scene, when a reptilian head appeared at the open door. Mesmerised, I lifted my feet off the ground while the seven-foot snake made a slow circuit of the hut, disappearing behind me for what seemed an interminable time, before sliding off in the direction of the main house. I raised the alarm, but immediately regretted having done so when the compound quickly filled with frenzied humanity swinging oil lamps, wielding cutlasses and assorted heavy sticks. The hapless cobra tried to climb the curved slope at the base of the house wall, making itself an easy target, and was decapitated. I felt something of a traitor and reproached myself for having overreacted – after all, it had only been searching for food and had not threatened me. After that, when I saw anything that might trigger a murderous hunt, I kept quiet.

The village policeman regularly accompanied a procession of women to a safe spot that he chose on the shore of the dam, where they could wash clothes and gather water for the day. Bearing on their heads a variety of receptacles, from calabashes and beautiful giant clay pots, down to buckets and chipped enamel bowls, the women complained loudly when his choice involved a longer walk than necessary, but they were in awe of his authority, so laughter was subdued and the spontaneous merriment characteristic of washing assemblies throughout Africa was absent. The proximity of three young crocodiles on the opposite shore did not noticeably worry any of them.

Each morning at seven the primary school children were taken to the edge of the dam for their morning bath: this consisted of the children stripping off and huddling in a compact group, over which the teacher threw several buckets of water. It was his duty to ensure that nobody urinated in, or defecated near, the water. Sadly, swimming in the dam was prohibited, as a means to limit transmission of bilharziasis and Guinea-worm infections. Any person with an open Guinea-worm sore was forbidden to enter the water at all. Bilharziasis is a debilitating disease, the severity of which depends on what Fergus cringingly described as 'the worm load'; but Guinea-worm disease (dracunculiasis) struck me as the more horrible of the two. A long worm can emerge from sites such as the lower leg, the nipple, the end of the tongue, or even the penis. With patience the worm can be wound around a matchstick, taking care not to break it, because to do so risks formation of an abscess. Control of Guinea worm is simple – just boil the drinking water. River-blindness (onchocerciasis), spread by a tiny black fly, was also widespread in the region. Added to repeated attacks of malaria and limited diet, the chances of survival to adulthood were low – many babies died in their first year, others before they were five.

After the initial cutting, there was little for Simbu to do, but still he reported daily with the two pups, which were quick to sense that in my company life was bountiful. Both were smooth-haired pi dogs with a white diamond on the forehead, and a white-tipped tail: the bitch, Fu-Fu, was a ginger-coloured sharp-witted opportunist wary of all humans; but the darker, brindle male, known as Simbu Dog – there being no possessive in pidgin English – was devoted to me and would lie blissfully contented in my lap, legs in the air, while I tickled his pink belly. His proportions were good and he smelled of clean young animal and wood smoke. Jealous of anyone who made rival demands on my attention, he would get between me and the intruder, snapping at his sister if she came too close. The two grew sturdier, thanks to hand-outs from the kitchen, more proof that I was a soft touch where animals were concerned. One of the laboratory assistants begged me to look after his young 'pet' sheep while he went on leave, but it was quite a while before it dawned on me that the animal was being fattened for slaughter, and leaving it in my care was an insurance against theft.

I had a makeshift desk on the terrace, where, with my Olivetti, I typed regular letters to my mother and coped with Fergus's secretarial work. The contract with the Ghana government and the UN stipulated that secretarial help should be provided at all duty stations, but this was seldom honoured, or if there was an efficient secretary, her services would be monopolised by the national counterpart. There were two official typists at Wa, but one was on leave and the other could not type, restricting his talents to clerking. I recall having to produce four copies of a report written for the regional office – I do not know how I did it, because these were the days of carbon copies.

At the outset I had feared loneliness, but soon settled to a routine of food preparation, writing, photography, sewing and resolving minor domestic crises. While we remained at Dorimon the only means of cooking was a Primus stove, so menus were not ambitious. Tomatoes, shallots, peppers and aubergines were never in short supply, nor was cooking oil, so we lived for some weeks exclusively on ratatouille and eggs in one form or another. A whole cow's liver, warm from slaughter, was delivered one morning with the sincere thanks and compliments of a local chief who had benefited from our taxi service. To dispose of this luxury without causing offence posed a real problem, as every activity within the compound would be known in the village by sundown. To feed bits to the dogs would be regarded as outrageous waste; to give large portions to friends and servants might be deemed ungrateful. The cutting-up process was unpleasant and I found myself remembering Fergus's account of a visit to an abattoir during his student days, looking for signs of liver fluke. Adda's return coincided with this gift and I gave bits to him, Da and Simbu, swearing them to a secrecy in which I had little faith, lavish trimmings went to the dogs, and some I claimed to have frozen. Any thought of burial at night was a nonstarter. I would either be discovered in the act or by some mortifying excavation of the site the following day.

Within hours of his appearance, Adda had established a hierarchical pecking order within the compound. Fergus, when on site, was number one; next was me; then Adda usurping Simbu, who was in charge when there was no guest in residence; Simbu reigned over the cowed Da and his wife, whose nominal duties were sweeping in and around the round-house. The only time Da's voice was raised in authority was when a team of compound cutters arrived from Wa and needed surveillance. Even then, Simbu was likely to appear from the village and take over command.

Nearly every day brought some drama, often involving mortality. Much to Adda's satisfaction the nesting house martins, whose droppings adorned the mosquito netting over our bed, were silenced by an unidentified predator after a night of restless chirping. A gun was stolen from a policeman who had carelessly laid it in the ditch while inspecting a headless corpse on the Dorimon–Wa road. There were two murders, and a near skeletal body had been found lying on a mat by the roadside. The drunken driver of an overloaded lorry killed nine of his passengers, all of whom had known he was drunk, but were anxious to get home quickly. Six prisoners awaiting trial died of suffocation in a crowded cell at Wa prison.

By this time we had become reacquainted with Karel and Marta Sin. It was Karel's first assignment outside the Czech Republic and he often consulted Fergus when he had suspicions about the background of cases brought to the hospital. He was learning fast, both at home and at work – so was his wife, who was in charge of paediatric care. In Prague they had lived in a small flat with shared kitchen and bathroom, their only means of transport a Vespa scooter. Now they had a house, servant and their first car, a Volkswagen Beetle. The car had been 'borrowed' by a friend of his steward, who then crashed it hundreds of miles away near Tamale. Reluctantly he sacked his servant, the intermediary, and embarked on the convoluted process of making an insurance claim. He had been called to examine the decapitated corpse found on the Dorimon–Wa road; it was already 'high', flesh remaining only on the hands and upper chest. He thought the pool in which it was half lying had dried up, exposing it to view, and that dogs had decapitated it. We suspected it was a cutlass job, and had been dumped. Nobody seemed unduly upset, and no person had been reported missing. On another occasion a woman with a huge belly swore, 'No not pregnant – last menstruation two months ago'; she was suffering intense pain, no heartbeat could be heard and the swelling was lopsided, so he decided to operate – giving a heavy anaesthetic. The incision revealed a full-term child, which survived the anaesthesia, but only just. Karel was furious, suspecting, as we did, that the woman had wanted an abortion.

Few callers disturbed my morning 'office' sessions, which, in any case, would become unbearably hot by ten, forcing my retreat to the shade inside the house. Dr Korabiewicz would interrupt a visit to the village to call for coffee and a chat: his usual greeting, a kiss sweeping from wrist to shoulder, was hard to receive with poise – particularly as I almost always wore an unflattering one-piece 'playsuit', combining shirt and shorts, flipflops and, by this time, no bra because I was a martyr to prickly heat. He made routine calls to some of the outlying huts, but foremost in his mind will have been to cajole some ancient artefact out of the chief: he was known to pay high prices, and some found their way to private collections or as museum exhibits in Warsaw. His wife had been known to countermand his advice and to tell his patients to halve the dose that he had prescribed for them. Of the pair, she commanded greater respect.

Nights became more oppressive, forcing us to sleep outside, but often gusts of wind, combined with distant thunder claps and forked lightning, indicated an imminent violent storm. Semi-awake, we would drag the camp beds inside, only to take them out again when the lightning had subsided and no rain had fallen. When that happened, the heat became almost unbearable. For our evening meal Fergus had taken to wearing a fetching pair of blue mesh underpants, while I wore one of my playsuits with gold brocade ankle boots because I had been unable to find any mosquito boots in Belfast – an outfit reminiscent of a Principal Boy in one of Jimmy O'Dea's pantomimes. Wearing boots was essential – I remember a painfully swollen insect bite on one ankle came to the attention of a field dresser whose job it was to carry out minor first-aid duties, who insisted on treating it with his 'secret' tribal tincture – 'We make a paste of squirrels' entrails or sometimes we use donkey dung'. All this with a straight face – he genuinely believed in its efficacy.

We remained at Dorimon until the rains had turned parts of the road into a morass. Work on the house in Wa was still not finished, but the risk of being cut off by flash flooding was too great. We had been happy in the round-house, and left with regret. We were also fond of Simbu Dog, who worshipped us, although he obediently trotted off with Simbu at the end of the day. We discussed the possibility of buying him for the going price of five shillings, but were deterred by several factors, chief of which was the amount of travel we undertook, and what to do with him when next we returned to Europe. There was also an element of not wanting to wound Simbu's pride. Having a salaried job, some sheep and goats, as well as two fine dogs, although, unhappily, no satisfactory wife, made him a man of substance in the village. Reflecting proudly on the growth of the pups, he voiced his intention to operate on Simbu Dog who had only one testicle: 'I will take the other one, then he get big and no go bush and get chopped by they Lobis.' Fergus, who had not long before heard agonised yelping coming from the village, where a small crowd was gathered around a bucket in which a dog was immersed, did his best to discourage such unprofessional intervention, threatening in jest to do the same to Simbu. He even extracted a promise that nothing would be done without employing the services of the vet at Wa, for which he would pay. We went back twice during September and October to collect vegetables from a small patch of garden, by then almost flooded, and to pick some grapefruit, which were rare in the north. Simbu Dog was overjoyed to see us, appearing in rude health, but I had a premonition that Simbu would not honour his promise.

I consulted a Czech obstetrician at Kumasi hospital during August 1962: he put on a surgical glove and did an internal examination, exclaiming, 'Oh, here it is' – a confirmation that I was at last pregnant. Then he wrote a letter to one of the leading obstetricians in Belfast, advising 'bringing forth' in the UK: not so much from the viewpoint of the mother as that of the child.

The regional office chose this time to defer decisions on almost all aspects of Fergus's project, implying that unless the Ghana government approved and signed a five-year plan of operations by the end of the year, he might well be out of a job. In the meantime, they proposed that he should undertake short-term surveys in neighbouring Ivory Coast, Togo and Dahomey. Although we did not know it, this stalemate was just the beginning of years of uncertainty about where and when the next assignment might be. Fergus considered returning to an academic career, but at that time there were few openings for biologists specialised in tropical parasitology. There were opportunities in Canada and the US, but I was prejudiced against the North American lifestyle. He was offered an interesting, but ill-paid job in Copenhagen, but we both had reservations about Denmark being the best country in which to spend the early years of raising a family, principally because of its notoriously difficult language. We hoped that ultimately a suitable vacancy would arise at the headquarters office in Geneva, although the system of 'geographical distribution' strictly limited the number of British appointees.

The kitchen in the old German house had been cleaned and painted, the rotten draining boards and sagging shelving replaced, and a capacious refrigerator had been supplied, although it proved to be just as temperamental as all the others. A new stove had been delivered, so after months of cooking on a Primus, I could at last produce a decent meal. The cockroach population flourished as before, and a flock of persistent hens was always in or around the kitchen, the door of which had to be left open much of the time to allow some circulation of air.

All our clothing was faded and threadbare, and while replacement shirts and shorts could be found or made for Fergus, my problems were more complex. Weighing heavily on my mind was the thought of what I would wear in December when we would return to 'civilisation'. I was still no more than a bit thick in the middle, although the baby began to kick during the week of our move. It had been decided to delay going to Accra until my departure was imminent because a curfew had been imposed between the hours of 6 p.m. and 6 a.m. and machine guns were everywhere, involving more police and military stops and inspections than usual. I would need a dress for any functions we might have to attend. At one of the Lebanese stores I bought a length of attractive material that looked like shot silk but was 100 per cent synthetic; a subtle dove's-breast pinkish brown, patterned with large, hyacinth-blue abstract flowers. It was fiendish to handle, slippery with a tendency to gather, and dissolved into spun sugar if the iron was too hot. However, teamed with the metallic winkle-pickers, it looked quite elegant and saw me through dinner at the Ambassador Hotel, some private parties and a reception at the University of Ghana, held by the vice-chancellor, Conor Cruise O'Brien and his new wife, Maire. We were invited to meet Dr Alan Nunn May, the English physicist and convicted Soviet spy who, nine years after release from prison, held a post as research professor in physics at the university, and his Austrian wife. Both were good company and easy to get on with, though there were awkward moments of constraint when some topic provoked an evasive response. We suspected he was still 'travelling' and part of a group then establishing a network throughout Ghana.

As my pregnancy progressed I bought a length of dark grey fine wool men's suiting and, crawling around on the cement, cut out and tailored a two-piece maternity suit, composed of pencil slim skirt with an obligatory U cut out of the front, and a three-quarter-length top. Worn with one of the first Khrushchev-style black fur hats bought at Harrods in Knightsbridge, a flame-coloured silk scarf, the Swiss Bally shoes and crocodile handbag, I felt I could still compete in the fashion stakes.

The three months before I flew back to Northern Ireland were packed with incident and I was also very ill with what was first thought to be another attack of malaria, but was subsequently agreed to have been blackwater fever. At one point my temperature rose to 103 and I was drifting in and out of consciousness, vaguely aware that the Kofi brothers were praying nearby. I vomited everything, including water, but Karel gave me an intramuscular injection, which lowered the fever, and I made a gradual recovery thereafter. Fergus was distraught, although Karel assured him that the 'parasite' would not be harmed. The same month he read in the *Observer* that his best friend, who had worked on tsetse control in Southern Rhodesia (now Zimbabwe), had died in a car accident near Gatwick on the first day of a long anticipated home leave; his wife and three children – one only two months old – had survived, but the eldest one lost a kidney.

Late in October Fergus succumbed to another hard-luck story: a child of thirteen looking for work told a pathetic and convincing tale of how he had left his village twenty miles away because, 'My father and mother both die and I have only sisters who cannot feed me. The people in my village are very bad.' He had such a frank and open countenance that even Adda was taken in, to the extent of allowing him to sleep in his quarters. He did a little daily grass-cutting in return for chop money, and of course I dished out drinks of milk and bananas to supplement his meagre diet. Part of the tale was that there was an uncle who might look after him, but that a new school uniform was required if he was to return to school, and the uncle could not afford it. Fergus made unfruitful enquiries, and cross-questioned the child, who looked hurt at the suggestion he might be lying. In the end it was agreed that we should buy the uniform in return for small services until term began. Then one morning a 'nephew' of Adda's spotted the boy and asked what he was doing on our premises, as he had absconded from school some months ago, taking with him the £4 his father (alive) had given him to buy the uniform and had apparently been living on this ever since. It transpired that almost all had been lies. Adda found one of our coffee spoons in his box, while another had already disappeared – presumably sold. He was escorted down to the MFU office and further grilled before being put in the care of the social welfare officer until his father should come and claim him. Tears came, and Fergus felt a brute, until Francis Kofi told him the boy had been loudly complaining that Fergus had promised him thirty shillings and had failed to pay up. So that was yet another 'last time' we were going to fall for a hard-luck story.

I stayed with my mother during December, January, and into February. We had more respect for each other by this time, and I enjoyed driving around the Ards peninsula with her, pausing near Mount Stewart House to watch a huge flock of wheeling lapwings and trying to interest her in watching the birdlife of Strangford Lough. In the evenings we watched the television I had introduced, against considerable resistance, to my mother's living room; she soon became an addict, and together we watched *That Was The Week That Was* and episodes of *Z Cars*, during one of which I went into labour. Meanwhile, Fergus was making surveys in Gabon, Cameroon and the Congo. A visit to Geneva, to discuss his future with WHO, was planned for early February, and it was hoped he would be in Northern Ireland for the birth.

11
Generation

My mother drove me to hospital during one of the heaviest snowfalls on record, and by this time I knew that Fergus would not be present for the birth. He was in Geneva attending meetings of the Bilharziasis Advisory Team, being briefed on what was planned for the next three years. Only on admission did it fully strike me how bizarre our situation was. The hospital staff did not make it any easier, making insensitive remarks about how much I must miss my husband, and I suspected a few of them doubted his existence. The contractions abated, so it was decided to give me an enema; while I was sitting on a commode waiting for the results, Matron made her routine visit to enquire how frequent the contractions were, but they had ceased. The next day Mr Boyd, my obstetrician, interrupted lunch to tell me that he intended to induce the birth – a procedure of which I had not heard – and did so on the spot, remarking brightly as he replaced the tray that I could now get on with my meal.

When the contractions began again, a new nurse resembling the infamous Irma Grese in appearance and manner remarked that were she in my place, she would refuse pain relief so as not to miss any part of the beautiful experience. Rapid riposte has never been my forte, but the urge to retort that she was unlikely to find herself so was strong. I took the pethidine. In the theatre Mr Boyd joined the chorus of exhortations to push harder, and soon the beautiful experience changed to a blurred image of forceps being brandished before oblivion took over. I woke slowly, feeling sore all over, then remembered where I was, and why. A cot beside the bed contained a tightly swaddled bundle, at one end of which was a small head. Glad that nobody was in the room, I lifted the bundle and undid the wrapping in a frenzy to confirm that the right number of legs, hands, feet and digits were present. The baby's face was pretty, not squashed and wrinkly, a proof that I had not, as had been implied, got my dates wrong: Katharine Ruth Siobhan was born, three weeks late, at five thirty in the evening of St Valentine's Day, 1963.

Next morning Matron swept in, accompanied by the breast-feeding expert, and a discussion ensued about whether or not I should attempt to do so, taking into account the small size of my breasts (the Czech doctor in Kumasi had assured me that 'many European women are like this, but still manage to breast-feed'), and the fact that a segment of the left one was missing where a benign tumour had been removed in 1958. In the event, the baby persistently turned her head away from the breast, and was persuaded only with great difficulty to suck at all. On enquiring why I was bruised and sore all over, the nurses said that, under the influence of pethidine, I had become violent. Fergus telephoned from Geneva, sounding relieved and affectionate, adding that he would celebrate at a dinner hosted by Dr Ansari's secretary that evening. The green-eyed monster struck, leaving me feeling very much alone.

The next day my mother, Aunt Rosemary and San came to visit, soon to be joined by some of Fergus's relatives with whom they had little in common, apart from pleasure in the arrival of a new member of the family. A wrong note was struck when Fergus's sister remarked on the yellowish tinge of the baby's complexion, but otherwise conversation was limited to banalities, and I was relieved when they had all gone. I had feared I might be devoid of maternal instincts, like captive apes whose infants have to be removed in the interests of their survival, but happily my fears were unfounded, so six weeks later, when Fergus first met his daughter, I was coping well.

My mother enjoyed the new baby, involving herself with it in a way she had been denied during my own early months. So competent and happy was she, it was agreed to leave Katharine in her care while Fergus and I spent a few days at Greencastle on the Inishowen peninsula. The weather was superb, the sandy beaches blinding white; the sea reminded us of Cephalonia, and choughs tumbled around the ruins of early Norman coastal defences. We explored what remained of the old Black and Tans barracks on Dunaff Head, where my mother, Rosemary, Johnny and I had taken shelter many years before, and we walked on the springy cliff-top turf, pausing from time to time to make love in some secluded hollow.

In all the literature I had devoured on the topic of pregnancy, childbirth and the recovery therefrom, I never came across a reference to the fact that it is all too easy to conceive soon after giving birth, even before the resumption of monthly periods. Shortly before Fergus had to return to Ghana, we flew to London for a weekend break. While we were there, I realised another child was due. This time I would not be feeble 'like most European wives', and would bring forth in Ghana rather than return to Northern Ireland. Despite my mother's unfortunate experience, her philosophy on marriage, based on acute observation of her school contemporaries, was surprisingly sound. Her comments were pithy: 'She's really let herself go since the birth of that child – concentrates far too much on it – he feels left out, and if she's not careful, he'll find solace elsewhere – always had a wandering eye.' I knew that the strength of my relationship with Fergus would be fundamental to the happiness of any children we might have, and that nurturing it should take priority, but it took courage to break the news of the indecent interval to my mother.

An ill-conceived impulse led me to get in touch with my old friend Celia, who was by then mother of five children, and living in an isolated mansion in the Ligoniel area of Belfast not far from the Ardoyne estate, later to become infamous during the Troubles. The house, a solid Edwardian one in nearly an acre of tastefully planted grounds, would in today's parlance have failed the location-location-location test. A granny flat had been added to accommodate Celia's mother, who continued to invade their privacy and freely criticise their boozy lifestyle of dinner and cocktail parties. The details gushed from poor Celia as she led the way to a sitting room stuffed with floral cretonne-covered sofas and capacious armchairs. She drew my attention to the fine quality of the wood and plasterwork, in contrast to that of the new red-brick executive style villa at Cultra in which they had begun married life fifteen years earlier. Their only son, a spindly five-year-old with red hair, freckles and an eye patch, regarded Katharine and me with ill-concealed suspicion, before resuming his Lego project. He brightened momentarily on the return of his sister, whose name eludes me, from primary school; without an embrace, Celia told the child to go and have a wash before joining us for tea, as she looked a grubby mess in that dreadful uniform. The older sisters, rejoicing in the names of Daphne, Wendy and Dymphna, were at boarding school. I was godmother to Daphne – or was it Wendy? Ignorant of what an honour it was, I had performed no useful function since attending the christening ceremony some fourteen years earlier.

A maid came with a tray on which were a silver tea service, delicate bone china cups and saucers, sandwiches, scones and fruit cake, as well as soft drinks for the children, who were listless apart from showing perfunctory interest in Katharine when she showed signs of waking. Afterwards, Celia took me on a tour of the ground floor, pointing out further fine details. In the kitchen she paused to offer me a drink, which I declined; only when she helped herself to a generous gin and tonic, did I realise she was quite drunk. Her mother had not appeared, which disappointed me, as she had been kind when we were children. Apparently sharp words had been exchanged about the previous night's party, at which much booze had been consumed, and they had not spoken since. In defence, Celia reiterated her old mantra: 'What's the harm in a little drink, if it makes the party go?' All the signs of solitary drinking were there, but it was another fifteen years before I identified with them. I departed with relief, pondering on what we had ever had in common apart from going to the same school. My impulse to meet again had probably been prompted by a wish to display our firstborn, and a need to demonstrate how happily I had emerged from a decade of social ostracism.

In the months preceding Katharine's birth I found two adjacent building plots at Craigavad, on the southern shore of Belfast Lough: they had an unimpeded view that stretched from Cave Hill to Knockagh summit and war memorial, below which was my grandparents' house, and further to Carrickfergus Castle and Larne. An architect was engaged to supervise the building of a flat-roofed bungalow for us, and my mother, who also designed her own house, took the adjacent plot, though dubious about living next to what she called a flat-roofed 'monstrosity'. My riposte was that considering the estate – for that is what it was – abounded with individual expressions of bad taste, one more would not make much difference.

That August, for the first time, I flew with a baby from Belfast to Heathrow; the plane was fully booked, so Katharine had to sit on my knee throughout the flight. She dispensed smiles all round, and it was fortunate we had a forbearing neighbour who did not flinch even when a sharp upper-cut landed our meal tray on the floor. Luckily no liquid spilled, but at floor level I could see a river of rose-hip syrup snaking its way down the centre aisle from the bag which contained disposable nappies, Kleenex, and my own toiletries. The cabin crew were very helpful, reporting broken glass in the bag, that it would be a job cleaning up the mess at Heathrow, and wasn't it lucky that our flight to Accra did not leave until nearly midnight. Understatement of the day: the syrup had reached my jewel-case, and there were sticky areas in the carry-cot; Katharine threw a tantrum in the baby changing room, where the cleaning-up operation had been protracted. She fell asleep as we were boarding the plane, with the engines at full throttle. There were probably no more than forty other passengers, so I was able to spread our belongings over several seats. Those were the days – the stewardesses were solicitous, nothing was too much trouble, and travelling with a baby ensured preferential treatment. I slept fitfully in an upright position, while Katharine, at floor level, despite icy air-conditioning, slept right through. Fergus and the WHO representative, who later facilitated us through customs, were there to meet us, and a UN driver drove us straight to a luxurious guesthouse owned by the West African Buildings Research Institute.

Fergus was fortunate to have left Brazzaville just a few days before violent fighting broke out in the town, but he had imported a filthy cold, which I caught, then the baby, though she suffered only a minor version. Spock was, and remained, my mentor; he wrote: 'baby seldom develops a severe cold during the first year'. What she did develop, however, was prickly heat a mere two days after we landed.

Accra in August was quite pleasant, with an ambient temperature below 80 degrees Fahrenheit, and overcast skies shielding the sun's glare. We took Katharine to one of the less popular beaches where the shore was rocky and bathing unsafe, but all beaches attracted gangs of accomplished boy thieves who flitted around the area between the palm trees and where cars were parked, waiting for any unattended item or unlocked car boot. I protected the baby too much, and myself not enough, so that my back got badly burned. Fergus, never a fan of beaches, and hating sand in the sandwiches, stayed in the shade of a palm tree, reading. His dislike was well founded, having twice had to rescue a child floating out to sea on an inflatable raft, while its inattentive parents sipped chilled drinks.

Our stay was protracted because of the many small things needing attention: car servicing, domestic and laboratory stores for Wa, identifying and claiming packing cases before arranging transport for them, getting new driving licences. I found the shopping excursions with an infant more complicated, although the Ghanaian girls were always happy to carry a white baby around. Twice we took her to lunch at the Ambassador Hotel and were not disgraced; at six months she was sitting steadily, and was transfixed by the collection of tropical birds, especially the South American macaws. Dinner parties were different: there would be no problem until we returned to the guesthouse, when she would wake and be lively and sociable into the small hours.

Katharine now saw more black faces than white, and unfazed by this, continued to dispense her usual charm to anyone who greeted us. Adda was back, although his duties were light because the guesthouse had a resident caretaker. His nine-year-old son, Yambah, was now with him, the child having travelled, with a friend of the same age, from Navrongo to find his father. A message had come from the nearby army camp saying that his son was there and please collect him. Yambah, when he came to greet me, was wearing a dirty dressing on his right leg to protect a wound, where 'a stone have hit it one month ago'. The bandages concealed an ulcer, like a miniature volcanic crater, provoking me to give off in true Northern Irish style, admonishing both father and son, and emphasising that gangrenous limbs are often amputated as a result of such neglect. 'Oh yes, we have seen in the north,' Adda said. Needless to say, an ulterior plan lay behind the visit. A list was produced of items to be purchased before admission to the Catholic Mission secondary school at Navrongo would be sanctioned, and financial assistance over and above Adda's monthly wage was expected. Fergus muttered a bit about being taken for granted, but coughed up the necessary amount, which was termed a loan, but was, in effect, a subsidy. Everybody knew this, but 'face' was saved.

It was rumoured that all the ferries in the north were flooded, but despite this news, a lorry, loaded with Adda, the driver, two field assistants and a heap of wooden crates, suitcases and general stores, left Accra at five one morning in torrential rain on the first stage of the drive that was routed via Kumasi and Kintampo to Wa. We followed in our own vehicle, but the addition of a baby delayed our start till nearly nine – quite good going really.

Adda's information about the ferries had been unduly alarmist, although, after overnight stops at Kumasi and Kintampo, we were forced to take the long route via Damongo because the Bamboi ferry was out of action. At the Buipe ferry the water was higher than we had ever seen it. Katharine behaved well, sitting in her cot on the bonnet of the car while we waited in line for our turn to board, a novelty for rural people who saw few European children, and some shyly touched her. We reached Wa before dusk, much relieved to find that Adda had worked hard to make the house comfortable – even hot water and ice cubes were available.

Early in September Fergus got a wire from Dr Ansari, proposing a one-day visit to Wa in mid-October: clearly he had not looked at the map, as he planned to fly from Geneva, land in Tamale at eleven in the morning, be driven to Wa the same day, spend the next day touring the project area, and on the third take the daily flight – which left early in the day – from Tamale back to Accra. No matter how the visit was scheduled, it would involve at least 800 miles on the road for Fergus. This was the first of many proposals showing how distanced some headquarters staff were from the reality of life in the field. Another wire announced an impending visit by the Bilharziasis Advisory Team.

Much progress had been made, thanks to Fergus's persuasive powers, on housing for junior as well as senior staff, as well as a rest-house for overnight visitors. The bungalow intended for us was nearing completion: it would be an improvement on the one we had at Kintampo, having three bedrooms and vinyl flooring throughout. There were even built-in cupboards, fans hung from the ceilings, and it was wired for electricity. This was a sore point, as we were to spend two dry seasons staring at motionless fans, before the generator went into action just before we left for the last time in 1965.

I loved having congenial visitors, though only a few of these realised how difficult it was to provide a succession of palatable meals. If they were working at the laboratory, I had to prepare breakfast, lunch and dinner; if the day was to be spent in the field, a packed lunch would have to be prepared. Some said: 'Don't go to any bother, just cheese and crackers will do' – the only cheese we saw was tinned and had a bland rubbery consistency, crackers did not crack for long in the rainy season, and the crumbs were a magnet for ants. My home-made bread was variable, and it was a while before I learned how to judge the right amount of yeast, so that the result was neither dense and heavy, nor full of large holes (not the best for sandwich production). Everything, chilled cans of juice included, went into a large red plastic insulated box we had been lucky enough to find in the UTC store in Accra. Thermoses of iced tea were always popular, but the casualty rate was high, and replacements obtainable only at Tamale or Kumasi.

We moved from the old German house to the new bungalow in early September. The Kofi brothers voiced their approval thus – Daniel: 'Oh Madam, it is very splendid'; Francis: 'As befits your status.' Five months only remained before we would have to leave for the Swiss Mission Hospital at Agogo, near Kumasi, for the birth of the new baby, and they seemed to pass quickly. On National Founder's Day, 20 September, there was intense activity on the football ground, and a bunting-draped pavilion had been erected for the district commissioner and other dignitaries. An arch proclaiming 'Freedom & Justice' went up, too, and the police band played a repertoire of old colonial tunes, 'A Hunting We Will Go' among them. I made a token appearance at eight in the morning but departed to attend to the baby, leaving Fergus to survive until ten thirty on the dais seated next to the district commissioner. The platform, while lavishly decorated, provided no shade, and faced directly into the sun. The parade consisted of government officers in MFU Land Rovers, a contingent from Agriculture and Pest Control, the sanitary squad (bucket collectors), a few heavily caparisoned horses, and finally some tribal dancers twirling giant gold-fringed umbrellas.

Dr Ansari's visit was postponed indefinitely, but the bilharziasis team, one American, one Albanian and one Briton, were the first visitors to occupy the new rest-house. They made a congenial trio, who regaled us with gobbets of gossip from the incestuous world of biological research. Our duty-free liquor allowance dwindled rapidly, and the evening meal always concluded with coffee (local beans laboriously roasted and ground by me) and liqueurs. Because of my pregnancy, I did not drink alcohol, but do not recall feeling in any way deprived. During this period, Fergus made his first serious efforts to stop smoking: in moments of frustration, when delayed yet again at a ferry crossing, there would be outbursts on the lines of 'I've had enough of this bloody country, its total lack of organisation and may its inhabitants roast in hell' – not politically correct, but after all, his association dated back to 1952, and it was symptomatic of his growing disillusionment with life in newly independent Africa. He began to negotiate for one year's leave to study for a master's degree in public health and hygiene in Boston.

The novelty of a white baby ensured that our house was never short of visitors, and Katharine loved their company. Yambah helped with feeding her when she was in a highchair messing around with solids, and neighbouring children battled for the privilege of pushing her around the compound in an antiquated baby carriage I bought second-hand in Kumasi. She adored Mousa Moshi, who was employed to keep the compound tidy and snake-free and to water any wilting plants. He could not bear to hear her crying, and carried her around while hosing the vegetables. Adda was less indulgent, resenting the extra work involved in boiling the daily load of nappies, which I insisted should not be mixed with the general wash. I sensed that our quarterly spat was approaching, but knew he would behave irreproachably until Yambah was fully equipped for school, and cash for his lorry fare back to Navrongo ensured.

Fewer Europeans were stationed at Wa than at Kintampo. The Russian geological team kept very much to themselves, although always courteous when encountered at the market. We were sorry for them because it was known they were forbidden to fraternise with other expatriates and had to report at two-month intervals to a senior party member in Tamale. American missionaries, with sallow, unhealthy-looking children, also observed exclusivity. The White Fathers, however, some of whom were stationed in places much smaller than Wa, were always grateful for hospitality, and provided useful, if hair-raising, information about local affairs. I felt humble in their presence, admiring their resourcefulness and cheerful optimism in the face of repeated disappointments. One Irish priest, whose roots were near Dundalk, on the border between the Republic of Ireland and Northern Ireland, had not been home for seven years. He came to mind every time we descended through low cloud to the lush green patchwork of small fields surrounding Lough Neagh and Belfast airport, and I was ashamed of ever having complained about bush conditions.

When I was six months pregnant, our only medical officer went on home leave. Katharine, who had just begun to walk, was pottering around while I worked on another maternity tent. Suddenly she began to scream and was inconsolable for a few minutes. My first thought was that she must have swallowed a pin, although I was scrupulously careful to keep them out of reach. By the time Fergus returned to the house for a lunch break, there had been two more similar outbursts, so he said, 'Pack everything at once, we'll have to take her to Jirapah Mission Hospital if we can get through.' The sky was steel-blue with fast-moving clouds, we could smell rain, and sixty miles of tortuous dirt track lay between Wa and Jirapah. The screaming fits had become more frequent, it was almost dark, and large raindrops were falling as we drew into the hospital compound. We were met by a surprised medical team, which did not wait for the results of a blood test, but took instant action on the assumption that it was malaria. In those days many doctors disapproved of such action, only to have patients die as a result. Within twelve hours it was evident the diagnosis was correct and Katharine, limp and exhausted, began to rally, and two days later we returned to Wa. Over the next few weeks there were violent electric storms, through which the baby slept soundly, while we cowered under the bedclothes, regretting that no lightning conductor had been fixed to the roof. In recent years several tragedies in the region had been recorded where the corrugated roof of a primary school had attracted a direct strike.

We now had to plan the trip to the Swiss Mission Hospital at Agogo, which had agreed to accommodate us before, during and after, the birth of our next child. Time taken away from his duty station, if it were not to be perceived as 'desertion of post', would have to coincide with discussions with Ministry of Health representatives, and allow for field surveys to be conducted in the area. Accurate estimation of the birth date was critical, as I did not want to waste days waiting to go into labour, nor did I want to leave it so late that Fergus risked being forced into the role of roadside midwife. Friends tended to levity, insisting the only requisites were a sharp knife and a bottle of brandy to sterilise the knife: after cutting the cord, drink the remainder, then drive to the nearest hospital.

In mid-November we made another trip to Accra, during which Fergus met UN and Ministry of Health officials, and managed to trace a wooden crate from Northern Ireland, which contained, among heavier articles, a supply of towels, nappies, and the ubiquitous Wettex cloths. (In the end it did reach Wa, having been sent to Tamale, where it had lain unclaimed for several months.) I enjoyed these restful days at the West African Building Research Institute guesthouse, spending mornings on the veranda with the baby, trying to tame the large blue and orange lizards that abounded in the Achimota area: we used cornflakes as bait, and they came nearer by the day. A variety of butterflies and birds, such as pied crows and glossy starlings were always around to keep Katharine entertained. Another stinking cold struck, again affecting the baby minimally, but I took so many codeine tablets that I vomited blood, to Fergus's horror. It was during this stay that we heard the news of President Kennedy's assassination on the BBC World Service.

In the end it was decided that Fergus would deposit me and Katharine at the hospital, before going to Accra to meet his cousin Dorothy, who had agreed to help us for a few weeks after the birth. Shortly before we reached Agogo, Fergus had braked to avoid an errant goat, resulting in the baby's head hitting the steering wheel. Seat belts were not in use in those days, so Katharine spent long journeys asleep in her carry-cot on top of a pile of luggage in the rear, if awake on my knee, or when showing signs of boredom, on the driver's knee. We were greeted warmly, although I detected unspoken censure when the staff saw the egg-like swelling on Katharine's forehead, and the fact that she wore no clothes other than nappy pants.

The verandas of the two rooms we had been allocated overlooked a garden, which merged into nearby forest. Bougainvillea bushes, canna lilies, flame trees, oleander and zinnias bloomed against a backcloth of royal palms, amongst which were some delicate conifers, like those on Japanese wood-block prints. Egrets settled to roost there every evening and a faint breeze was almost always detectable. The noise of squabbling vervet monkeys, the occasional bloodcurdling scream, and unidentifiable cackles came from the forest, while fruit bats swirled overhead as dusk turned to night.

We joined the long communal table for the evening meal, which began with grace being said by the house mother. It was clear that punctuality was expected – any latecomer sat down in an atmosphere of silent disapproval. Conversation, for the most part, was in Swiss-German, which, despite having a rudimentary knowledge of German, I found incomprehensible. None of the women, apart from visiting patients, wore any make-up, and though the rule of changing for dinner was observed, the dresses worn reminded me of the immediate post-war era: limp floral prints with heart-shaped necklines and sparsely gathered skirts, frumpy footwear, even, in one case, boots with ankle socks. I saw no jewellery other than a crucifix, and almost all wore their hair screwed into a tight bun. Herr Doktor was monosyllabic and confined any exchange to other medical officers near the head of the table. It was expected that older children would be fed earlier, then left in the charge of an ayah, while the adults ate at the big table. Adda was accommodated in the servants' quarters, where the hospital expected him to take care of our laundry: not among Katharine's favourites, he was never called upon to baby-sit.

Fergus departed the next day to meet Dorothy at Accra airport, while I counted the hours until their arrival two days later. Despite the fact that we had adjacent rooms – one for Dorothy – and the run of adjacent verandas, it was difficult to prevent the baby straying into the corridor and other patients' rooms. The fridge we used was communal, a disadvantage when we wanted, after the birth, to prepare celebratory cocktails of gin, Cinzano, Dubonnet or Campari. No notice prohibited the consumption of alcohol, but we felt it would be regarded with disapproval. I remember the furtive way I sneaked ice cubes for sundowners, and the dread that a chilling bottle might be spotted by the house mother.

While Fergus was away, a Belgian doctor inoculated Katharine for smallpox. When I asked him to do it in an unobtrusive place, he argued that it was always better on the upper arm, and made two long scratches with a scalpel, rather than the half-inch one recommended. For mass schemes conducted by MFUs in primary schools, Francis Kofi used a multiple punch; afterwards, we regretted not having asked him to immunise Katharine, who had first been done while under six months old, when antibodies may not be formed. She had a serious reaction to both scrapes, running a temperature over 103, and I was affronted by a Dutch paediatrician, who in an offhand tone said, 'Oh, just put some talcum powder on the rash.' When I persisted, she reluctantly prescribed some medication to ensure the exhausted child slept soundly.

Katharine was happy to see her favourite Irish aunt, and Dorothy, having been educated at a Masonic school, quickly adapted to the spartan regime. On the predicted day – 25 February 1964 – I went into labour at three thirty in the afternoon and Mary was born, 'naturally', two hours later. Fergus stayed with me until we were in agreement that the fashionable trend for fathers to be present was neither natural nor helpful, so with relief, he retired from the increasingly messy scene, to join Dorothy who was trying to interest Katharine in a tin of Heinz Beans and Ham. Unlike my mother, who claimed to have given birth noiselessly, I screamed, recalling a friend describing the 'beautiful experience' as like shitting a grapefruit. I hyperventilated, but knew the hospital's policy of no pain relief was well founded when exhortations to push harder were superfluous, and the baby's head was already showing. Within minutes a nurse held aloft something which Fergus subsequently likened to a skinned rabbit, pronouncing, 'You have another beautiful daughter.' (Francis Kofi, that master of well-meaning tactlessness, later said to Fergus: 'Oh, sorry, doctor, but the next will be a male, and after all, girls are more serviceable.') Delivery had been so rapid there was considerable tearing, so I was taken to another room to await the arrival of Herr Doktor, who would stitch me up. I was left, feet strung aloft, an adjustable lamp directed on the damaged parts, with the assurance that he would be along when he had finished his dinner, and would I like a cup of tea in the meantime?

That night Fergus and Dorothy celebrated on the veranda, while Katharine slept fitfully because of the smallpox reaction. I slept scarcely at all, hearing the distant wailing of the new infant, although the nurses assured me she was quite all right. On the second night, when everyone was asleep, I got painfully out of bed to search the rooms for the crying baby: I found her, plainly in need of maternal solace, in a small room near the kitchen. In retrospect I realise that I was distressed by not having been allowed to bond with the baby after delivery, and incapable of controlling my emotions. The house mother found me trying to soothe the baby and told me, sharply, to return to bed. I rounded on her, using four-letter words to the effect that the hospital's rules were inhumane, and calculated to drive mothers insane. For the first time in my life I was hysterical. Next morning the paediatrician implied that I was a neurotic mother.

Fergus, who was conducting field trials in the neighbourhood, was equally distressed, muttering imprecations about typical continental insensitivity and the arrogance of the medical profession in general. A breast-feeding routine had been established despite initial setbacks, and Katharine slowly returned to her normal cheerful self. Leaving Dorothy in charge of both infants, Fergus and I went to Kumasi to amass supplies, which were to go ahead of us under Adda's supervision in the Land Rover. But back at Agogo we found Dorothy unwell and in great pain. Despite a grumbling hernia, her doctor had pronounced her fit to undertake the trip. Examination the next morning revealed a strangulated and inflamed hernia needing urgent surgery. All things considered, we were in the right place – how much worse it would have been in Wa.

The two months of Dorothy's stay at Wa, during which she made a rapid recovery, were remarkable – after 'small' rains, the climate reverted to extreme heat and harmattan conditions during the days, but without the cool nights which mostly accompany that wind. Then there was the saga of the termite nest in her bedroom: we thought she was being neurotic – and said so – complaining about 'things' crawling around and over her at night, until I opened the bottom drawer of a built-in unit and a lava flow poured out: thousands of termites, big ones, little ones, winged ones, some carrying unhatched eggs and empty egg capsules. Quickly they spread in all directions, so I grabbed the spray and attacked, while Dorothy and Katharine watched frozen in horror. I hated destroying such a sophisticated community: the insecticide was lethal, but many continued to twitch in a futile effort to escape the mass; later we found straggling survivors all over the house. Apologies were due to Dorothy, for whom more traumatic experiences were to come.

Fergus was summoned to Tamale to collect two WHO consultants and bring them to Wa for three days, where, in addition to assessing the Bilharzia Research Project, they were to meet other experts working locally in the field of river-blindness. Both were German and one was tolerable, the other a complacent chauvinist with a tendency to monopolise all discussion. During intervals between infant-feeding and bottom-wiping, Dorothy and I slaved to prepare a succession of varied meals, including dinner on three nights; after our day's toil, our repartee was not sparkling, but that will not have been noticed as long as the *hausfrauen* came up trumps with the food. When they left, admittedly amid profuse thanks and hand-kissing, with Fergus at the wheel, in lieu of an MFU driver, we subsided, freed from drudgery, with cups of strong coffee laced with vodka.

Nights were interrupted by one or other infant, frequently both, and such was my fatigue that one night Fergus and Dorothy implored me to go to bed early. Having fallen into a deep sleep by eight thirty, I was woken at eleven by Fergus going outside to investigate a suspicious noise. He found a shrew trying to eat a toad, which had blown itself up to an unswallowable size. Having managed to separate them, he was soon asleep again, leaving me wide awake. Next came a storm, accompanied by what sounded like giant hailstones striking the roof, so the windows had to be closed, babies tucked up, and a drink fetched from the kitchen, where, groping around in the dark, I stepped on a damp Wettex cloth, causing an adrenalin rush until I saw what it was. Mary woke at four in the morning for a feed, then peace till six thirty, when tea was brought in by Adda.

When Dorothy and Fergus departed for Kintampo, I waved

them off with mixed feelings. Her stay had been invaluable and we would miss her, but now I was strong enough to cope with two infants, although apprehensive in the knowledge that Karel was still on leave, and I would be on my own for almost a week. At dusk an overloaded Volkswagen driven by a female missionary appeared with a white-faced Dorothy who had spent most of the day roasting in the car, by the roadside, no more than sixty miles from Wa. There had been three punctures, two ruined inner tubes and one shredded tyre. Fergus left her to experience what it is like to be alone in the bush, the temperature mounting as the day advances, silence broken only by the call of a distant bulbul, or a rodent scuttling for cover. He walked some miles to the last village they had passed, where the family of one of his assistants lived, and an urgent message was sent for the MFU mechanic, before he got a lift back to the marooned car. Dorothy later confessed to never having been so scared in her life. She saw only one person – a scowling man who had looked into the car but made no greeting, before melting into the scrub, cutlass in hand. The fortuitous appearance of the missionary ensured Dorothy's return to Wa, while Fergus remained until the Land Rover came to tow the car back to the workshop. He arrived home at two in the morning. Dorothy eventually got away, driven to Accra by Martin Odei, a Ghanaian biologist appointed to the project by the Ghana Ministry of Health.

The next few months saw a succession of conflicting letters and wires either from headquarters or the regional office; liaison was poor between the two. Staff working in the field, officially answerable to Dr Alfred Quenum, the autocratic director in Brazzaville, were sometimes driven to break protocol and write directly to headquarters – thus putting their careers at risk. Fergus was granted permission to attend a conference in Rome late in September, so we made plans to accompany him and go to Geneva by road afterwards. This permission was then revoked on a minor technicality, only to be approved again some weeks later.

In the meantime, as a result of the Ghanaian minister of trade having revoked all import licences for 1964 because 'certain irregularities' had been discovered in the granting of same, some basic commodities, already in short supply, had disappeared from the market altogether. Spare parts for cars were unobtainable, and the tyre and inner tube shortage worsened. The question of whether or not I should return to Wa with the children after home leave was debated, but if so, Fergus was determined it would not be for any extended period.

In the end he attended the conference and visited Geneva on his own, joining me and the children in Ireland for a three-week break in the autumn of 1964. He was still trying to stop smoking, but a bad bout of bronchitis, which his GP pronounced might be his last if he did not stop, added to his determination to win the battle. It took a further eighteen months before he finally gave up.

My mother had moved to her new house, happy to breathe clean air after the fog-pocket of Knock, and delighted by the ever changing view to the Antrim side of Belfast Lough. Our own house was full of imperfections, but preferable to a rented one, and the children loved having their indulgent grannie next door, to whom they could run for solace and complain about my harsh discipline. But for Fergus and me this time marked the start of a lengthy separation, during which he was sent on surveys to several French-speaking parts of West Africa: Cameroon, the Congo, Gabon, Brazzaville and Kinshasa. The children, who were happy to see Dorothy again, spent Christmas and New Year with me in Ireland; and my mother was more relaxed than she had ever before been in child company, taking particular pleasure in Mary, with whom she formed a protective bond.

Fergus returned to Wa alone in January 1965. A Ugandan kob we had jointly raised by bottle had been well looked after by Daniel, but instantly resumed its dependence on Fergus. It had the full run of house and surrounding bush, but returned to the summons of one of the children's squeaky toys. It was never house-trained, so there were often lakes on the floor. On a visit to Dorimon, Fergus heard that Simbu Dog had died as a result of the broken promise we had foreseen. Rage was profitless, but we both felt we should have rescued him, despite the fact that what we could have offered was not ideal. I am certain dogs have souls.

On the domestic front, Adda had been sacked after twice getting so drunk that he became impertinent and abusive. Sobered up, he admitted to regularly smoking hash, which accounted for his red eyes; looking back, I think he had been on hash for as long as I had known him. When I returned with the children in March, he had been replaced by Abdulai, who was an instant success with them, and the atmosphere in the house was much more pleasant. Katharine spent a lot of time in his quarters demanding her cut of whatever food was on offer, and eating with her fingers: 'I *want* to eat with my fingers, I don't like a spoon.' She and three slightly older female friends were singing on the veranda one day, chanting 'Ai Ai Assin' over and over again; when we asked for a translation, they looked a bit sheepish – 'It means, "Do not urinate on the meat,"' they said. Mary joined a group of adults who gathered daily at the back of the house for the equivalent of a coffee break: Mousa Moshi, an itinerant woman who sold roasted plantain and other delicacies, Abdulai, and a couple of servants from nearby houses. Both children loved to be carried in a cloth on someone's back, but Katharine, already rather too heavy, could always rely on Mousa for a lift. We had come back during the month of Ramadan, when he would have nothing to eat or drink between the hours of sunrise and sunset, and I felt irrational guilt to see him carrying her around while he used the hose. It also lessened my enjoyment of a morning coffee break, or cool drink during the day. On the day that marked the end of Ramadan, Abdulai did some washing, cleared up our breakfast mess and made the beds, before departing in ceremonial dress for the mosque. Many goats and sheep had been slaughtered, and a repeat of the previous year was predicted, when Mousa had suffered from belly palaver, which Fergus termed 'protein poisoning': his usual midday meal was boiled cassava sprinkled with red chilli powder, and maybe a drizzle of palm oil as a treat.

Fergus's interest-free money-lending attracted some bizarre applicants. One, asking for £20, admitted it was to bribe the police to discontinue an action that his wife was taking against him, as the couple had agreed, when the heat of the moment had passed, to patch up the quarrel out of court. What was the dispute? 'Oh, she refuse to do my washing, and when I made a row she pull my testicles and they have swell. Then I was angry and somehow her ear got in my mouth and I bit it.' The loan was refused. Even Abdulai had 'finish with women'. His first wife had drunk and smoked wee (Indian hemp); the second had been too lazy to prepare meals, preferring to pass time gossiping with neighbours – sadly an only too familiar pattern.

We entertained the members of the tennis club with their wives and girlfriends – it was an exercise of the E.M. Forster 'bridge party' sort, because almost all the females – Daniel's woman, who was a teacher, apart – were awed by the grandeur of the scene and contributed nothing, exchanging soft talk and giggles among themselves. When it became clear that our sojourn at Wa was really coming to an end, Francis made arrangements for a farewell party to be held at the Love All Canteen in the centre of the town. This was a more relaxed gathering, although again the women, who had worked hard to produce the feast, appeared only to serve dishes before melting into the background. There were many side dishes of aubergine, okra, grated coconut, pineapple, nuts and chillies, but the *pièce de résistance* was an enormous stew containing virtually all the fish and meats locally obtainable. There was muddy catfish from the Black Volta, giant land snail (very rubbery), chicken, mutton and goat, the hairy ear of which, protruding from a vast bowl, was offered to me as a special delicacy. I am sure it was rude, but I demurred, saying I thought it should go to my husband. Fish eyes, too, were held in high regard, and neither Adda nor Abdulai could understand why we let them have the heads of any fish they prepared for us.

Late one afternoon the house was invaded by a swarm of something, to this day, unidentified – a cross between a lobster with big hairy pincers and a six-inch spider. Again with reluctance we used the spray to prevent them invading the bedrooms. It was about this time that I wrote to several European zoos, asking if they would be interested in the kob, whose horn buds were beginning to show and when fully grown would be an elegant two-foot lyre shape. Its skull was concrete hard, and it had the habit of thrusting its head up between my legs. As the day of our final departure approached I had a letter from Hanover Zoo, saying they would be glad to take it. A travelling case was made for the journey, but in the end, because it was suffering from travel stress, we left it at Damongo Game Reserve, where its chances of survival were better.

I returned to Ireland with the girls while Fergus was at Geneva attending conferences and debriefing sessions prior to starting his master's degree course at the Harvard School of Public Health and Hygiene. Shortly after our arrival, the children and I turned varying shades of yellow and were diagnosed as having hepatitis. My mother did not succumb, so it was assumed she must have had it as a child. None of us was violently ill, but as soon as Fergus told his classmates in Boston, I was the recipient of much long-distance advice from well-meaning neighbours in the International Student House, where we had been allocated a two-bedroom apartment on the Fenway opposite the Boston Museum of Fine Arts. A list of foods to be avoided at all costs began with coffee, eggs and alcohol, all of which I had been consuming regularly. I never did confess.

12

New World Interlude

In mid-October 1965 the children and I flew from Belfast to Dublin before transferring to a 707 transatlantic flight to Boston. Before our long flight I took them for lunch in the airport restaurant, where they picked and messed with a delicious meal; however, the woman at the next table remarked on what a delightful pair they were. At this time children were not only tolerated, but received special attention from the flight attendants: crayons, colouring books, games and toys were offered, but thankfully not the plethora of digital games, audios and videos of current times, which assault the senses simultaneously, without concession to silence, peace and tranquillity. It seems that before I was forty I was already a grumpy old woman. Both children went to sleep for a while, and I drifted off, too, until awoken by an announcement that we would soon be crossing the Labrador coastline. Having thought, Good, we're nearly there, it was a shock to hear it would be three and a half hours before touchdown in Boston.

Fergus and his Iraqi doctor friend Edward met us and exerted their joint charm to such effect that the Aer Lingus stewardess facilitated us through customs with minimal delay. The airport was so hot and noisy we might as well have been in West Africa. It was dark, lights were flashing and sirens screaming, as Edward's Cadillac was swept into multi-lane traffic, and we headed for the International Student House, where we were to live for the next ten months. The children were barely awake when we put them to bed in their day clothing, and in the morning had little time to enjoy Fergus before he left for the first class of the day. They explored the apartment, commented unfavourably on the taste of the milk, and squealed with delight at the antics of squirrels stock piling nuts in one of the trees directly opposite.

Our block dated from the turn of the century. The living room was large with a bay window overlooking Fenway Park, so we moved the dining table to take advantage of the view; the rest of the room was so gloomy that the lights had to be kept on during the day. The view from the galley-shaped kitchen and our bedroom was of a dark chasm soaring from the basement, and ending at the third floor where a rectangle of sky could be seen – we were on the first floor. The bathroom, and a large closet intended for coats and cleaning materials, completed a total of six doors leading off the entrance vestibule. Worn, dirt-engrained wood-block floors were throughout, the exceptions being the kitchen, where there were holes in brown linoleum, and the bathroom, which had once-white tiles with a black mosaic trim. I spent a lot of time, sweating because the radiators had been turned on early in October, scrubbing these floors, which afterwards looked little better.

The girls were impatient to explore their new surroundings, so I took them down to the entrance lobby, where the postboxes lined one wall, and a wide flight of steps led to street level. We walked a short distance to the playground, which was empty, but soon raucous cries of dispute signalled the arrival of other children accompanied by child-minders or, less often, by their mothers. One of the latter joined me and introduced herself. Tall, good-looking and unconventionally dressed, her brood of four, three boys and a girl, ranged from seven years to a one-year-old baby. Refreshingly forthright in manner, Carolyn confided how hard it was to retain sanity in the present circumstances. She was a Mormon from Salt Lake City, a professional artist, seeking an outlet in painting when the shackles of motherhood allowed. Her husband was a professor at the School of Public Health. I did not realise quite how liberated she was, nor how disturbing her opinions were to some members of our small, largely conventional community, the southern state missionaries in particular.

The birds in the park were unfamiliar, I found the local speech difficult to understand, and the brilliant casual clothing worn by the younger generation was in advance of what was worn in Ireland. Fergus and I realised that we had been missing out on the swinging sixties (though I suspect we would never have swung), had never been to a rock concert, nor had we smoked pot. We enjoyed the songs of Tom Lehrer but we were puzzled by Beatle mania, which was sweeping both sides of the Atlantic. Middle age and entrenched attitudes were rapidly approaching.

The playroom in the basement led off the communal laundry room, where sooner or later I encountered all the resident wives. Sitting, quietly reading in a corner of the playroom, was a neat little figure with a solitary male child the same age as Katharine. She looked out of place, quite why was hard to define. It was not the clothes, as she wore blue jeans and a horizontal striped T-shirt; maybe it was the hair, worn like a ballet dancer in a knot tightly scraped up from the forehead. She did not look American – nor was she: both she and her husband were Scottish. I pondered on what constituted not looking right, and realised our family came into the same category. Our mouths were not big enough, and our teeth, while not neglected, were not uniformly even and white. Our clothes tended to be tweedy and of classic cut, and I abhorred flashy costume jewellery. In the street people turned to stare at us. Sybil Wilson was to become a lifelong friend, but at the start our shared loathing of the house mother, and wariness of the American lifestyle, were enough to form a bond. Unfortunately she did not like my Mormon friend, quite why I could not understand – I suspect they were competitive in the field of arts and literature, or maybe Carolyn's appearance at evening functions in a purple silk sari, which did not suit her pale northern hemisphere skin, was to blame.

The welfare of residents in the house was the responsibility of a formidable widow whose husband had been US ambassador to one of the smaller Middle Eastern states. Despite her background, she retained narrow parochial attitudes and was discomfited if she sensed these were not shared: I took an instant dislike to her, and while the niceties were strictly observed, I sensed the dislike was reciprocal: unfortunate, considering Fergus was class president and chairman of the house committee for the year.

Our neighbours on the first floor were an East Coast Jewish MD, who was studying in the same class as Fergus; an earnest Canadian sexologist and his nice but humourless wife, with one child whose conception, as everyone sooner or later was informed, had been planned with the aid of a bedside thermometer; and a Brazilian doctor, Celso, his wife and two daughters. The Brazilians were friendly and helpful, but their command of English so poor that Fergus wondered how Celso was able to follow lectures. On the ground floor was a family of southern state missionaries who had also worked in West Africa; both parents were doctors and they had three pasty-faced children. Goodwill was exuded, but there was an underlying zeal to take charge of any situation. Not long after our arrival, my back seized up while I was hauling large bags of shopping and the children up the stairs from the basement: medical advice was to remain in a horizontal position for three days, so I could not escape their solicitous visits and gratuitous advice. Thereafter, if any of us developed a sore throat – we had on average one per week, the suspect source being the playgroup – they proposed a throat swab. My firm refusal of this, as well as anal suppositories, labelled me as negligent in matters of health; worse still, they suspected we were unbelievers.

Anything found faulty in the apartment – windows that would not open, curtain rails that did not run smoothly, electrical problems, leaky taps or blocked drains – was to be reported to the janitor, who lived a troglodyte existence in the basement with his gigantic wife and overweight daughter. Warned of his prickly character, and tendency to take umbrage, I trod warily, conscious that my accent was thought to represent unwelcome 'foreign' demands, but anxious to ensure our problems did not go to the bottom of his priority list. The interior of his dungeon was full of plastic flowers, imitation stone-wall screens, Murano glass *objets d'art*, chairs with lace antimacassars. The TV was permanently on, there was a pervasive smell of deep-fat frying, and someone was always eating at a big table amid an assortment of sauces and pickles. Only much later did I see some of *The Flintstones* cartoons. Probably because of Fergus's position on the house committee, we got through the year without a major dispute, although I was impatient with such inefficiency at basic levels – hard to reconcile with US dominance in space research.

Most of our shopping was done at the neighbourhood A & P (Atlantic and Pacific) corner store, where I was impressed by milk packaged in waxed cartons rather than glass bottles, and we all became addicted to ice cream, available in varieties we had never dreamed of: mocha, chocolate chip, pistachio, mint, treacle toffee, forest fruits, raspberry ripple – in Ireland we had been restricted to vanilla, chocolate or strawberry. In Africa I had made my own, best forgotten, variety.

By the end of October autumn was turning to winter, and a penetrating wind from the east swept down the Fenway, stripping the trees bare, and the squirrels had found the food intended for birds on our windowsill. I took the children to feed the ducks and watch baseball practice, and drew their attention to the beautiful Russian Orthodox church and a striking modern office tower on the skyline. At the other extreme, the park boasted the ugliest public convenience I had ever seen. To mark its opening a plaque dated 1928 had been engraved with the names of benefactors and the architect: vaguely Spanish, the roof was flat with numerous small battlements and decorative grilles protecting the windows. Our Scottish friends, who had a car, took us to Franklin Park Zoo, but we found it as depressing, as did its miserable, hunched animals in their cramped cages: the pools were filthy, and there was litter everywhere. We also visited the house where Nathaniel Hawthorne, of whom neither of us had heard, set his novel *House of Seven Gables*. (Confession – I still have not read any of his books.) I think it was the following spring when we visited Salem and Thoreau's cabin at Walden Pond, further highlighting our joint ignorance of American history and literature.

By the time the first snow fell, the children's vocabulary included 'cookies', 'candy' and 'sidewalk'. The temperature plummeted so dramatically that the frame of Fergus's glasses snapped, and we all took to wearing earmuffs, and, in the park, the children cried to go home because of the cold. Halloween and Thanksgiving loomed, and I was inundated with literature inviting me to join the Society of Harvard Dames, as well as sundry groups and 'programs'. I got roped in for the Library Committee and for the Arrangement Committee of a Pot Luck Supper – I reckoned that was better than the Clean-Up Committee. The children were invited to the birthday party of a four-year-old boy, whose mother, between sorting out quarrels, gave me a lecture on the importance of instilling a sense of leadership and achievement at an early age. Po-faced, earnest, well-intentioned, all frivolity would have been alien to her nature; I wonder if her son enjoyed his party – neither Katharine nor Mary did.

One evening, after the children had gone to bed and Fergus had settled to his 'homework', I decided to walk to the nearest Sears department store. The neighbourhood, despite its academic population, had a reputation for thuggery and violent crime. A man had recently been murdered, and women were advised not to walk across the park after nightfall. Before we left, a body was found among the bins, at the bottom of the chasm in our block. Despite being advised against my solitary walk – it was along the busy, well-lit, main route to the store, after all – I set off alone and arrived in one piece. I expected something like Harrods but the reality was far from that: it was loud, it was vast, and its claim to stock everything was probably true, but I found it difficult to locate not only the elevator, but the right level on which to start my search for dress fabrics. After the open markets and ramshackle stores of West Africa, I found it repulsive; 'Rudolph the Red-Nosed Reindeer' and 'I Saw Mommy kissing Santa Claus', piped throughout the store, were proof that the festive season was in full swing. I wanted to replace our ancient Christmas tree decorations, but could see only balls made of fine glass which would shatter on the parquet floors. Forget about good taste – I settled for a flat-pack white plastic tree with tiny coloured lights, which Katharine and Mary thought was the most beautiful thing they had ever seen – apart from the one in the window of the A & P store.

Later I was advised to take a whole day off – possibly thanks to a reciprocal child-care programme – to visit the better stores in downtown Boston. Our budget was restricted because Fergus had brought us over at his own expense, so I was overjoyed to discover Filene's Bargain Basement, where top quality, and some designer, goods were marked down on a daily basis: a grey Aquascutum rainproof, bought for ten dollars and later known as Dad's flasher coat, lasted into the student years of our (as yet unborn) son. I bought high fashion shoes and good quality clothes for the girls. We also patronised the Salvation Army shop, where Katharine pounced on a huge stuffed tiger unloved by some rich kid; she still has him. The windows of Jordan Marsh were enough to convey that the exquisite luxury goods on display were beyond my range, or indeed ambition.

Drinks parties mostly began at six thirty with lethal cocktails accompanied by insufficient snacks, and we were seldom invited to stay for dinner. Our novelty value as (a) being Irish and (b) having lived in the wilds of Africa, wore off after we had 'performed' a few times. One invitation, however, is memorable: we were invited to a reception at the house of the faculty dean in an exclusive part of Boston. He had an eclectic collection of paintings and sculptures, and Caucasian rugs and Afghan carpets covered the floors of a succession of open-plan rooms, in each of which a blazing fire burned. His wife was charming, allowing each person more than perfunctory time. The guests ranged from very old parchment-skinned academics, Daughters of the American Revolution, members of the diplomatic service, down to students at the School of Public Health, and others, like Fergus, already advanced in their careers, who were studying for a master's degree in public health and hygiene. I do recall feeling ashamed by having to admit to being a wife and mother, with no academic qualifications, in the company of so many leaders and achievers, and wanting to show that I was not quite brain-dead. Women's liberation and protest groups were in their infancy. Only very recently have I realised that I was a women's libber from the start, always swimming against the tide.

Pumpkins carved to make lanterns, pumpkins stuffed, the whole panoply of traditional feasts dominated the scene in International House in the weeks leading up to Christmas. I bought an Elna sewing machine, which was to do service for the next fifteen years. Our Iraqi doctor friend Edward, who had not brought his wife to Boston, was a frequent visitor, often sharing our evening meal before he and Fergus embarked on their study of epidemiology or statistics, which often continued, joined by other students, into the small hours. He was enthusiastic about my casseroled leg of lamb with vegetables, but told me how wrong it was to use garlic and onions in the same dish.

I felt it behove Fergus, as house chairman, to make some seasonal gesture of hospitality for those unfortunates, far from their homes, who would be remaining in Boston over the Christmas holidays. He did not feel the same, at least not so forcibly, but gave in when I pointed out that most of the stress would fall on me – he would only have to foot the bill. It was a huge success; I did not count the heads, but over thirty packed into our small space, screaming at each other through a smoke screen, against a background din of Beatles records I had borrowed for the occasion. Drink flowed from the cramped bar in the kitchen, where some guests spent the entire evening. We found the Chinese and Japanese difficult, inclined to sit together in self-protective clumps and leaving as early as they decently could. I felt bad about this, as some brought gifts in gratitude for lessons in English. The girls fortunately slept until after midnight, when both woke and joined the party.

We had a warm invitation to visit Hartford, Connecticut, where Grandma's cousin Helen, a retired professor of history at the university, and her two brothers, Charles and Homer, lived. We were to stay with Charles and his wife Carleta, the parents of my putative pen-pal, Jane, now married with two children. Memories of my duplicity returned, and I dreaded our meeting.

Edward, who was going to stay with friends at the embassy in Washington, said he would be happy to drive us to Hartford. It was our first experience of a turnpike system and spaghetti junctions, and I was terrified by the many drivers who defied regulations, blithely swinging in and out of lanes, and the enormous trucks belting along at 60 m.p.h. The countryside between Boston and Hartford struck us as tame – gently undulating and densely wooded with young birches, and studded with small lakes and reservoirs. There was housing almost all the way, but because the houses were not built in rigid lines, and most were clad with cedar shingle, the general effect was pleasant: we liked the fact that each owner was not constrained – as in UK – to fence his patch, which was in any case much larger, so that the houses appeared to nestle naturally on their sites.

We located Helen's house only after much argument over the minute map she had scribbled in pencil on a torn-off sheet of notepad. She rushed out to greet us, quite a small figure, her face reminiscent of a benign gargoyle, but with a mass of pretty white hair. There was a definite resemblance to Grandma, and the family penchant for purple was evident in Helen's clothes. (The gene was first noticed when Eileen reached the last stage of the full mourning she adopted on the demise of 'dear Dav' in 1921. The first stage was all black, which she wore with a long widow's veil, through shades of grey in the thirties, to variations on a lavender, lilac and purple theme at the time of her death. During visits to Belfast, she always took me along to appointments with 'dear Mr Dunne', her tailor in Wellington Place, to help in choosing suiting for two new costumes she ordered every year: towards the end, the purple verged on vulgar. Her favourite ring was a large antique amethyst, reputedly once owned by a bishop – sadly the original stone had been replaced by a dishonest jeweller, so what I inherited was well-worn glass. I recently had the stone replaced and the ring looks glorious. The gene is very persistent: I am fond of the colour; Katharine, whose birth stone is amethyst, loves it; and my design-conscious only granddaughter is not averse to wearing the royal colour.)

Helen was an uninhibited extrovert, chattering nervously throughout a nice lunch she had prepared, but she quieted down gradually, and before Edward made his escape to Washington found time to tell him how well she thought some of these Middle Eastern countries were coming on! She had a collection of ornaments from her travels, some very nice, others truly awful, and it was nerve-wracking to keep an eye on the children lest curiosity should tempt them to touch. We were relieved when she decided it was time to drive us to Charles's house, and more so to get there in one piece – erratic driving was another thing she had in common with Grandma. Snow was falling steadily when we got there, and Charles came out to give instructions on how and where to park, but she ignored his gestures and parked where she wanted. We could see from his expression that he was accustomed to this, sighing perceptibly as he helped us through ankle deep snow to the porch, where he had cleared a space for the car.

Inside, the house looked like the cover of a Christmas edition of *Ideal Home*, and plump Carleta came trotting out to give us a genuinely warm welcome. We were taken into a large sitting room with a blazing log fire, and introduced to Jane, her stolid husband, and two children – a girl of eight and a five-year-old son. There followed a ritual opening of children's stockings, containing token offerings only, and we were presented with a book of lovely photographs of fine examples of New England architecture. Fortunately I had brought two expensive cakes and small gifts for Jane's children, otherwise we should have been overwhelmed. Snacks and delicious dips were handed around, and a giant antique silver bowl of warm punch sat on a side table.

When I left to put the girls to bed, Carleta scuttled off to the kitchen, having put on a professional-looking apron over her cocktail dress, with which she wore a tiny black plate hat with a veil reminiscent of Jessie Matthews in a thirties film. Fergus was left to make polite conversation, which he did not find easy, as common interests were few. These were hard-headed businessmen: Charles a stockbroker and Jane's husband in real estate, their sports were baseball and American football, and neither played golf. Politics would be dangerous, as Fergus had no idea where their sympathies lay, although he suspected Republican. Helen sounded as if she might be a Democrat, but she had gone quiet and nodded off from time to time. Medicine, and the control of diseases encountered in tropical zones, were topics about which they knew no more than could be gleaned from the pages of *Reader's Digest*. Fergus's relief was plain to see when I returned to the room and Carleta announced that dinner was ready.

We returned to Boston by Greyhound bus, relieved to be back in our dreary apartment. I had managed to liven it up by sticking my version of Mondrian paintings made from stiff coloured paper on some of the doors in the entrance hall, but nothing could compensate for the lack of daylight. Sybil and I decided to organise a New Year's Eve celebration, without prior consultation with the house mother. We played Scottish and Irish music, much alcohol was consumed, and it was acclaimed a great success, but it had been noticed that we had 'borrowed' some of the Christmas decorations. We were summoned to the house mother's office where we were carpeted like sixth formers – 'pained to have to say so', 'should have known better', 'surprised that you of all people', and so on. That Fergus had been a participant was not mentioned – she had a soft spot where he was concerned.

The next trouble I got into was the result of organising a skating party on a pond in Fenway Park. This was a popular event but illegal because of dangerous currents under the ice. A great pity because the natural ice had a delightful spring in contrast to the alternative flooded and frozen football pitch littered with bottle tops, fag ends and twigs. I felt guilty because one of the wives, a nervous woman, bulldozed by her husband into taking healthy exercise, fell just minutes after talking to me about her fear of falling. Going at a snail's pace, she tripped and went down heavily; clearly in great pain, her husband took her to hospital, where examination revealed a double fracture of the tibia and severe muscle tears. After an operation, she returned in plaster from thigh to foot and remained so for six weeks. Their children, about the same age as Katharine and Mary, were looked after in turn by all the females in the house. I had them for a couple of days, doing all their smelly, unrinsed washing: mercifully her mother, from Oregon, came to the rescue.

The Japanese ladies, who had begun to emerge from their shells, organised classes in the formalities of Ikebana flower arrangement. They emphasised that to master the art would take many years, so we would learn only the basic rules. We were to report with a selection of blooms, twigs, berries, dried grasses – anything we thought had potential. They were, without exception, as delicate as some of the blossoms, and I was not alone in feeling gross and clumsy; they never verbalised criticism, but would quietly remove an offending flower or twitch a twig to another angle. There were also Chinese cookery classes, and most of the American women who attended, belonging to the Constance Spry generation, were ill at ease. Unlike the flower-arranging classes, the cookery sessions were led by a massive matron, whose family had settled in Vancouver at the turn of the century. She was a tyrant, displeased when I queried the length of time taken to steam little parcels of minced pork and was tactless enough to mention the risk of tapeworm from undercooked pig meat.

The stress of cramming for forthcoming examinations continued to permeate the building – students from outside the US did not relish having their grades posted on a board for all to see – and many, including Fergus, were unsure where they would go during the next year, and by whom they would be employed. Fergus was again offered the job of biologist on the Bilharziasis Advisory Team, although it had not been decided where it was to be based or, more importantly, who the other members of the team would be. Vague offers abounded: 'Oh, you must come to Jamaica … Iraq … Iran … Thailand … my father is the minister of health and will fix it all for you', and so on. All nebulous, and with the threat of continued life involving suitcases, boxes and furnished apartments, we felt that much of our exhaustion and nervous irritability was due to uncertainty about the next move.

The succession of letters sent to headquarters over the winter months and into the spring resulted in more positive signals from Geneva. There were two jobs in Africa – one on the Jos plateau in Northern Nigeria, the other in Tanzania – one in Geneva, for which Fergus had been shortlisted, and one based at the regional office in Alexandria, which would have been preferable to the regional office at Brazzaville. He was also offered a career service appointment, meaning he would no longer limp along on a two-year-contract basis; the drawback being that WHO could, in theory, send their 'expert adviser' to some hell-hole in the middle of a desert.

By the end of March we were all suffering from 'cabin fever', having been confined too long in an overheated, infection-laden atmosphere. There were subtle signs of spring, but I was worrying about the onset of summer – the interval between seasons in Connecticut is short – and the urgent need to buy or make suitable clothes for myself and the girls. With Sybil and her husband, Iain, we booked a chalet on Cape Cod for two weeks at the end of June, just after graduation day. Once the ceremony was over, Fergus planned to visit his older brother, Woodrow, who had settled near Toronto, before driving down to join us at Cape Cod with Edward, who had decided to hang onto his car until the last minute before returning to Iraq.

At the end of May, while sharing one of our evening meals, Edward looked at me and announced without preamble: 'You're pregnant.' I denied this, but he insisted, saying, 'It's something about the eyes – you'll see, I'm never wrong.' He wasn't.

Sybil bravely drove me, Katharine, Mary and her own child, Angus, for hours through the outskirts of Boston before we reached anything approaching open countryside. Cape Cod, in my romantic imagination, would have crashing waves and black towering cliffs, but was in reality limitless beaches and dunes, sparsely vegetated with poison ivy and sea holly. Rarely one glimpsed, at the end of a drive marked 'Strictly Private', a cluster of dwarfed conifer surrounding a holiday home owned by one of Boston's super-rich. We visited Provincetown at the northern tip of the Cape, where for the first time I used a supermarket trolley; our local A & P store used brown paper bags. We went to the famous aquarium where many monstrosities of the deep appeared to be in good health: Katharine still recalls a menacing wide-mouthed, sharp-toothed specimen which eyeballed her through the thick glass. We all remember the hairy caterpillars which abounded around our cabin, the sting of which induced a red, intensely itchy reaction, and the inland pond where a small sea-plane landed just before Mary waded out of her depth, with me, a poor swimmer even in salt water, squelching through the soft mud in pursuit, yelling 'Come back' to the heedless child.

Only when I was back in Ireland did I gather courage to tell my mother that another child was due. In the autumn of 1966 Fergus joined me and the girls for a short break in our new house at Craigavad, before flying to the regional office in Brazzaville, from which he was to conduct surveys of snail populations in Gabon and Cameroon. Afterwards he was to report at headquarters in Geneva for briefing on a new bilharziasis pilot control project to be started, at the request of the Tanzanian Ministry of Health, in March 1967. Officially called the WHO/ Tanzania Schistosomiasis Pilot Control and Training Project, it was to be based at the East African Medical Research Institute in Mwanza on the southern shore of Lake Victoria, with Fergus as project leader. His national counterpart, the director of the institute, would be Dr Valentine Eyakuze, a brilliant clinician but renowned for indiscriminate outbursts of vitriol.

Early in the morning of 12 January I woke up in a wet bed – it was the first time my waters had broken, so I knew the birth was imminent. Leaving the girls with my mother, I drove to the hospital at Dundonald, on the outskirts of Belfast, where I was given a room next to one that had been occupied by Mrs Ian Paisley a few days earlier: the nurse confided this in an awed tone, as if the establishment had the royal seal of approval. Alone again, I suffered solicitous comments on how hard it must be with my husband not present – always detectable an element of doubt that he actually existed. Remembering the agonies of Agogo, I asked to be given pain relief. In the theatre the clock showed three thirty, and I was assured that Mr Boyd was on his way. I fear I remarked waspishly that he was having a protracted lunch. Shortly afterwards, everything merged into a haze from which I surfaced at five to be told that I had a beautiful boy weighing 8lb 12oz.

Three hours later, on hearing that my husband was on the line, I hobbled to the phone to impart the good news. The green-eyed monster flickered once more when he said he would celebrate that night at a dinner hosted by the long-time partner of the less offensive of the two Germans who had stayed at Wa, who was currently absent from Geneva. A few days later I drove home with Michael Fergus rattling around on the rear seat in the same blue and white carry-cot that had done service in Ghana. My mother and the girls, then four and three, waited on one of those sunny winter days when the warmth of the sun is just perceptible, and the winter jasmine in flower, to meet the first male to be born into my side of the family for almost seventy years. They were ecstatic, but Mary so extravagant in her display of affection that I had to restrain her by explaining the delicate structure of a baby's skull, and how the fontanelle gradually closes to protect the brain. Looking back, I realise I never treated them as children, and expected far too much in terms of comprehension. Katharine cites books read in early childhood, saying, 'Don't you remember *you* gave me that when I was only nine?' – Laurens van der Post's *Lost World of the Kalahari* was one; another anthropological work was about the Ik tribe in Uganda, which had some repulsive habits, and more suitably, Gerald Durrell's *My Family and Other Animals*.

Fergus first saw his son two weeks later, at the start of three weeks' home leave before flying to Tanzania to inaugurate the project in Mwanza.

13
Kenya – Uganda – Tanzania

The federation of Kenya, Uganda and Tanzania was by this time demonstrating that Francis Kofi's firm conviction that 'All Africans are brothers' was patently untrue in East Africa. Indeed, ten years earlier, when Fergus conducted school surveys in Ruanda, he had been present at silent 'morning after' scenes in village compounds where Tutsi teachers had been massacred overnight by Hutu raiders. In early 1967 there was border tension and sabre-rattling in the Bukoba region, from which Dr Eyakuze came, on the western shore of Lake Victoria, and General Idi Amin was at the height of his power in Uganda. Jomo Kenyatta still reigned in Kenya and Julius Nyerere – an exceptional leader – ruled in Tanzania, where technical collaboration with both Russia and China was much in evidence.

The BOAC flight from London via Cairo landed at Entebbe in torrential rain; the children's raincoats had been left in Ireland, everyone was shouting in Swahili, and Fergus was not there to welcome us. Katharine and Mary, excited at the prospect of seeing their father, kept repeating plaintively, 'Where can Daddy be?' Michael was bawling, and his bottle of milk, entrusted to a hostess with a leopard-skin hat, was now on its way to Nairobi. A corpulent but amiable Idi Amin lookalike led us to his office; despite his seniority, his English was rudimentary, and there being no equivalent of West African pidgin, I was unable to communicate our plight. I tried unsuccessfully to contact David Bradley at the university, with whom the East African Institute for Medical Research and WHO collaborated, and with whom Fergus had co-authored several papers on bilharziasis. The noisy downpour continued and Mary, having found a pair of blunt-nosed scissors, was quietly littering the floor with fragments of white paper. Mugs of thick sugary tea were offered. Then

Fergus appeared: there had been a long delay on the road, due to a lorry having crashed axle-deep into a pothole – it sounded all too familiar. We had a token breakfast of fusty cornflakes and watery milk, and I prepared a fresh bottle to placate the baby. In the three years since Mary's infancy I had forgotten the tyranny of preparing sterile feeds under testing circumstances – on the bonnets of cars, inside Land Rovers, in semi-darkness in unfamiliar rest-houses, often aware that our large container of sterile water was running low.

Our combined baggage amounted to seventeen pieces, all of which were loaded onto an old DC-3 aircraft, which took off at ten in the morning on a direct flight over Lake Victoria to Mwanza. The lake's immensity was immediately apparent, and for a while we might have been over the Pacific, until we started to lose height and saw small islands with little sandy coves, and a hilly coastline with huge sculptural rocks topping some of the summits. The pilot announced that we were nearly there and drew our attention to Saa Nane island zoo, on which, to the children's delight, several giraffes could be seen; then he indicted Bismarck Rock in the bay, and Buganda hill, on top of which a fine new hospital was under construction.

A welcome delegation, consisting of Dr Eyakuze, and several field and laboratory assistants recruited to work on the new project, met us at the rudimentary airport: the names of the latter – Hermann, Reinhardt, Klaus and Dieter – a reminder of Tanzania's years under German rule.

A small cavalcade of vehicles, headed by us in the director's Mercedes, took the main road to Mwanza town. The vegetation was lush and most of the flowering shrubs were familiar from Ghana. We turned right onto a branch road leading to the residential compound at Bwiru, and met, for the first time, herds of cattle with humps and wide spreading horns driven by turbaned men or small boys. The tarmac degenerated to deeply rutted laterite before a sharp left turn up a slight incline led to a circular parking space beside the bungalow that was to be our home for the next six years.

The garden, though neglected, had been landscaped many years earlier, and Fergus had already recruited a shamba boy to help him restore some of its former glory. The lake could just be glimpsed, and the kopje, directly above the house, was topped by a giant cone-shaped boulder on which the leader of a pack of baboons often sat contemplating his territory; a colony of rock hyrax lived at its base. During fierce electric storms, the children would ask: 'What if the lightning strikes the rock? It will tumble down and hit our house.' We dismissed their fears with explanations of the geological time-scale – 'It has stood up there for millions of years …' – but there were times when I too felt a bit uneasy. Some dangers would be real enough, however – a hyaena crunching bones under the guava tree just outside the children's room, a leopard coughing as it passed under the window beside Katharine's bed, a giant python coiled in the ancient fig tree.

But this was all in the future. For the moment, the contents of our cases were strewn around, the children were demanding the whereabouts of favourite toys last seen in Ireland, and I was getting to know Stephano, a cook/steward who had worked for 'Webbo' – Gerry Webbe, a Medical Research Council scientific officer who spoke fluent Swahili and had specialised in schistosomiasis transmission. Stephano came with glowing references but spoke almost no English, so I would have to acquire a rudimentary vocabulary in Swahili. Under the colonial regime, all government officers had to pass an examination in written and verbal Swahili if they were to advance in their career; it had not been obligatory for wives, but most acquired what was termed 'kitchen Swahili' if only in order to survive. By this time only a few such wives remained; one or two had come from Kenya or Nigeria, and regarded Mwanza as the sticks. They insisted their servants wore a white uniform, cummerbund and fez, and were notoriously demanding – one, for whom Stephano had worked for a few months, had asked him to wash the kitchen ceiling. His flat refusal had led to dismissal not long before our arrival. The lady in question called on me, emphasising that I should not take any nonsense from the 'natives', who were without exception lazy, unreliable and dishonest. Her manner was condescending and I was frosty, intimating that five years of living in Ghana had led me to form my own opinions: thus effectively ensuring that we were not invited to dine.

The house bore the signature of German rule, similar in many ways to the one that had reduced me to tears in Wa, but this one had not been neglected to the same extent. However, after a few days only, many imperfections revealed themselves. Malodorous man-holes half hidden in the vegetation, and old cans and discarded tyres harboured stagnant water in which mosquito larvae thrived. The concrete floors of the bedrooms were the familiar red Cardinal, and the living room was battleship grey with areas of red showing through – I later compounded this mess by using dark blue paint which failed to key with the underlying layers. The kitchen was enormous, but the windows so high that one might as well have been in a prison. Two Belfast sinks with sodden and stained draining boards, an ancient gas cooker and yet another kerosene-fuelled fridge completed the equipment. There was a capacious store cupboard with ample shelving next to the back door, from which a track led to Stephano's quarters, and over a ravine to our neighbour's bungalow. There was a separate lavatory and the bathroom had the usual temperamental gas-fired water heater. The WC was far from pristine, and blocked within hours of our arrival; a suspect trap, topped with disgusting brownish froth, lay below its window, and that of the kitchen. Fergus arranged a meeting with the clerk of works, who came with his team in several vehicles, noted the many holes in the mosquito netting, counted the mosquito breeding sites, then left without actually doing anything, or giving any promise of intent. Memories of the painters at Kintampo were revived.

The cot we had asked for duly arrived, with a fitted net, but after a night of restless sleep for Michael, I found little specks of blood on the net, and something that looked very like a bed bug, which I sent to Fergus for identification. It was positive, so an intensive scrubbing session with Dettol, kettles of boiling water and a toothbrush ensued, annihilating the bug population that had thrived in the wooden slats under the mattress. An Italian electrician came and pronounced the wiring in the house potentially lethal.

The climate was pleasant and the girls played outside in their paddling pool with a hose, while Michael lay on a rug on the veranda watching. Katharine made friends with the five-year-old flaxen-haired daughter of the German vet; she was a stolid unresponsive child, but Katharine did not seem to mind. Mary preferred the company of Salome, one of Stephano's six daughters, whom I overheard her informing, 'Rolf Harris has got three legs, you know.' The girls soon picked up a basic vocabulary of Swahili nouns and could count up to ten, but like me, had little concept of sentence construction. The children of our Australian friends – John and Rosemary McMahon, both doctors – by contrast spoke fluently, having spent much of their time in the care of a massive, light-skinned ayah who came from the coast. Their daughter Sheena already attended the Anglican Diocesan Primary School, which was the only option other than the state primary, at which all lessons were in Swahili. So by the end of July, Katharine joined a large class of mixed Asian, African and European children. Bishop Wiggins and his wife, both from New Zealand, were the founders, and their son taught the higher grades. I never heard of any application being refused, but Mrs Wiggins was quoted as having said of us: 'Such a pity, we hear they are heathens.' Katharine really enjoyed singing hymns at morning assembly, and once, when I enquired what they had sung that day, the reply was 'Oh, we sang about vicious cement' – it took me a while to work out that it must have been 'fishers of men'. For a while, until firmly discouraged, she would return from school chanting: 'Did y'ever say Yes to Jesus, did y'ever say No to the Devil?' The uniform was a cotton dress of harsh blue with small white polka dots; boys wore a shirt in the same material, which could be obtained from one of many stores owned by a member of the Alibhai family, who also owned the largest general store, which stood on a prime corner site in the centre of the town.

A young entrepreneur – Nur Mohammed – owned a specialist shop offering many surprising things not otherwise obtainable without making a visit to Dar es Salaam (former capital of Tanzania), Kampala or Nairobi. I found melamine 'unbreakable' tableware, odd bits of Hornby train-sets, including rails, and he sold me a Rolleicord twin lens reflex camera, to which I later added attachments enabling me to photograph maps and diagrams for the project. He talked about his hope of settling in Canada, and I often wonder, as I arrange my breakfast on a pale blue plastic tray bought from him, if his dream was realised.

The Elna sewing machine bought in Boston came into heavy use during these years when the children were growing rapidly, and the lifetime of garments, due to sunlight and frequent washing, was short. I made shirts for Fergus and almost all my own dresses, not to mention one or two for Stephano's six girls. His wife spent much of the time on the coast at Tanga with their only male child, Joseph, while his eldest daughter Joyce, 'married' to the librarian at the institute and living in another of the houses nearby, kept an eye on her father.

Stephano knocked on our bedroom door each morning at six: he would call 'Hodi' and if the answer was 'Karibu', entered bearing mugs of tea; then while we all got washed and dressed he laid the breakfast table with packets of cereal, a jug of milk, freshly squeezed orange juice and a slice of pawpaw for each of us. This did not vary over the years, and I still miss the fresh pawpaw with a little slice of lime. Shopping was more complicated and time-consuming than it had been in Ghana: in addition to the Land Rover, we had the Peugeot 504, which, after dropping Fergus at the institute and Katharine at school, I drove to Alibhai Stores and the main market, sometimes, if I could face it, stopping at the Somali butcher's shop on the outskirts of the town.

Good meat could be obtained from this butcher. He had an immense gap between his front teeth and dealt with customers while giving sharp orders to his assistant, who wielded a variety of choppers and knives. An entire fillet of steak, costing three EA shillings and sixpence, had to be ordered in advance, but one still had to join a queue stretching from the shop, down a flight of steps, which ended near the malodorous wayside drain, to claim and pay for your moist blood-stained brown paper parcel. The chopping block was an ancient tree stump stained with the blood of many years. One particularly repulsive incident lingers clearly in my brain: a cow's head, black and white skin, ears *in situ*, was targeted by the axe-man while teeth ricocheted off walls and customers. On another visit I stood wedged in a line of overweight, pungent-smelling women, while a cascade of greenish liquid flowed down the steps from a stomach, laid on the floor of the shop, which was being hosed before being cut into portions for sale; tripe was a great delicacy. The overpowering pong of blood, body odour, charcoal-burning stoves, dried fish, roasting plantain and roadside drain varies little throughout Africa, and is fixed on my 'memory stick'.

Mwanza was a thriving cosmopolitan centre at the railhead of the track that led from the coast, the construction of which had cost many lives, African, Indian and not a few Chinese, during the latter years of the nineteenth century. It was also one of the ports at which the MV *Victoria* stopped – the others were Bukoba, Entebbe, Kisumu and Musoma. Mwanza had spread rapidly, and was a magnet for hopeful illiterates who had little to offer in the way of skills, and often spoke only the language of the Sukumu tribe, which inhabited the hinterland between Mwanza and Tabora, the capital during the days of German rule. Lepers were more numerous than in Ghana, and many cripples with wasted limbs begged on the streets. The Somali men were strikingly tall, thin, very black, and wore heavy turbans; their regal women sometimes wore heavy gold jewellery. Ismali women wore clothes and ornaments exotic in comparison to the simple batik prints favoured by the indigenous women, and the older men tended to be overweight, sometimes illiterate, but oozing prosperity. One patriarch in particular took a regular Sunday afternoon drive, in a cream-coloured Rolls Royce stuffed to capacity with family members of all ages, along the lakeside, passing Bismarck Rock, the dusty golf course, the Mwanza Club, with its swimming pool and tennis courts – once an all-white bastion, it now had a few Asian members – before returning at a speed that must never have exceeded 15 m.p.h. to the town centre.

Alibhai Stores strove to satisfy the demands of a rapidly growing expatriate community. A textile factory had recently opened and employed managers from the UK: I remember the shock of hearing a rasping Ulster accent bewailing the fact that she could not find any cornflakes. The only milk available was the Ultra Heat Treated (UHT) kind, which the girls condemned as undrinkable, or Carnation in tins. The shelves were packed with tinned guava, pineapple and pawpaw from new canning factories in Nairobi or Kampala; they were regarded as luxury, and held in high regard by both the African and Indian population, presumably because of the sugary syrup. Tinned mandarins, frankfurters from Eastern Europe, and crab from Russia also sold well. A Lebanese bakery produced white *bâtards*, which went stale very quickly, so again I made our bread. An elderly German woman and her son ran a farm on one of the islands in the sound, and had a small depot in the town where they sold pasteurised milk as well as large eggs in lieu of the problematic local ones; pork could be ordered, though often it tasted a bit boarish. Delicious tilapia fish could be bought at many wayside stalls, but even then supplies were declining due to over-fishing, rafts of water hyacinth, which made parts of the lake inaccessible to fishermen, and, of course, pollution, to which the new textile mill contributed. The farmers were liberal in their use of pyrethrum, which they could buy freely at the Agricultural Depot, and this, too, found its way to Lake Victoria.

Shopping excursions were possible only after we had employed an ayah to look after Mary and Michael. Maria's complexion was very dark, and her countenance scowling, but Michael, happy to be carried around on her back, did not have to look at it. Stephano excused her surly manner by explaining that she was the single mother of five, who worked to provide for them and her own mother, who had a small farm in the valley on the other side of our kopje. Stephano, the new shamba boy, Joseph, Maria, and 'Mzee', a desiccated, wall-eyed ancient who lived in a hovel near the foot of our drive, congregated near the back door every morning for a protracted tea break. Sometimes the group was joined by another ancient who made beautiful, finely woven baskets with an integral purple design; a few have survived the years, but the purple fades in time. Our wall-eyed Mzee was so old that he had worked as a stone-breaker for the German army during the 1914–18 war. He told how harsh the soldiers had been with any labourer suspected of malingering or dishonesty: a lash had frequently been used and serious crimes resulted in execution – heads being displayed on stakes by the roadside. No free tea and sugar in those days.

It was not long before we found ourselves involved in a drama precipitated by Joyce returning to live in her father's already overcrowded quarters. The librarian had agreed a bride price with Stephano, who claimed that some of this was outstanding, that his son-in-law had shown disrespect and was taking advantage of his position at the institute to avoid coughing up the remainder. The situation was a tickly one for Fergus, the librarian being a colleague who thought this conferred an advantage when divulging his side of the story. This he did at length, seated at ease on our veranda, downing companionable pints, while Stephano lurked resentfully in the back regions. He claimed that he had taken the pregnant and indolent girl off Stephano's hands; an exorbitant price had been asked and he had done her family a favour, while demeaning himself by marrying beneath his station. Other accusations involved the borrowing of a paraffin stove, which had been returned only under duress, and then found to be damaged beyond repair (enquiry revealed that the stove had, in any case, belonged to the institute). More disputes concerned scraggy hens which ranged around both compounds, a tethered goat, and suspected ill-treatment of the librarian's affectionate dog, Bobby, which was already devoted to me. Further complications involved two children from the librarian's first wife, who, when the inscrutable Joyce decamped, were left in his care.

In some ways the stalemate suited Stephano, allowing him more time after work to slope off and drink too much pombe, after which he would return in a belligerent mood. Often raised voices would echo across the compound as he harangued his beautiful, if bovine, daughter before sleep overcame him. With bloodshot eyes and a hangdog expression, he would appear the next morning, apprehensive about how much we had overheard. He was also aware that I was not quite as gullible as he had first thought, being ignorant that the years spent in Ghana had given me a fair understanding of African attitudes, and the intricacies of the extended family system.

I discouraged the use of 'memsahib', settling for 'mama' rather than 'madam', favoured by the Kofi brothers. Yet again, I did not fit any comfortable category. I liked to do a lot of the cooking myself, but finding that Stephano could make excellent curries, as well as preparing fish irreproachably, I allowed him to make many of our midday meals. This freed me to deal with secretarial work connected with the project, in the office space I had set up in a corner of our vast bedroom. The only competent secretary was in theory to be shared with Dr Eyakuze, who monopolised her when she was not absent on a training course, or on maternity leave. There were two typists at the laboratory, but their skills left a lot to be desired, so Fergus had expropriated an Imperial machine for me to replace the old Olivetti portable. I had also made enquiries about access to the darkroom at the institute: there had been an English photographer, but he had resigned, leaving a hopeless trainee in charge of what little equipment there was. However, permission would have to be obtained through the director; on hearing that I had run a university department, he made no objection, particularly when he saw that my work might well enhance project reports and would cost him nothing.

We joined the Mwanza Yacht Club – another reminder of colonial rule. The modest wooden clubhouse was almost on the sandy shore beside a very old gnarled tree, the roots of which were often under water; it reminded me of an Edmund Dulac illustration. One of the traditions was that female members would take turns to prepare a Sunday lunch for an unknown number, usually in the region of thirty. I recall how on one occasion I managed to make stuffed pancakes for fifty diners. We had acquired an electric fridge freezer from a departing Canadian couple – it was old and the star-rating allowed survival of the occasional cockroach, but far superior to anything we had previously owned. I also had brought from Ireland one of the earliest food mixers with attachments for kneading dough, mincing meat and grinding coffee. A large quantity of steak was minced, and I spent the previous day frying and stuffing pancakes, which were then covered with cheese sauce and put in dishes ready for reheating at the club. A circular letter from the chief engineer, also commodore of the club, to the effect that there would be an electricity cut from 9 a.m. to 4 p.m. arrived the same day. Fears of putrefying pancakes and guest mortality were not realised, and my effort was appreciated even by an Italian family. Mass catering is not for me, but I wholeheartedly admire those who can and do, like the finalists in *MasterChef*.

These tasks terrified me, but the children so much enjoyed their visits that I suppressed my fears. They clambered over the rocks, climbed the tree, were taken out in the rescue boat, and to my surprise, accepted that they were not to paddle in the water because of the threat of contracting schistosomiasis. It was safe to swim in deeper water, and many adults did so from their boats. Few crocodiles remained in this part of the lake, but hippos were seen from time to time in the bay near Bismarck Rock.

The girls pleaded so relentlessly that I succumbed and a visit to Saa Nane zoo was arranged. A lone pioneer had dedicated his life to establishing it between the wars, but tragically, at the age of forty had suffered an incapacitating stroke while on leave in Europe, and had never returned. When we visited, there were no obvious signs of deterioration, but later reports indicated many problems had arisen due to no suitable director having been appointed. Apathy, declining visitor numbers, shortage of animal feed, and ignorance cast an all too familiar shadow on this small enterprise. An ancient Masai attendant, one of whose ears had been slit and elaborately coiled around the orifice, took our ticket money and let us through a turnstile. The giraffes were a bit too matey for my peace of mind and had to be shooed away with sticks; I was afraid of back-kicks when they did shift, or that they might take off through our party. They were, however, in good condition and really beautiful, as were several zebra. Gazelles lay around like so many cows, and an evil little dik-dik sprang on to small rocks, from which it then charged us, head down, with short sharp horns. The rhino, about which we should have been warned, stood immobile, wearing a supercilious expression: the girls suggested prodding him, unconvinced when told that rhinos can move at great speed. Most of all they were thrilled by a pair of large torpid crocodiles, insisting on sitting as close as possible on the wall surrounding their enclosure.

The western corridor entrance to the Serengeti reserve is about eighty miles north of Mwanza: Fergus and John McMahon decided to explore the possibilities of staying inside the park at a recently abandoned research camp that had been built for two German vets working for Bernhard Grzimek, the animal conservationist, the project having folded after much money had been spent on housing and laboratories. *Plus ça change.* Currently it was being used by a young zoologist friend, Richard, as a base for his research. It was decided to delay our first safari by a few weeks, by which time the treacherous black cotton soil near the entrance to the heart of the reserve should have dried out.

Meanwhile, the Schistosomiasis Control Project area had been chosen at Misungwi in Sukumaland some twenty miles south of Mwanza. Twice weekly Fergus and his team of field assistants spent a full day listing water-bodies, groups of dwellings, estimated population, species of water snail found and likely transmission sites. In the absence of a statistician, the data had to be tabulated by Fergus, although one was soon to be seconded from Nairobi for a few weeks, and WHO hoped to recruit a public health engineer. Together we dealt with a mountain of paperwork, much of which had to be sent to the regional office, with copies to headquarters.

Early in August Fergus flew to Nairobi, leaving me alone with the children for the first time in East Africa. The institute would have provided a night-watchman, but I declined and slept with a cutlass beside the bed. I knew that I could never bring myself to use it, and would have felt more secure if I had had a small gun, like the pistol my mother kept until the Royal Ulster Constabulary's regular inspections during the Troubles annoyed her so much that she handed it in. Nothing disturbed us at night apart from the howls of our resident hyaenas. At night their eyes could be seen in a group at the bottom of the garden. I remember a gruesome incident involving these animals, which took place during a barbecue held by the German vet, whose terrace overlooked the same gully as ours. An antelope was being spit-roasted, the air redolent with appetising smells, when our host's dachshund, which had wandered out of the pool of light, was snatched almost literally from under our noses. Subsequent howls of feasting ensured the party began on a sombre note. There were far too many hyaenas in our area, and the hungrier they got, the cheekier they became, but old-timers assured us they ate human meat only if it was carrion, or comatose from drink. Not long after this incident a body was found, its face entirely eaten, by the roadside not far from our house.

Inevitably, sooner or later, whatever their prejudices, almost all Europeans, particularly those with children, joined the Mwanza Club, which had a swimming pool and two tennis courts. It also had a library with some interesting books on the dusty, sagging shelving, but nobody was officially in charge of it, or bought new books. I managed to revive it to some extent, opening for two hours on Sunday mornings, arranging the shelves more logically, and wheedling some cash from the committee for new purchases, as well as appealing for donations of money and unwanted books. Damp had already damaged some books dating back to the late nineteenth and early twentieth centuries; almost all were foxed and some old engravings were missing, probably taken to be framed. An early edition of Livingstone's journals was incomplete: before we left in 1973 I 'liberated' the remaining volumes, which bear the purple stamp of Mwanza Club Library, remembering how Fergus spoke with regret that he had not done the same for a valuable first edition set of *Bannerman's Birds of West Africa*, used to raise the seat of one of the clerks in Kintampo. At the poolside were a number of rusting metal chairs and chipped tables with malfunctioning canopies; a few bar staff, retained from pre-independence days, would bring orders and wipe the tables.

It was here that we met another couple who became lifelong friends. Donald Gilchrist, a tall, spare Scot with skin of the type that never tans, had worked at mission hospitals since graduating in medicine just after the war; some years later he qualified as a surgeon, and now worked at the old hospital in Mwanza. His wife, Jean, was a radiographer and they had two sons, Robert and Mungo, about the same age as Katharine and Mary. Donald is a philosopher manqué, and he and Fergus spent hours thrashing out world affairs, while ostensibly in charge of the children. Thankfully our girls could swim confidently from an early age, but other users of the pool needed constant supervision and there were several instances of near drowning while we were there.

Each month a film was flown in from Kenya to be shown in the open – no matter how liberally insect repellent was applied, one always returned home badly bitten. Some of the films came under the heading 'family entertainment', but others, memorably *Spartacus*, were for adults, and I do not recall how Katharine persuaded us to let her see it – maybe it was later, when she was on holiday from boarding school in Kenya – but she was taken home in floods of tears after seeing Jean Simmons on her knees at the foot of the cross bearing the crucified Kirk Douglas.

One of the narrow roads along the shore led to an overgrown cemetery with weathered headstones, some recording the death of young men from England who had died within months of arriving at Mwanza; others in memory of pioneers who had reached a ripe old age before death. One of Mwanza's most colourful residents, Gertie Brown, lived on the road to the cemetery with her partner, a geologist who had spent years searching fruitlessly for the diamond pipe he was convinced existed at a specific location south of Mwanza. Gertie remained a striking woman with high cheekbones and lovely skin, although by the time we met her she must have been about eighty and had put on weight. She was vivacious, and it was easy to believe that she had been a Gaiety Girl in the twenties. We were asked to afternoon tea, served in fine porcelain cups and poured from an ornate silver pot; there was juice for the children and thin cucumber sandwiches. We were introduced to her pet pelican, with which we had already had an encounter: I had stopped the car to admire the scene when I turned to find myself eye to eye with a small red orb – clearly the brute expected a hand-out. I wound the window up just in time to avoid the first thrust of that incredible beak; when no fish was forthcoming, in frustration he attacked the headlights. The girls, safely out of range in the back of the car, were thrilled. We met Gertie's geologist once only before he killed himself in a particularly messy way, blowing his brains out in her chintzy living room just before dawn one morning. Thereafter she became a recluse, joining him after a few years among the headstones in the cemetery.

Fergus went to Dar to meet the WHO representative, but we did not accompany him, as the coastal climate is similar to that of Accra – more often than not humid and conducive to prickly heat. Indeed, we never visited the capital, though later we spent time at Tanga, a coastal town south of Mombasa, when we had to leave Mwanza during Amin's hostile attacks from the air.

The garden rapidly rewarded Fergus's attentions. In addition to judicious pruning of flowering shrubs, he scraped a sandy bank bare to encourage kingfishers, and by late July one pair was nesting. We considered making a pond in a natural hollow where water tended to collect, but were discouraged by pessimists who predicted that ants would eat any rubber or synthetic lining. Plans for the Serengeti trip continued and Fergus hoped to revisit some of the places where he had conducted school surveys in 1957 in south-west Uganda; we were deterred, however, by reports that three Belgian tourists, who had accidentally crossed the border into the Congo, had been marched off by militia and summarily shot.

Despite the demands on my time, I continued writing to my mother and a few really good friends in the UK: among these were Sybil and Iain, our Scottish friends from Boston, who had returned to work at the Medical Research Council at Mill Hill in north-east London. Iain had a contract to spend two years at their research centre in the Gambia, and a letter from Sybil sought information about what they might expect. From what little I had seen of the Gambia in 1960, I could think of few less desirable places to be stationed, but did not say so, rather, listing the things I had found indispensable such as Wettex cloths, muslin nappies, insect repellent, an ample number of towels and, assuming they would have a generator, a fan and a sewing machine. I complained to my mother that most people were lazy about letter-writing, not realising how welcome letters from home were.

During the last week in October, as soon after dawn as possible, we set off for the Serengeti in the Land Rover, with the children, Maria and her six-month-old baby, plus Stella, Stephano's third daughter, to look after Maria's child, and help with what would be an enormous load of washing. The road to Musoma was tarred for the first twenty miles, then the laterite began. As we crossed a bridge cobbled together of widely spaced wooden planks, which rattled as we lurched to the other side, a swarm of bees filled the interior of the Land Rover. Fortunately I was the only one to be stung; it was very painful and the lump lasted several days. Gradually the land became more fertile, with banana and sugar cane plantations, and we could see the range of hills that juts into the lake south of Musoma. Soon a scattering of dwellings appeared on the lake side of the road, an indication that we were nearing the entry gate to the western corridor of the Serengeti at Ndabaka. We knew that many of the local inhabitants, even some park rangers, were dedicated poachers, operating on quite a large scale, despite the heavy penalties they faced if caught.

On arrival, a ranger checked that we were legitimate, took the payment, and gave us permission to park under a jacaranda tree, which provided the only shade. We all wandered off to pee and stretch our legs, returning to drink lukewarm pineapple juice and eat peanut-butter sandwiches. Michael's sodden nappy went into a big plastic bag, in which dirty items stayed until washing facilities were available. Disposable nappy design was still in its infancy; in any case, their use was a guarantee of developing a sore bottom, so inside plastic pants were an outer layer of terry towelling, an inner muslin nappy lined with Kleenex to take the worst, and the skin liberally plastered with a barrier cream. I never discovered how Maria coped with her own baby, but the breast-fed infant was content and there were no unpleasant smells other than the pervasive body odour we had come to accept as part of life in Africa.

After a few miles the track changed to black cotton soil, which after rain would turn into a treacly morass, dreaded by all travellers. We were fortunate, unlike Dutch friends, who two weeks earlier had been forced to return to Mwanza. Soon we began to see small groups of Thomson's gazelle, several giraffes, a pack of hyaenas, bunches of four or five warthogs scarpering off, tails erect, waterbuck, a few ostriches, many baboon troops and hundreds of gnu. Katharine spotted a group of vultures bouncing up and down on a heap of something that attracted myriad flies, insisting on closer inspection despite Fergus's protest that at this rate we would not reach Seronera by nightfall. The heap was a gnu – its ribs already exposed.

We stopped at the camp beside the Grumeti River, and were lucky to find the young zoologist 'at home'. We had brought contributions for Richard's larder, tinned sausages from Czechoslovakia, a can of rubbery orange cheese, a dozen cans of beer and some fresh fruit. One round hut was his bedroom, another the office/laboratory, and a row of outbuildings contained the kitchen, cook's room and a modern bath, which had to be filled by hand with grey-green water from the river. This same water was what one drank after boiling and – I hoped – filtering, though I did not see a filter. The loo, perched over a deep hole in the ground, prompted the girls to ask if it led to Australia. They sat on a low branch above the silky river, and pronounced it heaven. In many ways it was.

Maria and Stella had remained impassive throughout, and Katharine and Mary had become blasé about the more commonly seen animals, complaining that they had yet to see a rhino or elephant. Richard patiently explained that they were rare in the area, but we might see some hippos in a nearby pool. Leaving Michael with Maria and Stella, we set off in Richard's vehicle, lurching over a mile of deeply fissured track, before he stopped, announcing that now we had to walk – in total silence.

Fergus had sensible desert boots, but the girls and I wore only flipflops. For a while the quiet was broken only by the distant call of a bulbul shrike, and faint rustlings from the surrounding bush. A large flock of wood ibis clattered into the air, giving away our presence just before we reached a round soupy pool no more than fifty feet in diameter, where several crocodiles immersed themselves immediately. After a short interval, about fifteen hippos of assorted sizes surfaced, little ears twitching, to inspect the intruders. A fully grown elephant silently crossed the stream on the opposite side of the pool; only then did I feel a tremor of fear, realising that Richard did not carry a gun, and my faith in Fergus, though considerable, did not extend to imagining he would be of the slightest use should we be forced to take evasive action.

On leaving, we thanked Richard sincerely for having allowed us a glimpse of his Mara paradise. (From what I have read recently this area is now at the centre of luxury lodge accommodation, which makes me even more grateful to have been there before mass tourism, and continued poaching, made their mark on yet another site of special scientific interest.) Travelling on to Seronera, we made a stop for drinks and leg-stretching. Then, while Fergus and the others stayed in the Land Rover, I climbed a slope overlooking a bend in the river, hoping to get a picture of a somnolent crocodile. A child's voice floated over the stultifying air: 'Watch out, Mum, there's a lion.' 'Shut up, Mary,' I replied; 'bad-taste joke.' Then Fergus, in measured tones, said: 'There *is* a lion, just walk back slowly, don't run.' I glimpsed a dead gazelle on the riverbank and quickly realised I had disturbed a meal.

Late in the afternoon, hot, exhausted and engrained with red dust, when the sun was turning to a red ball, we reached Seronera Lodge. It was a relief to find that we were expected, and that two self-catering rooms were ready for occupation, but accommodation for Maria and her baby had to be arranged at the servants' quarters, near the laundry. Stella was to stay in our second room with the children. Formerly these rooms used a communal kitchen with a steward to lay tables and do the washing-up, even cooking if requested, but rumours had been rife over the previous eighteen months of a marked decline in standards and they turned out to be all too true. The cot requested for Michael was nowhere to be seen, and when one was produced, it was encrusted with bat dung. There was no fridge for the food I had brought in our now warm ice-box, no cook and no means of cooking until six in the evening, when a fire was lit to warm bath water. Luckily we had brought a Primus along, so it was back to the old Ghana regime of making up baby feeds on the dressing table among hair brushes, melting butter, hardening lumps of bread and our precious tin-opener. The kitchen was filthy, such pans as there were blackened and misshapen – fortunately I had brought one along just in case. There were no aids for dish-washing other than a slimy rag, which I incinerated as soon as the fire got going. We found an assortment of cutlery and china in a cockroach-infested meat safe; most of the cups had a layer of hardened sugar at the bottom. The dining room was some distance from the kitchen; grimy cloths covered the tables, which bore crumbs from the last meal, and there were several Kapok mattresses on the floor, indicating it was a multi-purpose room. (I wrote a letter of complaint to the National Parks manager at Arusha, who was English and probably well aware of the situation: Seronera, the main lodge in the largest reserve, was one of the worst.)

We had hoped that after the children had been fed and had gone to sleep under Stella's care, we would dine at the main lodge, mostly patronised by rich Americans, but we were refused, owing to a new rule that no meals would be served to tourists staying in the self-catering rooms. They graciously agreed to serve us with drinks and nibbles in the amphitheatre in front of a stone-fronted bar. A large fire was blazing and beyond lay the vastness of Serengeti under a clear star-sprinkled sky.

After a good night's sleep, we woke to see two giraffes delicately nibbling the tops of some nearby acacia trees, and tame glossy starlings, their iridescent oil-slick-coloured plumage brilliant in the soft early light, hopping around outside: all the effort suddenly seemed worthwhile. The children discovered a colony of tame rock hyrax, and wanted to visit the museum. A sad and dusty place it was: stuffed, moth-eaten specimens of smaller animals were displayed under flyblown glass, the labels curled and brown at the edges. There was a collection of pallid snakes and frogs in formalin and a few hand-axes and arrowheads said to have come from the Olduvai gorge. Faded sepia photographs of nineteenth-century pioneer hunters, standing proudly with attendant askaris beside a kill, hung crookedly behind cracked glass. The children were unimpressed, but strangely often referred to it afterwards. Leaving Michael with Stella and Maria, we hired a guide for the afternoon. Driving his own vehicle, he took us first to see a family of lions at their ease in the shade of an acacia tree. The male lay prone, legs in the air, while two females watched several cubs at play nearby. Then, alerted by seeing another of the park vehicles stopped near a large solitary tree, he drove to see what the attraction was: wedged high in a fork in the branches, a fine leopard stretched out, long tail dangling, guarding his kill –a Thomson's gazelle, its head also dangling from a long neck. Nowadays, thanks to the mixed benefits of digital technology, all the rangers have mobile phones, so such a kill would be surrounded by four-wheel-drive vehicles, each sprouting video cameras and telephoto lenses. Buffaloes we found about as entertaining as domestic cows, but we knew they were among the most dangerous animals, liable to close in on and trample any interloper. Visitors were warned on no account to leave their vehicles, but in practice many did.

Gradually we learned to indentify the less common antelopes – kudu, topi, gerenuk and hartebeest – but by the time we set off on the journey back to Mwanza, we were all sated by sightings of baboons, zebras, warthogs and troops of green vervet monkeys. We stopped briefly at Richard's camp, where his cook contrived a meal using some of our remaining canned contributions. Fortuitously one of the Land Rover's tyres chose to develop a slow puncture just as we approached the camp, for a search revealed that the institute's mechanic had not replaced the tool-set in its usual place under the driver's seat.

As we were on the point of leaving, one of the rangers implored us to take his heavily pregnant wife to the hospital in Mwanza, as she was thought to be miscarrying, so she managed to squeeze herself into the back of the already overloaded vehicle. Steely blue clouds had formed behind us, flashes of lightning shot over the horizon, and distant peals of thunder could be heard. When we got to the black cotton soil area, it was much softer than it had been on our way in, so we decided that I should take over the driving while Fergus walked ahead to test the surface, to a chorus of anxious voices: 'Look Mummy, there are big drops of rain, and why does Daddy have to get out so often, and what will happen if a lion, or rhino comes?' What indeed. We made the gate with about fifteen minutes to spare before the downpour started in earnest. (Two weeks later a young couple were stuck for forty-eight hours before deciding they had no option but to abandon the car and walk the remaining eight miles to the exit. The girl told me she had been terrified – they had seen three rhinos and a large herd of buffalo.)

We deposited the pregnant woman safely at the hospital, then, mission accomplished, on reaching Bwiru, collapsed with stiff drinks. Stephano had the house in good order, beds made, table laid and a curry prepared. He announced that the cat, recently consigned to our care by a departing European family, now had six kittens: the girls were thrilled, Fergus and I less so, as we faced having to tell them that we could not keep them all. Eventually two handsomely marked males were kept, and the mother spayed. It was thought a wild cat was responsible, and indeed the one we retained matured into a fiercely independent character with a large bushy tail, which spent days away from home. The other we managed to foist on a missionary family living in the project zone.

As the end of the year approached, a succession of minor incidents occurred. An unidentified insect bit my 'bad' leg, which swelled to elephantine proportions and broke out in small blisters – the agony subsiding only after a couple of days. Mary spent time with Stephano's wife collecting termites from a previous night's swarm, hopefully bringing a cup of them for us to try. Fergus bravely did so, pronouncing them rather like shrimps, but I declined, feeling much as my mother did about lobsters. The girls, together with John and Rosemary's children, Peter, Sheena and Andrew, had collected a number of large land snails (*Achatina spp.*), which were housed in boxes all over both houses, even on the dining table at breakfast, to Stephano's disgust. They marked them with nail varnish and held races in the garden. I drew the line at a vacated tortoise shell in the house until the ants had removed all traces of its dead occupant. Mary started to attend a nursery school that had opened on three mornings each week; unfortunately it was short-lived through lack of demand, and she had to wait until March 1969 to join Katharine at Isamilo Primary School. Our insensitive German neighbour annoyed a black mamba by injuring it with a stone; Fergus then saw it near our car park, chucked a large stone at it, and missed completely; we were astonished how quickly nine feet of snake could disappear into the rockery. Much ineffectual hue and cry ensued, all neighbouring cooks and shamba boys joining in the fray. I hoped it would get the message that it was unwelcome, but it didn't, and was seen from time to time on the track crossing the gully up which cattle were driven daily by a little boy no more than ten years old.

By mid-November I had recovered from the Serengeti trip enough to contemplate taking our entourage to Uganda by lake steamer. Fergus had been asked to attend a schistosomiasis expert committee meeting early in January, followed by the annual medical conference the following week. John and Rosemary, with their three children and their ayah, planned a similar excursion. I had in mind to visit the Queen Elizabeth and Murchison Falls game reserves in western Uganda at the conclusion of the conference; Fergus was less enthusiastic, having been there in 1957 unencumbered by family. It must be hard for readers to imagine how difficult communications then were between countries in the East African Community. Any attempt to make steamer reservations by telephoning the central booking office in Nairobi was guaranteed to provoke a rise in blood pressure. The alternative was to send a letter, which in theory should arrive the next day, but never did. So unable to visit the office in person, chances of booking return tickets for our family and vehicle from Mwanza to Jinja, near Kisumu, and back were slim.

The situation became farcical: Fergus had a personal invitation to go to Kampala, but the regional office in Brazzaville refused permission, saying they intended to send the regional representative (who had not been invited, and had nothing to contribute) as an observer. The secretary of the East African Medical Association then intervened, asking Brazzaville to reconsider its position in view of the valuable contribution which Fergus would make to the special committee on schistosomiasis. He was determined to go, even without official travel authorisation, but this was dangerous territory and might have resulted in days being deducted from his leave, and refusal to pay travel costs. More seriously, he risked arousing the wrath of Dr Quenum in Brazzaville, and seriously jeopardising his future career. As the time approached for our departure, John and Rosemary, their children, the youngest of whom was Andrew, a year older than Michael, and ayah, had their return journey, including their car, confirmed by Nairobi, but not the outward trip; in our case, it was the reverse – between us we had a full booking. Our reservation covered the Peugeot 504 brake.

We liaised with the McMahons when it came to festive catering: our servants, being nominally Christian, wanted Christmas Day and Boxing Day off, while the McMahons' cook, shamba boy and ayah were all Muslim and did not mind working on those days, provided they got two days later in the year or could add them to the celebrations at the end of Ramadan. I had bought a tree, bearing little resemblance to any northern hemisphere conifer, from the forestry department's nursery, insisting that the roots should be preserved. Decorated with old baubles, including those bought in Boston the previous year, it looked authentic when surrounded by small presents for the children, including Stephano's brood, and the ten-year-old son of one of the administrative staff, to whom Michael had taken a liking – John Leugobola. There were soft drinks for the children and hard ones for the parents. Father Christmas provided two dolls in wicker cradles for the girls, proudly displayed to all visitors, but played with minimally thereafter, as predicted; I suspect they were of status value, as all their friends had frilly dolls and cradles. The Barbie craze had yet to reach Mwanza. I was determined to prepare a better Christmas dinner than those we had suffered during the Ghana days, and ordered a free-range turkey from the island farm; ingredients for stuffing posed no problem, in fact the only traditional items missing were Brussels sprouts and potatoes; cranberry sauce and a good variety of dried fruits and nuts were on the shelves of Alibhai stores.

In late January 1968 we travelled to Kampala for the conference and arrived at Makerere University guesthouse exhausted by the trip. We had found the MV *Victoria* unsafe for children and constant vigilance had to be kept lest any of them were tempted to sit on the rails or crawl below the lifeboats, beside which there were no rails at all. The lifeboats were, of course, on the upper deck, and the stairs up and down to this area provided an irresistible round circuit. By now Michael had a fair turn of speed and tried to keep up with the older children. The cabins were comfortable but exceptionally small; the girls and Fergus slept well but I had to share a bunk with Michael, who was wide awake at intervals, humping and thrashing around all night. David Bradley, seconded from the London School of Tropical Medicine, of which he later became director, and joint author with Fergus of a paper to be presented at the conference, found us an excellent temporary ayah who used to work for his family.

The food at the guesthouse was excellent, and the accommodation almost luxurious: we had two enormous bedrooms, two bathrooms and two loos all to ourselves for £6 per day – food included. While Fergus was at the conference centre, I was able to find many things that had been unobtainable in Mwanza, where austerity was beginning to bite with a vengeance. Even rice, which we bought by the sack, was in short supply and riddled with tiny fragments of quartz, so many washings were needed before cooking; even then, tiny bits were liable to surprise the unwary diner. David took us to the botanical reserve, where the variety of exotic butterflies surpassed even those in Sierra Leone. In the end, our five-day safari to the game reserves proved quite legitimate, because the steamer service was unable to honour our return booking until a week after the conference ended; even then we had to accept second-class cabins – sexes segregated even within families, but happily we were allowed to use the first-class dining and bathroom facilities.

We reached Mbarara, where we checked into an Agip motel, in mid-afternoon. We would have preferred a small privately run hotel overlooking the Queen Elizabeth game reserve, but did not dare risk it, as the road was bad, they had no telephone, and might not, in any case, have had any vacancies. An early start the next day was more prudent, even though nine in the morning was the earliest we ever managed. The sky was slightly hazy and it was not too hot on our journey north to Kichwamba, on the edge of the escarpment overlooking the plain, where we stopped for coffee and soft drinks at a small hotel/restaurant owned by a Swede and his Finnish wife. Forty years on I wonder how their enterprise fared under Amin's reign of terror, and whether our Tutsi ayah, some of whose children were still in their teens, survived the atrocities perpetrated by his troops.

On the second day we checked in at the main lodge in the middle of the reserve. Any view of the Ruwenzori range was obscured by dry season haze and smoke from bush fires. One early explorer spent six months at Kasese, without realising the Mountains of the Moon existed, and we saw only a faint shadow of them on the day we left. The park was totally different in character from Serengeti; but we saw any number of elephants and hippos, the birds were more varied, and we saw a pride of seventeen lions – in fact, we parked right in the middle of them. Hordes of warthog, vast herds of buffalo and a serval cat – the last mostly nocturnal – crossed our path. A bull elephant wandered around the staff quarters at the park, searching for fermenting pombe, to which he was addicted – nobody seemed in the least perturbed. There were many chimpanzees in the area, but we were told that we would have to stay at a campsite to have any hope of seeing them.

On our last two days we drove down through the south end of the park, which bordered on the Congo. Elephants were everywhere, while the roadworkers worked on, apparently oblivious of their proximity. Outside the park we came on vast herds of topi, before starting to climb steadily into the famous Kisengi province of Uganda, where the mountains reach eight-thousand feet. The road was rough and the precipices almost alpine in character. Everywhere the steep hillsides were neatly cultivated, or in some places forested with coniferous trees interspersed with eucalyptus: a formidable feat of planting if one considered the distances, gradients, and stultifying heat during the day. There were small compounds on even the steepest slopes with plantations of bananas, beans, maize and even strawberries. We stayed at Kabale, which is famous for its pleasant climate, but unfortunately did not have time to visit Lake Bunyoni or Kisoro some fifty miles away on the border of Ruanda-Burundi and Congo, where the ascent to mountain gorilla territory begins. The final day was just a straight batter back to Kampala, which we reached early in the evening in time to take the girls for a swim in the university pool. On this trip Fergus had, technically speaking, 'abandoned post'.

When we eventually boarded the MV *Victoria* again, the

children and I were conducted to a nine foot by six foot second-class cabin, to be shared with two Indian women, one African woman – all immense – and six assorted children. The Asian ladies got on board at Bukoba, and amid much thumping and loud discussion, filled the available floor space with huge tied bundles. All the lights were ablaze, and at one time the cabin door was filled with voluble male relatives of assorted ages, giving advice, while I lay in my 'negligée' on the top bunk, my head about eighteen inches from the ceiling. Michael, beside me, slept through it all, but Katharine and Mary in the lower bunk added their views on where things could best be stowed. Outside the cabin, the floor was packed with recumbent bodies shrouded in blankets and cloths; between them a narrow route led to other cabins and several bicycles chained to the rails were a hazard to our shins. In the other cabin Fergus and John McMahon were trying to discourage a nervous elderly Asian, who thought his bunk was dangerously high, from laying his mattress on the floor; also in their cabin was a doctor from Dodoma mental hospital, who helped us by taking the older children up to the first-class deck and reading them stories. Michael celebrated the journey by doing five 'smellies' en route, so I spent a lot of time in the foetid bathroom trying to clean up, before adding the rinsed nappies to the huge load we had accumulated over the previous few days. Rosemary, whose younger son was still in nappies, was fortunate indeed to have her ayah on board.

During the latter part of February Michael was very ill for three weeks. It began with loss of appetite and persistent thrush which did not respond to treatment with gentian violet, followed by teething problems and a chest infection resistant to all the drugs prescribed. He was miserable and, because even sucking was painful, would not drink enough fluid to prevent dehydration. It was emotionally and physically draining all of us, but he rapidly regained lost weight, and soon was back to normal, dishing out orders to his peer group. I fear Stephano's brood had been told not to thwart the boss's son. Lucy had inherited Joyce's inscrutable countenance, and unlikely to rebel, little Joseph clung limpet-like to his mother, while Margaret, Salome, Elizabeth and Hilda, who saw themselves as trainee ayahs, were happy to carry Michael around. Stephano, unknown to us, had negotiated the sale – for that is what it was – of Stella, by this time fifteen, to a policeman in Dar for 400 EA shillings. A previous attempt to 'marry' her to a middle-aged local man had provoked her to seek shelter with the family of a school friend. 'That girl is always troubling me' was what Stephano thought about the matter.

Maria of the scowling countenance continued to look after Michael in the mornings, but I had unspecific reservations about her. One day I returned to find Michael at the front of the house, one foot wedged between the blades of the lawnmower, while Maria gossiped with the shamba boy at the back door. Michael was not distressed, and probably would have extricated himself, but I blew a fuse in Swahili, which no doubt sounded ridiculous. The message got through, however, that this was the final straw, and her services were no longer required. She did well out of it, getting three months' severance pay, but no glowing reference. Katharine and Mary were pleased, Stephano enigmatic, and the shamba boy more industrious after the incident. Stella took over in the interim period, before, to our regret, moving out of our life, to live with the policeman after Stephano got his final payment later in the year. I hope the man was kind, as Stella had a nice nature and would have preferred to stay at school for another year.

In mid-July we all went on home leave to Northern Ireland; Fergus for a month only, while the children and I did not return to Mwanza until November, in good time for the festive season. On New Year's Eve I gave a party for more than twenty with turkey, roast pork, all the traditional trimmings, and lots of booze. I do not remember whether it was before this party, or a subsequent one, that Fergus found me late at night crying into the stuffing for the cavernous bird. His reaction was: 'Throw the bloody thing in the bin if that's the way you feel about it.'

14
Debilitating Afflictions

The early months of 1969 saw a succession of 'Mwanza Special' respiratory ailments and fluctuating fevers, the cause of which was never established, usually followed by a fruity cough lasting several weeks. Conventional medical advice was that no current drug was of any benefit, so 'just sweat it out'. In the end I took a drug recommended by the Asian pharmacist; it may have just been a coincidence, but by April I felt well enough to return to the tennis court. Malarial attacks, or the suspicion thereof, in our family as well as in Stephano's brood, were a regular occurrence. Lucy was brought to me one afternoon, limp and with eyes rolling heavenwards, so I rushed her to the institute, where she was treated for malaria without a preliminary blood slide being taken. Katharine got the same treatment, although her symptoms were not so alarming. Regular de-worming of Stephano's children was done partly as insurance against our children getting an infestation. Fergus, being a parasitologist, took the view that 'it all depends on the load', but I was appalled when Margaret, then about six years old, sicked up on the 'lawn' what looked like an entire stomachful of parasitic roundworm (*Ascaris lumbricoides*). Incredibly, of our children over the years, only Mary got a light infestation of threadworms.

In mid-February a Russian clinician/parasitologist recruited by WHO joined the project, by then officially in its second phase. Jarockij often returned with Fergus from the laboratory for afternoon tea, which he drank, peasant style, hand around cup, forefinger holding the spoon in place, making no secret of how much he enjoyed joining in the family scene. He had been allocated living quarters nearby, in a small stone building with a corrugated iron roof, which had once been a prison. Periodically he would invite us to his version of afternoon tea; vodka, white bread and a tin of Beluga caviar, with biscuits, Fanta and Coke for the children. I am grateful to him for educating me in what caviar should be like; the vodka, too, was good, probably sixty per cent.

My return to the tennis court coincided with a match against a team from Mwadui diamond mine about halfway between Mwanza and Tabora, the administrative centre in German colonial days. Fergus and a West Indian judge, recently come to Mwanza, had taken on the task of upgrading tennis facilities at the club and shocked the Asian members by undertaking some of what were regarded as menial tasks themselves. This was a subtle move to encourage the club employees whose job it was to maintain the two clay courts: weeding, sprinkling and rolling had long been neglected, and unused to direction or discipline, they passed much of the day chattering in the shade of a mango tree outside the kitchen. News quickly spread that the visitors would expect entertainment on a lavish scale, accustomed as they were to standards at the largest diamond mine outside South Africa. There was a general improvement in attitude, and Mwanza Club was not shamed on the day, providing a buffet luncheon and not, for once, running out of ice cubes. It was quite an event and I remember Maude Lyonnet, enviably elegant as always, joining the spectators with her two sons, one in a silk-canopied pushchair. Her husband, Roger, was a WHO doctor specialising in smallpox – his previous posting had been in Afghanistan. Roger became a faithful friend, utterly loyal and dependable over the next twenty years, although his ineptitude as a tennis player was a severe test of Fergus's patience.

As a result of our having provided a bed for one of the visiting team, who knew Fergus from the mid-fifties in Accra, before the Gold Coast became Ghana, we were invited to visit the mine at the end of May. The pipe had been discovered by a lone Canadian geologist, John Thoburn Williamson, in 1940, after nearly five years of fruitless prospecting. The site was a vast concentration camp for the mine employees, with maximum security regulations in force, despite which some gemstones did get out. In contrast, senior staff enjoyed just about every material advantage within the boundaries: yacht and tennis clubs, cinema, school, swimming pool, shopping centre, hospital and an air service to fly staff or their dependants to Nairobi for the equivalent of £5. Notwithstanding these delights, some of them were happy to escape to Mwanza from time to time. We were taken on the official visitors' tour and proudly shown a replica of the Williamson pink 23.6-carat round diamond which Williamson had presented to Princess Elizabeth as a wedding gift, and which had been set at the centre of a hideous flower brooch. The design was a single daisy on a two-leafed stalk of white diamonds set in platinum – so undistinguished, not to say trite, it might have been drawn by a child. My comment that I wouldn't wear it if paid was tactless, and did not go down well with some of the women. Poor Fergus winced, saying, not for the first time, 'Will you never learn?' But we had spent an enjoyable weekend in an unreal world, to which we were to return two years later in quite different circumstances.

The Schistosomiasis Control Project was progressing satisfactorily. As it was scheduled to end in 1972, Fergus explored job possibilities within overseas development agencies, schools of tropical medicine, and universities both in the UK and America. A vacancy at headquarters, for which he was ideally suited, was filled by a candidate from Atlanta; Fergus heard that he had been second choice. John and Rosemary were to leave Mwanza in August for home leave in Australia, followed by an eighteen-month contract in the highlands of Papua New Guinea. Katharine was devastated at the prospect of losing her best friend Sheena, but things were soon to change for her in any case. Many parents had become uneasy about standards at Isamilo Primary School, where the state had begun to interfere in what had hitherto been an independent school, answerable only to the Anglican Church. New teachers had been recruited whose spoken English was suspect, and all pupils were expected to line the official route to cheer and wave flags on Young Pioneers Day, Independence Day, or the visit of any minister from Dar. As no event ever began on time, this involved standing for hours in the heat. I mostly excused the children on grounds of sickness.

Fergus had accumulated a number of local leave days, which if not used before a certain date would be sacrificed – accordingly plans for another safari began to take shape. He would, of course, intersperse pleasure with official visits to other specialists working in the field on schistosomiasis or related rural health issues such as irrigation, wells and water supplies. This would ensure it was not just a holiday, and he would earn per diem expenses to help towards the considerable costs of overnight accommodation for the whole family. The *Victoria* had been in dry dock for three weeks for its annual service. Rumours were rife of delays in obtaining spare parts: cracks, literal and metaphorical, were widening in the hitherto notably efficient East African Railways and Harbours service. Liaison with the booking office in Nairobi had worsened to the extent that now they flatly refused to confirm reservations. In the end, the *Victoria* came on a trial run to Mwanza in June and we sailed back with it to Kisumu a few days later, hoping that it would not sink on the way. (Horribly prescient in the light of the disaster in 1996, when a more modern vessel sank between Bukoba and Mwanza, with the loss of over five hundred lives.)

My recall of the journey from Kisumu to Lake Naivasha is dim, but whichever route we took would have involved at least eight hours' driving: the 'scenic route', for which I always pleaded, via Narok, was probably overruled in favour of the longer, but better-surfaced road via Kisii and Kericho. To recover from the battering, we stayed two nights in a timber lodge at the southern shore of Lake Naivasha, from which we walked into Hell's Gate, notching up the great bustard and secretary bird en route – the Lammergeyer bearded vulture did not oblige. We spent three nights in Nairobi at the Fairview hotel, which was a good base for families with young children, although the city was crowded, noisy, dusty, full of tourists and the traffic frightening. Next we took the Mombasa road, heading for the Amboseli reserve, stopping to eat a memorably uncomfortable picnic in rhino scrub country. The ground was scattered with small sharp rocks, there were thorns underfoot, which pierced our flipflops, and the temperature was so high the horizon was a quivering mirage. Little stirred, apart from thousands of ants scurrying around the crumbs, but we spotted a solitary rhino in the distance, and at close range, the rear end of another one browsing in the scrub. Bibiana, an ayah recruited locally, accompanied us on this trip. She was a little older than Stella and more appreciative of the wildlife, and she was invaluable in coping with our load of washing and ironing, as well as helping to tidy up the children's mess and keeping an eye on Michael, by now two and a half. Fortuitously his major 'toilet' breakthrough coincided with this trip.

We stayed at Marangu on the slopes of Kilimanjaro at a lodge from which many climbers began their assault on the peak, which, from my photographs, was heavily snow capped. Here we met a couple from Tucson, Arizona, who became lifelong friends. Lillian was a Superior Court judge, inveterate adventurer and reliable correspondent; her husband, Bernie, was an asthmatic with high blood pressure, which precluded mountain-climbing, but Lillian had completed her ascent of Kilimanjaro a few days earlier. She added this triumph to several descents of the Grand Canyon, and white-water rafting through the rapids long before it became a popular pursuit. We visited them in Tuscon in 1993 and travelled to the Grand Canyon in the luxury Lexus saloon they lent us, getting to the rim just after dawn. It was bitterly cold, with snow on the ground, and there were scarcely any people around other than lodge staff. I am grateful to have seen the canyon before the scene was violated by the building of a viewing platform, which extends, like a diving board, from the crater rim.

From Kilimanjaro we travelled to the Lake Manyara hotel, perched on the edge of the Rift Valley escarpment, overlooking the national park directly below. From the beautifully planted garden, one could see elephant families, herds of buffalo, and a scattering of giraffe in almost constant movement on the stage below – it was like having a front row seat in the upper circle of a theatre. The swimming pool was pristine, the accommodation superior, but the atmosphere was dour, and the staff uninterested in visitors because of the average twenty-four-hour turnover, coming in coaches chartered in the US or Germany. The baboons at the entrance to the park were importunate to the point of being dangerous, sitting on the bonnet and reaching in through any open window, making negotiations for tickets hazardous. Mary in particular was nervous, her sunhat having been snatched by a colobus monkey at von Nagy's small zoo near Moshi, a refuge for orphaned semi-tame animals that had been hand-reared.

Leaving Manyara, we began the long ascent to the summit, which overlooked Ngorongoro crater. The air grew perceptibly cooler, and the vegetation changed to tall trees, from which curtains of Spanish moss dangled in the mist. Several elephants crossed our path, one bull stopping in the middle of the road to inspect us, before, to general relief, disappearing silently into the forest. We stopped to gaze over the vastness of the crater towards Jaeger Summit – l05 feet higher – and two other ancient volcanic peaks, knowing that lakes Natron and Magadi lay in the vastness beyond, promising ourselves that one day we would visit them too. We never did, having to content ourselves with seeing the flamingos at the better known, more easily accessible, Lake Nakuru. Descending to the plain, we were soon choking in clouds of dust as we neared Olduvai Gorge on a track that bore notices advising how best to cope with shifting sands. I revised my view, expressed once to an Australian water engineer recruited to Fergus's project, that air-conditioning was for wimps. He had boasted about his duty-free Mercedes, which had this benefit. Our admiration of the Leakey team of archaeologists, who depended on water coming in by road from Arusha, was, and remains, profound. We saw them patiently scraping, softly brushing, and sifting under the relentless sun, scarcely a bush in sight, but they stopped work to describe what they were doing to interested, largely uninformed, visitors. Our visit was five years before the four-million-year-old fossil remains of Lucy, our earliest ancestor, were discovered. The children were too young to appreciate the significance of it all, but intrigued by the lavatory, which in this instance was a three-sided wooden structure perched on a little hill overlooking the main site: the fourth side was a sack flapping in the faint breeze, the wooden seat over another bottomless shaft to Australia.

As a result of my letter of complaint two years earlier, we spent two nights and a full day as guests of the management at Seronera, receiving VIP treatment, including palatable meals. We inspected the self-service section and found it much improved, though still without a refrigerator. Highlights on the last lap to Ndabaka were seeing a 'congregation' of crocodiles and, for the first time at close range, three cheetahs resting on a small hummock. Now that Serengeti can be viewed on television screens worldwide, I appreciate more fully the chance I had to take pictures with a hand-held Exakta camera, changing telephoto lenses under adverse conditions, mostly using Kodachrome II film, which has borne the time-test surprisingly well. This film went out of production early in 2012, to the worldwide regret of many professional photographers.

October brought the long school holidays, the object of which was to release children back to their family farms to help with planting the before the rains began, but on 16 October they started with a vengeance. I was in the main market when the first downpour fell and water rapidly rose to ankle depth. I got back to the institute, on a hill about half a mile from the town centre, in time to collect Fergus and the children, who now looked healthy, having regularly been out in the morning sun. Michael adopted Stefano's daughter Salome after Lucy was returned to her father, the librarian, and they all had great fun on the big orange bouncy ball with ears, bought in Nairobi. We had inherited a primitive barbecue from John and Rosemary – a metal drum sawn in half with holes in the bottom, which rested on stones in the garden. Charcoal was cheap and plentiful, and we never lacked advice on how best to achieve and maintain a constant glow; Jarockij proved invaluable, always joking about his horror at having seen me trying to cheat with a sprinkling of paraffin. As the year drew to a close staple foodstuffs rocketed in price after the State Trading Corporation took over distribution. Effectively this resulted in spasmodic deliveries only, thus creating ideal conditions for both black and brown profiteers. Shades of Ghana yet again.

In November Fergus attended a conference on all aspects of schistosomiasis held in Geneva, returning via Dar, where he gave a talk at the annual general meeting of Medical Missionaries. He felt that the Geneva talks had not been productive, despite the vast cost of getting so many experts together around one table: yet another example of conflict between ivory tower administrators, who spend a few days only visiting field projects, and those who actually work there. He had met the chief personnel officer, who admitted that a number of staff members in similar positions to ours wanted to return to a more temperate climate. He said that the organisation was examining ways to deal with their 'issues', and that there would be no question of sacrificing valuable long-serving staff members. All very cordial and chummy, but it would soon be fourteen years since Fergus began his career with WHO at the remote field station near Fort Rosebery in Northern Rhodesia.

The conviction that we were likely to remain at Mwanza for at least one more duty tour, added to our unease about continuing

The mosque at Dorimon

Dancers at Wa

With Simbu dog outside the guest-house at Dorimon

With Katharine at Wa, 1964

Outside our house at Wa: (L–R) Fergus with Katharine, Daniel Kofi, me and Mary, and Francis Kofi

Katharine with Mousa Moshi

Our house on the East Africa Medical Research Institute Residential Compound at Bwiru, near Mwanza, Tanzania

Rocks above the house at Bwiru (small figure Mary)

Mwanza Yacht Club

Herding cattle at Bwiru

The Bismarck Rocks, Lake Victoria, Mwanza

Ndabaka Gate, Western Corridor, Serengeti

Masai women near Lake Manyara

Mary and Michael on the deck of
the MV *Victoria*

Hyaenas near Seronera

Michael, Mary and Katharine at the Naabi Gate, at the eastern end of the Serengeti

Katharine and Ainda Sidwell at Lagg Strand, near Malin

state interference at Isamilo Primary School, led us to explore the possibility of sending Katharine to a co-ed preparatory school near Eldoret in Kenya. We would not think of sending her to board in the UK, but Kenya was worth considering, involving only an overnight boat trip to Kisumu, followed by a reasonably short road trip to Eldoret a few miles north of the equator. We stayed at Eldoret in order to meet the headmaster of Kaptagat School, to which children of many UN parents and ex-colonial officers went: the head – ex-Dragon School in Oxford – had prudently taken Kenyan citizenship in 1956. Much would depend on events in newly independent Kenya. The arrival of Sven Christiansen, a Danish statistician from the WHO Epidemiological Centre in Nairobi, was fortuitous in this regard. His task was to make sense out of the wealth of facts, percentages and figures emanating from the Schistosomiasis Control Project. He and his wife, Kirsten, became good friends who gave us invaluable help during 1971–73 when Katharine was a pupil at Kaptagat in the highlands. She sometimes arrived in Nairobi by train with a group of fellow pupils from the school, and they met her off the train, having her for overnight stays before putting her on a plane to Mwanza.

In January 1970 we celebrated Michael's multicultural third birthday party. He joined a nursery school, which our young neighbour, Herta, had taken over. Strictly speaking, he should not have been at the school, being too young, and not near the top of the waiting list, but we hoped nobody would spot this and complain on grounds of racial discrimination or influence. Herta, whose husband, Peter Kilala, was deputy director at the institute, made the case that there were far too many Asian children in the group, who gabbled Gujarati at each other; their parents were keen that they should become fluent in English, thus raising their chance of entry to an independent primary school, and Michael's presence would be an asset. It crossed my mind that the Asian parents might be less appreciative were their offspring to air some of Michael's favourite expressions, such as 'You are a stupidy gorm' or a 'greedy gorb', used in defence when in dispute with his sisters.

In February we were visited by Dr Ansari. By this time we had a better measure of the man within, fuelled by reports from colleagues working at headquarters, who complained of his duplicitous behaviour and erratic moods. The American appointed to the job for which Fergus had been second choice, reported that he was unhappy, and little more than the departmental lackey. Notwithstanding, I pulled out all the stops, providing good meals, although disappointingly his appetite was never good; but he always brightened when the meal ended and a choice of liqueurs was offered with the coffee I had freshly roasted and ground. He was almost fulsome in praise of the project, saying it had the soundest baseline data, and best presented reports of all he had visited, and was insistent that Fergus should remain in charge until it had run its five-year course. Our inclination to remain with WHO was also strengthened by dawning realisation that the children's educational costs were only beginning; there were rumours too that retirement age might be reduced to fifty-five with increased benefits, and the possibility of consultantships thereafter. Dr Ansari implied that Fergus could have at any time one of the WHO academic professorial appointments in member countries, and that in his case, because of his vast experience of Africa, it would probably be in Nairobi; also hanging fire was a vacancy on the Bilharziasis Advisory Team, requiring three suitable candidates.

With all this in mind, the thought of sending Katharine to school just north of the equator did not seem so radical. We had visited the school and liked the headmaster: the climate was good and, because of the high altitude, it was situated above the malaria zone. Dormitories were spartan, with iron beds and small lockers, but the children appeared cheerful, mannerly and in rude health. The uniform was hideous: grey pleated skirts, a crude blue Aertex shirt, maroon sweaters, grey socks and brown shoes; a straw hat, like the one I had worn during the war, was obligatory when travelling – a cap for the boys. They would be happy to welcome Katharine in mid-September.

Sweden had approved a generous loan to Tanzania for the improvement of rural water supplies, and had sent a number of water chemists, engineers, and an epidemiologist to assess the project. An inadequate three weeks had been allocated to this task, so we had a lot of entertaining to do that spring. The Swedish team stayed in a variety of small hotels in Mwanza, most of which would not qualify for a one star rating today, so a visit to the delights of Bwiru made a pleasant break from the dusty, evil-smelling town centre.

The German community organised a dinner dance at the club, at which, under pressure from Herta, we put in an appearance. She was a Sudeten German who regarded herself as Czechoslovak; the northern Germans dismissed the southern ones as ignorant peasants, and the southern those in the north as irredeemable snobs. Herta was outnumbered by three to one, and there had been friction among the members of the organising committee. My part was to roast joints of pork and transport them to the club as a contribution to the main table. In addition, Herta had prepared schnitzels, sauerkraut, various salads, mango strudel and a rich trifle.

The unavailability of staple foodstuffs continued to be a problem, as was the rising cost of living and the fact that our post adjustment was one of the lowest in the organisation. Fergus's monthly salary, which had allowed us to save while we were in Ghana, was by this time insufficient, and I felt that unless the UN created a commissariat in Dar, to keep a store of goods not available locally, prospects for our next tour were dire. Meanwhile, I was helping Fergus to prepare a series of lectures, which had to be stencilled, as well as making slides of pollution and transmission sites in Mwanza and its environs.

A Pakistani public health engineer had joined the project team, and an independent American research worker in schistosomiasis, Margaret Magendantz, had offered to work in parallel with the team: she was a strange girl who could have been a professional violinist but had chosen biological research instead. Fergus said her work was irreproachable, but suspected she was making a token rejection of the US way of life. She had taken over the 'prison' vacated by Jarockij and lived frugally. Tall and good-looking in an androgynous way, her long fair hair was tied in a pony tail and her clothing never varied from a shirt worn with a navy-blue divided skirt, and leather sandals held together with bits of wire; irrespective of the weather, she cycled daily to the institute on a second-hand bike bought in the market. Naïvety led her to leave her Stradivarius tied to the luggage carrier at a wayside duka; unsurprisingly it disappeared while she was inside. She was devastated by the loss, while our emotions were a mixture of sympathy, impatience and anger that such a beautiful instrument had been carelessly sacrificed: none of the locals would have had any idea of its value, and after some artless strumming it would have succumbed to the climate, probably ending as firewood. She became reclusive, seeing few people outside working hours, and was a constant worry to us – particularly after she contracted schistosomiasis through wading bootless in shallow water. Fergus, puzzled by her unexplained absence from work, had called at the prison and found her barely conscious. After hospitalisation, she made a slow recovery. It should be said that she was not the exception among research workers, who were notorious in taking risks where their own infection was concerned. I remember even Fergus showing me cercariae swimming in a test tube, his forefinger in the swarming soup.

Violent protest was erupting worldwide; this was the decade during which innocent populations were under attack by extremist movements, and terrorism and tribalism in one form or another began to plumb new depths of inhumanity. Air travel was no longer a luxury mode of transport, but a tedious process not unlike sheep-farming. Security gates, electronic checks and body searches became the norm, and flights to Northern Ireland were under particular scrutiny. Many letters from home contained increasingly depressing news about events in the North: intemperate proclamations from both nationalists and unionists fuelled outbreaks of violence not only on the streets of Belfast and Derry, but in the border towns of Strabane and Lifford, and smaller towns in all six counties. Republican extremists used the Inishowen peninsula as a refuge after committing some criminal act in County Derry, and arms were regularly ferried from Greencastle, to the sands at Eglinton, not far from Coleraine. All RUC barracks were protected by coils of barbed wire, army and police patrols wore flak jackets, and the centre of Belfast had to be entered via security gates. Friends wrote that in Letterkenny, Culdaff and Carndonagh an atmosphere of wary suspicion was palpable in pubs and hotels; furtive glances were exchanged, and visitors got a guarded, rather than enthusiastic, welcome; male footwear was scrutinised – a high shine might indicate a British soldier in civilian clothing.

Despite my uneasiness about the conflict, I wanted the children to have a long stay in Northern Ireland during the summer, because soon we would be tied to school or university terms for at least fifteen years. Fergus was not due for home leave until June, but even that was subject to postponement if the regional director in Brazzaville was minded to keep him in post awaiting the recruitment of a temporary project leader. In the end, I flew with the children in April via East African Airways from Nairobi to Frankfurt–London–Belfast. Seasoned travellers though they were, the children slept for almost twelve hours after we reached our house at Craigavad, next door to their indulgent grannie: if ever I did anything right, it was providing her with grandchildren, an outlet for the love that had been so long repressed.

Fergus joined us in June, and through an agency called Irish Aunts, we engaged a Donegal woman to help my mother look after the children for a week, while we visited Dublin. This was the longest break we had taken from full-time parenting, and I found it difficult to banish all feelings of guilt, though logic told me they were unfounded.

We rented a chalet near Malin for two weeks, and the children saw, for the first time, magnificent stretches of fine sand backed by high dunes down which they could toboggan. Towering Atlantic rollers broke relentlessly on Lagg strand, where their kite flew higher than ever before, and when the wind was chill, they could bathe in warm rock pools near the foot of the cliffs, from the top of which the view extended over Doagh Island and its ruined castle, towards Errigal and Muckish, and the promontories of Dunaff, Fanad and Horn Head, to the Rosses and Aranmore; Glashedy Island stood like a little cake near the mouth of Trawbreega Bay. The girls, who could just remember their year in the US, were impressed when told that only the Atlantic ocean divided them from Boston.

In one of my more insane fantasies I asked Johnnie McLaughlin, who owned the hotel in Malin, if he thought Glashedy could be bought; ever the optimist, he promised to look into it. But with his help, and that of Matt Doherty who owned the general store, we did buy two plots of land, one overlooking the harbour at Glengad on Lough Foyle, the other at Ineuran Bay near Malin Head. I went to great lengths to obtain planning approval from Lifford, eventually getting it for a one-storey house at Glengad, and for Ineuran 'a structure of outstanding architectural merit with concessions to local tradition'. The former we sold to a solicitor whose wife had been born on Inishowen; the second I still own, but outline permission has long expired, and it would take a genius such as Frank Lloyd Wright, plus huge capital investment, to do credit to this site, which is little more than a rock pocket with a stupendous view. Some day one of our descendents may pitch a tent or caravan there, or more likely have a picnic and reflect on Grannie's many impulsive purchases.

Fergus took the children to visit his mother in Comber, County Down. She had survived a severe stroke some fifteen years earlier and was, he said, a sadly diminished version of the woman she once was. She still wrote a daily diary and regularly attended her church, but was in many ways childish, with an embarrassing tendency to play any piano that came into orbit. His sister, Elsie, a radiographer, devoted her life to her, ensuring that the old woman got such good care that she lived long enough to get a telegram from the queen, and a visit from Rinty Monaghan, the flyweight boxer, with whom she was photographed. Also living in the inharmoniously extended eighteenth-century farmhouse, were a much older brother, his young wife and only child, and another reclusive bachelor brother, Eric, who was a gifted artist. The children loved these visits, returning late in the evening covered in straw and dust, having spent much time messing around in the hayshed. To say the farm was running down was an understatement – it had long run down, and any income came from renting out many of the fertile acres that surrounded it. By all accounts, Fergus's father had been a reflective man, more interested in reading than in tilling the land: his life had been shattered by the death of their eldest son, Jack, from TB while at an agricultural college in County Tyrone in the late twenties. He felt that negligence had been involved and diagnosis delayed. The family had suffered during the depression from 1929 to the mid-thirties, and after the war, when many subsidies were available to farmers, he had not taken advantage of them. In consequence, the long rocky lane from the main road remains untarred to this day.

San, now suffering from arthritis, came to visit us, and I took the children to visit her and Murray in the subsiding little house at Neill's Hill my mother had been instrumental in their buying some years before. Murray looked unwell and his skin was a sinister waxy yellow, but he brightened instantly on meeting Michael, pronouncing him 'a fine little fella'. Michael was well behaved, pottering around and making friends with their tabby cat: it was a concession to age that they no longer had a dog. Our visit had been a surprise one to preclude San making a special effort, but she insisted that we have some of her featherweight scones spread thickly with butter and her own raspberry jam. A slender silver fluted vase of the sweet pea that Murray continued to grow stood in the middle of the table. Two months later, when we were back in Mwanza, I got a letter from San with the news that they had been allocated a flat in a new housing development at Dundonald, but that Murray had been admitted to the new hospital in the same area. The flat allocation, which may have resulted from my having drawn their case to the attention of the Down County Welfare Committee, came too late for Murray, who died of prostate cancer at the end of November. We implored San not to allow grief to scupper the plan to move, so she accepted the offer of the newly built first-floor flat in Dundonald with a resident warden early in 1971. It was in a quiet neighbourhood devoid of street violence and graffiti, unlike some of the offers they had rejected, which had caused Murray to complain: 'They just don't listen to us when we say we want to remain in the neighbourhood we have known for fifty years.'

She adjusted slowly and her sister Molly continued to make the effort to come from Carrickfergus, sometimes staying overnight, her compulsion to dispense advice and criticism in no way lessened by the passage of time. These purgatorial visits gave San something with which to entertain loyal friends from Knock and Holywood Arches, most of whom had been victims of Molly's criticism in the past. My mother, whose sight problems had yet to force her off the road, had an Austin A40 and came regularly to take San either to Craigavad or Holywood, or shopping in Bangor and Newtownards. Sometimes they would tour the Ards peninsula, visiting Portaferry and Donaghadee, of which San spoke sourly, having lived there in a caravan for a while when Murray's garage in York Street failed, and he had been forced to sell their house on the Gilnahirk Road. Auntie Dodi (the name the children affectionately gave Dorothy), who had trained as a social worker after her divorce, now worked from an office in Bangor, and kept an unofficial eye on how things were.

In September Fergus walked to the departure lounge at Belfast airport holding Katharine, in a too-long navy-blue raincoat, by her left hand; with the other she clutched her tiger bought in Boston. When they turned to wave before disappearing, I felt for the first time the enormity of the decision we had made to send her to school in Kenya: more than a lump rose in my throat, and I was thankful that Mary, Michael and my mother had said their goodbyes at home. San had held her counsel, but I knew quite well what she thought.

Six weeks later we were reunited for Katharine's half-term holiday. We stayed in a lodge at Soy near Eldoret, where a tame crowned crane patrolled the garden, and herds of giraffe and baboons thronged the surrounding countryside. We joined the Eldoret Club on a daily basis so that the children could use their clean, little-used pool. A girl from Katharine's dormitory joined us, having been left out of an invitation her elder sister had to join a family living nearby; possibly they did not know of her existence, but we felt the school should have intervened, particularly as it was the child's first term. When the holiday ended, we took them back to school and Katharine left us without a tear, preoccupied by the fact that *The Sound of Music* was to be shown that night. Afterwards we battered, in rapidly fading light, the considerable distance to Kericho Tea Hotel, where Michael cracked up, saying he hated us all, the food, his bed, the hotel, and wished we were dead. However, next morning he had recovered enough to horse around with Mary and enjoy the beautifully maintained aviary and pond, which teemed with giant goldfish and tadpoles. Then the relentless pounding back to Mwanza, broken only by a short picnic and customs stop, plus our customary puncture near the exit from Serengeti. The tyre was quite new, having been bought in Nairobi, but Fergus found the inner tube unfamiliar, having been patched many times – it had been substituted by some unknown mechanic. In future we marked all inner tubes with nail varnish. Mary and Michael were incredibly good, showing signs of extreme fatigue only as we neared Mwanza and clanked over the noisy planked bridge, through the wide gaps of which one could see a rushing torrent: Michael's timely comment was: 'Say the bridge falls in?' Within days our Irish holiday was a distant memory, referred to only when my skills with Lego were compared unfavourably to those of Grannie, and the reproach added that, anyway, I was always busy doing something else.

Project data had accumulated during my absence, Fergus's quarterly report was due, and graphs of infection rates in all ages of the population in the suburbs of Mwanza had to be photographed. Many guests, including a consultant who had been booked into an awful hotel in the town, came to us for an evening meal – Dr Eyakuze, as usual, not having offered any hospitality. Meat, no longer in plentiful supply, was now expensive when obtainable. Our Somali butcher opened twice a week only because the government had idealistically fixed prices so low that many farmers were not sending cattle for slaughter. Despite visits to Nairobi, our clothing continually needed replacement or repair and the Christmas holidays were approaching. Katharine would be back in no time at all, from December 6 to January 10, and travel arrangements had yet to be decided.

On 25 November, our tenth wedding anniversary, a letter came from Brazzaville saying that the director general had approved Fergus for a career service appointment, first put forward four years previously, but turned down each time because of the 'nationality quota' rule. He decided to accept it, because it would end the uncertainty of limping along from one two-year contract to the next; it did, however, limit his work to the African region, and anywhere therein they might choose to send him. The greatest plus was that it would remove the very real fear of being out of work, something that was happening to many well-qualified scientists at that time.

When Katharine arrived by steamer, she was accompanied by two Norwegian girls, Anna and Edit, from school. Their father, Paul Jenset, was one of the ship's engineers, whose wife was said to have committed suicide by wading far out into Lake Victoria, leaving Anna, Edit, and their brother, Peder, without a mother. She had indeed attempted suicide, but the Norwegian embassy took over, and she was sent back to Norway, where care services took over her case. All that the children were told, when they got back from school one day, was: 'Your mother has gone away.' She later divorced Paul and remarried. The children were undemanding, and surprisingly happy, and we were grateful to their father for having added Katharine to his responsibility list while she was aboard the *Victoria*. On Christmas Eve we gave a party for twelve children, with Fergus in the role of Santa, wearing a red candlewick bedspread and white cotton-wool beard, its Sellotape fixing provoking derisive mirth from all present. I opted out of full-scale catering for adults, and let it be known that the house would be open for drinks and nibbles for anyone inclined to drop in. Our own feast was planned for Boxing Day, when I could expect little help from Stephano, whose reactions would be slow after over-indulgence in pombe on Christmas Day.

15
Turning Point

Early in January 1971, I dropped my art deco hand-mirror on the concrete floor of our bedroom. I was not superstitious, but the thought that this might presage seven years' bad luck crossed my mind. On the same day I found cockroaches scuttling around the drawer where I kept make-up, and moth holes in a Liberty woollen suit, which had – or so I thought – been protected in an air-tight bag, and it was obvious that I was going prematurely grey.

Once, during an alcohol-fuelled confessional, I confided to the Poet that life had yet to deal me a crippling blow. His unhelpful response was to liken me to a chocolate-coated marshmallow – 'hard and brittle on the outside, but mush within'. Odd how such trivial remarks endure. My mother's 'He's far too good for you', apropos Fergus.

What lay in store was insidious, progressive, terrifying and potentially terminal. It would dominate my life for the next sixteen years.

Fergus transferred Katharine into the care of her form mistress on the Nairobi–Eldoret train. She was relieved not to see, as she had feared, the sadistic swimming teacher who 'keeps us in the water for ages when it is cold, never comes in herself unless the sun is shining, and she is *fat*'.

Fortuitously Fergus had decided to postpone his trip to Uganda for the conference of the East African Medical Association until the second day, as he was not programmed to speak until the third, thereby missing the turmoil that accompanied Idi Amin's well-calculated assumption of power during Milton Obote's absence at a conference of Commonwealth ministers in Singapore. Other delegates who had travelled by boat and road during the previous week had found themselves confined to halls of residence or hotels in Kampala. The conference venue was the Parliament Building, at the hub of activities, where seven people were reported to have been killed. A curfew was in force from seven in the evening until six thirty in the morning, and a bomb had been pitched into the main entrance to Entebbe airport, which was closed. Telephone lines were more chaotic than usual, and Dr Ansari was a prisoner in the Apollo Hotel in Kampala. To cap all this, Fergus got a wire from London asking him to attend an interview for the post of assistant director of the Commonwealth Bureau of Helminthology – a job he had applied for so long ago that he had forgotten about it; BOAC had been paid for his return fare. Meanwhile an indefinite postal strike was in operation throughout Tanzania.

Information gleaned from an ex-colleague, who was likely to be on the interviewing committee, revealed that the post was blighted by the incumbent female director, who had seen two assistant directors off the scene in the last decade. The advertisement had sought someone to 'bring the Institute into the twentieth century computerized age', but the director, a notorious technophobe, did not want to be brung, so the job could be deemed a nonstarter. Fergus had ethical reservations about using the air ticket, but it would allow him to visit headquarters on his return flight and continue discussions with Dr Ansari about his future in the tropical diseases division of WHO.

For Katharine's half-term holiday, I took the *Victoria* to Kisumu, accompanied by Mary and Michael. When the boat docked early in the morning, neither passengers nor crew were allowed ashore until they had been searched for Tanzanian paper money. There had been an Ealing comedy-style robbery earlier in the week, when three million EA shillings had disappeared from the hold, but cold feet and incompetence ensured most of it was soon recovered, leaving half a million untraced. According to the previous timetable, the boat would have docked a day earlier, which had been ideal for the half-term, but after the coup in Uganda, the sailing was changed to include an extra stop at Bukoba. Rumour was that the boilers of another ship belonging to East African Railways and Harbours, the *Usoga*, were no longer safe, dating as they did from 1912. The vessel, now in dry dock, looked just like the Bogart/Hepburn steamer in the *The African Queen*, so it was probably true.

Katharine and the Jenset children, Anna, Edit and Peder, had been escorted from the school by a pleasant Asian girl who was sister-in-charge of a health centre near Kaptagat. But the whole exercise had been so fraught with uncertainties and abortive telephone calls, it was not until we actually went ashore that I knew the children were there. We all stayed at the Jensets' house, and I had the task of feeding eight at each sitting during the weekend. There was a cook/steward in residence, but he was not in the same league as Stephano. We took the children to swim at the Kisumu Club, and for a picnic in the Nandi Hills, indulging them with a continuous supply of ice cream, which was unobtainable in Mwanza.

Quite often interesting items appeared in the main market in Mwanza: Chinese influence brought cheap blue and white chinaware in the form of teapots, rice bowls and soup plates, some of which were hand painted with remarkable fluidity in a fish design: although mass produced they were very attractive – only three have survived the years. Sometimes little woven baskets, finer than those locally produced, could be found, some originating from as far afield as Malawi, or the Congo, judging by their purple interwoven designs. Cages of noisy black-faced lovebirds from the plains around Tabora were often on display. I tried to ignore them, knowing the occupants were doomed, and to buy them would encourage the trade. In the wild these busy little birds fly fast and low in large flocks like budgerigars. However, while Fergus was away, I weakened and bought six, which were temporarily confined in an old parrot's cage wrapped in mosquito netting, on which they exercised their hard little beaks. An aviary, the cost of which was escalating by the hour, was being built in a semi-shaded area at the rear of the house.

Early in March of that year the nightmare began. It was Sunday morning and Fergus and I were taking the children to the club for an early swim; Mary and Michael were in the back of the car and I was driving. Just past Bismarck Rock, where we had seen a large Nile monitor lizard cross the road, Fergus said he thought he was going to faint, turned very red in the face, then pallid and cold before breaking into a heavy sweat, and losing consciousness. He had told me that as a child he had fainted several times, and twice as an adult, but nothing had prepared me for this. I put his seat into the reclining position, and drove as quickly as possible up the hill to the hospital, holding his right hand with my left when not changing gear, at the same time assuring the children that Daddy was just in a faint, that it had happened before, and there was nothing to worry about. Fortunately our friend Donald was on duty and admitted him immediately to the so-called Grade I inpatients ward; his blood pressure was very low, his heartbeat barely perceptible, but he had regained consciousness. Donald suspected a mild coronary, which was soon confirmed by a physician from one of the mission hospitals. Fergus was, and remained, in total denial – protesting that it had merely been another fainting incident. The cardiologist who flew in from Nairobi was impressed that all the right procedures had been followed, and the medical team was united in prescribing a three-week period in bed under mild sedation, followed by return home to a quiet atmosphere, before resuming mild activity. He was put on phenobarbitone, but was highly resistant, needing three times the prescribed dose, so the cardiologist advised a switch to Valium, which he hated, arguing it made him slow-witted, and could be addictive.

This incident came as no surprise to me, as it was a matter of days since his return from a three-day visit to Dar to a mountain of project-related work; he was anxious about our future, and maintaining good relations with his national counterpart was an ongoing exercise in self-control. Dr Eyakuze was prone to second laboratory and field assistants, as well as project transport, without prior discussion as to whether or not this would fit in with Fergus's work schedule. I lent an ear to many explosive outbursts, and unprintable epithets about this arbitrary behaviour during our lunch-time breaks.

It was a great relief when Donald agreed to discharge Fergus from the hospital, which dated from the early days of German rule. Working in the small kitchen where family members could prepare food for relatives, one day I found an uncovered stool sample on the draining board beside the sink; the place swarmed with flies and there was no mosquito proofing. Without the support of Donald, who would be the next one to collapse if he continued to work such gruelling hours, I do not know how I could have endured those weeks, and am eternally grateful. His advice as we parted on the day it happened was: 'If ye think ye cannae sleep the night, take a guid stiff whisky before ye go to bed.' I believe it was at that precise point that my relationship with alcohol changed to addictive dependence, though, because of genetic predisposition, inevitably it was going to claim me in the end. Not long after, I who had never used booze as a tranquilliser was taking a good stiff something or other to deal with any sort of stress, real or imagined. A tumbler always sat beside the typewriter in the corner of our bedroom, which passed as my office, while I typed project-related letters and reports. Often I had to hammer these out against time so that Fergus could collect them at lunch time. If I asked him to join me for an aperitif before our meal, he would decline, saying it would make him drowsy: so innocent are most of our nearest and dearest. In hindsight, I had a typical alcoholic personality, reinforced by a degree of tolerance not commonly found in females. The disease is, as the literature says, cunning, baffling and powerful – its progress relentless.

On the night that Fergus came home from hospital an attempt was made to break into our house through one of the kitchen windows. I heard the ping as the hinge was forced. However, when I went around flashing a torch, I neither saw nor heard anything. The next day we noticed one of the veranda chairs overturned and a window catch distorted. The police, full of swarming inefficiency, deemed the thieves sophisticated, as they had been 'very clever and worn gloves'.

The children accepted the need for quiet when visiting the sickroom – bouncing and horsing around on the bed being temporarily prohibited – and settled to their usual pursuits. Fergus slowly improved, and in fact looked so well that I was sorely tempted to let him get up. However, medical opinion was unanimous – he was to stay put, resting and heavily tranquillised, if he was not to become argumentative and stressed. But ultimately Fergus began agitating for a return to office routine, and took to wandering, secateurs in hand, around the garden, determined to work on a half-day basis the following week. In such extreme heat we both knew a return to the lab after lunch would be unwise: sometimes I found myself near collapse, while the children often dozed off during an enforced rest. Roger Lyonnet, now based in Dar with the smallpox eradication programme, was very concerned about Fergus, telephoning me almost every night about his progress.

When he came to Mwanza at the end of the month, we had a dinner party for him and his assistant, as well as Donald and his wife, Jean.

If the results of medical tests at Nairobi were positive, we hoped to have a better idea about the future, and possibly a recommendation for a transfer to Kenya. Fergus thought he could finish work at Misungwi, and produce a full report on the project by the time Katharine's summer holidays began in mid-July. I therefore wrote to my mother somewhat flippantly: 'We might come home to NI for a bit of bombing and rioting.'

The check-up two months after the heart attack was satisfactory, although one quirk remained on the ECG; the cardiologist said that Fergus should not remain at any station devoid of advanced medical facilities, but the final decision would rest with the chief medical officer in Geneva. Meanwhile, Fergus was back at the wheel again, so we went up to Eldoret to be with Katharine over the exeat break. The climate was deliciously cool, the mornings a delight, when heavy dewdrops shone like diamonds in the sun, and a fresh smell of eucalyptus made a pleasant change from the heavy pall that often lingered at lake level. Our return journey was uneventful and Mary and Michael had a wonderful time being taken down to the engine room of the *Victoria*, and up on the bridge to watch the radar screen.

Katharine, whose reports were glowing, had been moved to Form 3. Mary's progress in writing was slow, though she drew very well. (Remarkably Mary survived this and now writes a beautiful italic script.) Michael could recognise a few letters, but was definite about not learning to read 'until I'm ready'; he did, however, pore over books with an intensity that augured well. At the nursery school he stayed with a group of nonconformists who joined 'activities' only after close scrutiny to see if they were likely to be fun. They had my sympathy, as much time, paint, paper and Plasticine was spent making useless 'toe covers' to be borne home for the admiration of apathetic parents. His behaviour vacillated between charming spontaneous displays of affection and brainstorms over trivia; but compared with the repulsive behaviour of some of their peer group, our offspring were mature and well-adjusted.

San wrote that she was depressed, and that the social workers from the 'Welfare' were constantly on her back. No doubt there were many difficult, demanding pensioners on their list, but I sensed a failure to separate the dishonest or vicious, from those who were merely inept, or a bit senile. Many elderly people were terrified to leave their houses because of escalating street violence and gangs of youths wandering around the estates. Friends from home made me aware that events in Northern Ireland were more serious than what was described on the BBC World Service. One spoke of his sister who no longer went into central Belfast, having been badly cut by flying glass after an explosion in a pub in which several people had been killed and many injured.

The political climate in all three of the East African Community countries continued to simmer, the latest blow being sequestration, without compensation, of all property worth over £5,000 or more than ten years old. The justification being that the landlords – mostly Asian – had already made their pile, and it was time for the state and the common man to have his whack. How many of the latter would benefit was debatable, many small shops having already closed, and such Asians as were able, including professionals, had left the country. The Chinese contingent was active, beavering away on the railway project, and new Russian staff were seen at the office of the WHO area representative in Dar.

Late in June we made another gruelling trip to Katharine's school to attend open day. We did not reach the Kenyan border until one thirty in the afternoon, having been delayed by two young men dressed in untidy army uniform, who stepped into our path waving guns, and saying they wanted to inspect our luggage. It was a small settlement, they wore no caps, and no sentry box could be seen – they were probably poseurs. Fergus waved the UN *laisser passer*, and other documents claiming diplomatic immunity, but by the way they scrutinized the papers it was clear they had never heard of the UN. After an inordinate time spent going through our belongings, including the no longer cold insulated box, we were waved on.

At the official post Fergus, now tired and irritable because of the loss of time, aroused the wrath of the duty officer by omitting to remove his sweaty hat in the presence of an enormous photograph of Jomo Kenyatta. A severe ticking-off ensued, but Fergus appeared duly penitent, where I would have been explosive; he always feared that my ill-concealed exasperation would get us into real trouble. We reached Kisii by four thirty, but after a look at the crummy hotel we had stayed in two years earlier when a freak hailstorm had halted our progress, we decided to press on to the Tea Hotel at Kericho. The road was a single-track tortuous strip of tarmac bordered with loose chippings; to continue by the direct route via Sotik would have invited early demise – to meet another vehicle it would be a case of who would first lose his nerve and take to the sides. So we descended almost to Kisumu before taking the good road to Kericho, thus putting another eighty-five miles on the clock. For the last ten miles the petrol tank registered an unwavering empty as we climbed every steep hill.

It was the last week of convalescence for Fergus and the strain of the journey was clearly visible. Luckily the hotel had vacant rooms. In the gardens, near the tea plantations with their unique shade trees, the lawns were still well maintained, the aviary loud with healthy-looking inmates, the fountain in the pond working and the water lively with large carp. The food was excellent, and the charge little more than at the sleazy dump in Kisii, with its memorable scrambled eggs floating in half an inch of tinned margarine, accompanied by bloated, burst, undercooked sausages resembling roadkill.

Next morning we made our way to Kaptagat for the open day. Katharine looked healthy despite a badly sunburned nose, and was overjoyed to see us, quite unaware of what we had been through to get there. We were treated to displays of Scottish dancing, wrestling, boxing, rugger and tennis, but the swimming was cancelled because so many pupils had colds – tough on those, including Katharine, who excelled. While the parents were given an excellent lunch, the children were banished to the dormitories to eat sausage rolls, potato crisps and fizzy drinks. Mary and Michael were in the care of Anna Jenset, now eleven, and proud to be put in charge of younger children. Along with the Jenset girls, we stayed two nights of the exeat at Eldoret, where I developed the school cold, which quickly turned to bronchitis so severe as to require an intramuscular tetracycline injection in the posterior, followed by a course of antibiotics. On the final day I recovered enough to crawl around, so Fergus was in charge of the children for an afternoon only. Before returning to Mwanza, we stayed overnight in the Jensets' house, and did a massive shop for things like bacon, cheese, sausages and butter, and detergents to deal with our inevitable vast load of washing.

The political situation continued to deteriorate, with General Amin threatening to strike deep into Tanzanian territory. Nobody understood what he was up to, but he had closed the Ruanda-Burundi border and made a claim – patently untrue – to have killed six hundred or more Tanzanian troops near Bukoba. We were glad we had advised an enthusiastic young American water engineer, who had written at Christmas for advice, not to sign a two-year government contract. Even continued funding for the institute was jeopardised when Amin announced he would withhold his contribution to East African Community funds until such time as Tanzania 'shows a more co-operative attitude'. The headquarters of the community were in Arusha (Tanzania), making the situation even more complex.

I finished slides for a trip Dr Eyakuza was making to the US, and completed stencils for Fergus's latest paper, but he was seething because two papers sent to Brazzaville in February, to be forwarded to Geneva for publication in the *Bulletin of the World Health Organization*, had not even been acknowledged by Dr Quenum. Fergus wrote such a forthright memorandum on the subject, I was relieved that he now held a career service appointment.

In mid-July Fergus travelled to Nairobi with a load of data for processing at the Epidemiological Centre. I was keen to get a call from him, worried that Tanzania would be cut off from all neighbouring countries. We were no longer on speaking terms with Uganda, and the British government's recent loan of ten million quid to Amin hardly improved matters. So far there had been no official reaction – partly because Nyerere's policy seemed to be to ignore anything nasty, and partly because we no longer had a daily air-link with Dar, whence the newspapers came. Fergus did get through by telephone, saying he planned to bring Katharine down to Nairobi for two days, and would take her for a dental appointment.

During this time, Fergus developed a virulent skin condition which was never diagnosed, but was so severe he had to be hospitalised after arranging for Katharine to fly down to Mwanza, escorted by Peter Kilala. Fergus was in a hospital wing without a telephone, so I had to depend on reports from friends who worked at a nearby laboratory. He was covered in sores, like something between carbuncles and enormous blisters, which were erupting almost as one watched. It was thought to be an allergic reaction of some sort, and I later heard that on admission it had been deemed life-threatening. When he got back to Mwanza, he played down the severity, but I was appalled by the extent of the raised and angry reaction; his neck, both arms and part of his back looked as if he had been badly burned and large, red blisters were slowly scabbing over. He was not an allergic type – apart from when he had elephantiasis of the scrotum, later attributed to a tick bite. Eventually the scabs fell off, leaving marks that were slow to fade; afterwards he was on a cortisone regime, which had to be phased out gradually – he said it made him more than usually irritable.

We both had reason to be tense and irritable, due to the silence from headquarters, so in August we wrote to the chief medical officer expressing surprise at the delay, considering all reports and recommendations had been with them for more than two months. The lack of response was particularly galling in the light of WHO's lofty ideals about 'Man being only in a state of health when both *mind* and body are at peace …'

During the summer holidays, Anna and Edit stayed with us for a week, and the usual uproarious time was enjoyed by the children – exhausting for the adults, particularly me and Stephano. Their father was very generous and had brought piles of cheese, frankfurters and ice cream from Kisumu in defiance of an officious English customs officer who had spoken severely to another ship's officer who had brought bacon and butter for a friend. Officially foodstuffs were not subject to duty between East African Community countries, and there was a noticeable lessening of tension after the rabid editor of the *Tanzanian Standard*, a female Asian, was sacked. Thereafter fewer references were made to imperialist machinations, and 'our own pure maidens' being exposed to decadence. She was South African, and a committed Communist.

Orderly queues at the Somali butcher's shop were a thing of the past, and at the central market one had to push and jostle with the rest – a hard, unyielding back and capacious basket in hand were a help. Prices soared as never before, and two high-ranking officials had been jailed in Dar for offences relating to the trade. The abattoir workers, who did preliminary hacking, took many perks in the form of 'waste', so carcasses no longer weighed as much as previously, and often vital parts were missing – 'Sorry, this cow did not have any kidneys.'

The tense border situation continued, with both sides lying through their teeth, and there was good reason to think a move would shortly be made to reinstate Milton Obote: the spearhead was likely to be through Bukoba. Many lorries had been commandeered locally, creating a petrol shortage, but Fergus did his best to ensure that the project vehicles had full tanks. Chinese officials had been demanding unheard-of delicacies, such as frozen pork and bacon in the stores, provoking cynical comments from the old colonialist contingent. Almost all the shops were selling off stock, and newspaper deliveries were erratic.

Near the end of August I wrote to my mother, telling her that, for the first time, we both felt less than enthusiastic about the possibility of coming to Northern Ireland for our home leave. We were very concerned at the level of violence now perpetrated by both sides of the community in Northern Ireland. We were particularly appalled by the shooting of a priest giving the last rites – even if it was to a member of the IRA – which we felt just about surpassed all. Cardinal Conway's evasive platitudes shocked us and the pronouncements emanating from the Vatican were feeble – even devout Catholics were shocked by an attitude reminiscent of the silence during the years of Nazi dominance. The army had been either unfortunate or careless, on some occasions, but there was clear evidence that both the IRA and Protestant loyalists had been guilty of brutality on a horrendous scale. We may have felt detached by distance, and not committed to either extreme, but the situation was not possible to ignore. Nor was it possible to envisage a relaxing holiday at home when life there had become so unsafe, when timed devices lurked in multi-storey car parks.

Meanwhile, the sharp letter we sent to Geneva did not produce any concrete or satisfactory reply. What they said more or less shelved the main issues, pleading they were still awaiting further reports and a full check-up from another physician of Fergus's choice in Mwanza, 'in order to judge your reserves'. We wondered if that indicated if his reserves were thought to be slender, he would be considered a bad bet, and forced into early retirement.

In September we rescued a clutch of pied kingfishers, which the ball boys at the club had intended to eat. When we got them home two were dead; of the remaining three, two were almost fully grown, but their wings had been cut, and they too expired. However, the smallest, now called Dewey, whose wings were just starting to feather, thrived in its stinking sand box on frequent meals of tiny fish, soon emerging to fly around the house, perching on curtain rails and leaving a trail of droppings. Too humanised for its own good, it would settle on anyone's hand or head. When the time came to release it near a wild colony at the lakeside, it returned within the day, either on its own, or proudly borne by an urchin expecting reward. Our hope that it would learn fishing techniques from the flock was probably never realised.

Katharine's return to school for the Michaelmas term was imminent, and this time we chose the route by the Serengeti corridor to the new Lobo Lodge, Keekorok, and Narok to Nairobi. Our booking for Lobo was unconfirmed, irregularities about reservations were commonplace – mostly perpetrated by Asian travel agencies – and there was, of course, always the threat of arbitrary border closure.

The Serengeti corridor, desert-dry for weeks, suffered a localised downpour the night before we set out, so it took more than an hour to cover the first fifteen miles. I drove in first or second gear, while Fergus squelched ahead, indicating the best route. Since our first visit, the main track to Seronera and Banagi gate had been much improved by grading and laying of drains at crucial points. We stayed the first night at the Lobo Lodge, a beautiful building set high on a kopje; many of the rocks had been incorporated in the lodge by a female architect who had used locally available materials wherever possible. The central nucleus resembled a sophisticated mediaeval banqueting hall: towering timber pillars supported a timber roof, and mature trees, their trunks protected by glass enclosures soared upwards. A swimming pool was perched right at the edge of the cliffs overlooking a water hole and the vast plains beyond. It was a magical place to visit, but the company, whose chain extended to the West Indies and who held a large share in state tourism, had already priced themselves out of the local market, and catered almost exclusively for package tours.

Instead of treating the children as such, the waiters, all in full regalia – white with cummerbund and fez – ushered them to a formally laid dinner table, and produced the menu for the evening meal. After I explained their modest requirements, they took an inordinate time to produce some soup, glasses of cold milk, and plates of meat and vegetables, for ravenous children, eight, seven and four years old. Despite the brochure quoting a fifty per cent reduction for children under twelve, they charged the adult rate for Katharine and Mary, arguing they were too big to share our room. A leopard was regularly seen at dusk padding about near the swimming pool, and during the meal a terrified American woman rushed inside, complaining of having met it face to face on a narrow track. The children were thrilled, but despite going out very early the following day, we never saw it.

Happily the border crossing passed without incident, and we continued to Narok, passing the Longonot 'satellite tracking station' – the most surreal thing we had seen: a solitary piece of sparkling Western technology sited on a plain in the middle of Masai land. The road was passable in the dry season, but one of the dustiest we had ever travelled, and very dangerous where the dust lay in deep piles. The track plunged down to a deep gorge, at the bottom of which were a few stepping stones, where the river would be a raging torrent at times, with no possibility of climbing up the other side. It would have been no great feat of engineering to build a simple wood and metal bridge, but clearly there were other priorities – like satellite tracking. We gave a lift to a solitary, odoriferous, old Masai who managed to pack himself and his spear into the car without piercing the roof. Sitting silently in the back beside the children, he fondled a sharp knife, and I was quite relieved when he prodded me to indicate that we had reached his boma, and got out emitting a gracious grunt.

Fergus had meetings at the Ministry of Health in Nairobi, and with Sven, the project statistician, as well as another check-up with his cardiologist, while I took the children for dental checks, and to buy more hideous items of school uniform. The train, one carriage of which was occupied by Kaptagat pupils and several teachers, left Nairobi on Sunday morning, but did not reach the school until nearly midnight. On parting, Katharine was not tearful, which slightly assuaged my feelings of guilt after hearing the views of two Dutch women who exclaimed: 'We would never *dream* of sending our children away for schooling.'

For the return journey to Mwanza, we took the Nairobi–Nakuru road almost as far as Lake Naivasha, then turned west towards Narok. In the intervening week the piles of choking dust had grown higher, and we came upon a lorry straddling the road upside down with the driver's cabin shattered; miraculously nobody had been killed. We stayed a night at Keekorok: its position not so striking as Lobo just to the south, but the staff were more pleasant and better trained, so we felt we got 'good value for money', as *Which?* magazine would say. We arrived in time for lunch, then let the children have a swim and watch the antics of the too-tame monkeys, which raided the rooms for anything edible, and a few things that were not: when shooshed away, many did not shift. Several carried tiny babies, all pink and tender; the way the mothers cared for them leaving not a shred of doubt that Darwin got it right.

In the late afternoon we hired a not very expert guide – the good ones having already been booked – who prevented us from getting lost in the maze of tracks. In films located in Africa vehicles charge around seeming to know instinctively where they are, but reality is not like that. Our guide was an amiable Masai from Narok, who seemed to think the Peugeot could crash through young acacia trees as effectively as a Land Rover, so we dampened his enthusiasm and confined ourselves to two-wheel track routes with a high grass ridge in the middle. He led us to a scene of hyaena domesticity, some adults, as is their habit, trailing their genitalia on the ground in a gesture of submission to those higher in the pack. The endearingly fluffy babies were heavily tick infested, with encrustations at the tips of their ears. Only on an underfed bitch with a prolapsed uterus, which sometimes came to lie on our veranda at home, had I seen such masses clumped together, cheek by jowl, so to speak. We should have had her put down, but suspected she belonged to Mzee, the old man who lived at the bottom of our drive, who would have been affronted by such interference. Yet another memory I would gladly expunge, as it is another example of our joint ineffectuality.

Late in the evening large numbers of zebra and waterbuck came onto the floodlit grass area in front of the lodge and spent the night grazing quietly; in the morning an askari went round with a shovel collecting the heaps of dung. The evenings and early mornings were chilly, so throughout the night a crackling fire was kept alive to keep visitors warm, and discourage visits from hyaenas and the big cats.

Not daring to risk finding Ndabaka gate under water again, next day we took the Banagi to Fort Ikoma track, only to hear later that Ndabaka would have been passable. Eighty needless miles were added to the journey. The Fort Ikoma road was a mixture of every conceivable surface; its stretch of black cotton soil was at the start, followed by miles of what looked like flint hand-axes, then fine sand and open river-bed. The old German fort had been turned into a superior hotel, and on the day we called, it was swarming with German tourists and tsetse flies. Despite being within a game-controlled area, the lunch menu was eland steak – elands were relatively rare. We decided not to stay, and ate, with faint misgivings, leftovers from the previous day, hoping the cooler climate would have discouraged proliferation of nasty organisms – we got away with it.

Mary and Michael gave vent only rarely to outbursts of awfulness when their spirits ran too high for such sustained confinement. They were excellent travellers, and their resilience over what was often a seven or eight hour period was laudable: in some respects Katharine had a better deal.

When we got back to Bwiru, we found another dog on our list of dependants. Imaginatively named, Blackie had belonged to a biologist who had returned to her native Kenya. Her bungalow, and her dog, which had been left tied to a tree, were taken over by a young playboy doctor, who had stayed on the compound for only a few months, before quitting for the superior delights of Dar. The unfortunate Blackie had again been abandoned, tied to the same tree. Noggin, our resident dog, doted on by Michael, accepted the new arrival, and Blackie expected no more than some food if anyone bothered to dish it out, and a bowl of water. Ribby, cowering, wormy, and tick-infested, he flinched at any hand extended to pat him, but in our care he turned into a responsive, affectionate animal, though so conditioned he never expected to enter the house. He was a good watchdog, and slept on a mat in a corner of the veranda outside our bedroom.

In the following months air activity escalated and troops were known to be massing on the Ugandan border. President Nyerere was against military action, but some of his henchmen and the TANU league were pressing him to invade the neighbouring country and dispatch the 'traitor Amin', the 'colonialist puppet'. They estimated the job could be completed in twenty-four hours, but we felt this was optimism of the Francis Kofi sort.

Silence from Ansari's office at headquarters was unbroken, which did not augur well. WHO has a Board of Appeal to which staff can bring cases of (a) personal prejudice on the part of a supervisor or other responsible person; (b) incomplete consideration of the facts; (c) failure to observe or apply correctly the provisions of the staff regulations or rules. If Fergus was not appointed to the current post, the organisation would be guilty on all three counts. Our joint nerves were not in a good state.

By mid-November the political situation had further deteriorated, so much so that Fergus wanted to evacuate me, Mary and Michael to Nairobi, for the time being. There had been several border incidents and a specific threat from Amin to bomb – 'destroy' was the term used – both Bukoba and Mwanza, if the provocative incidents did not cease. My sympathies were to some extent with him. This was the statement of a man who felt insecure both within and outside his own country, who had had, and would continue to have, further provocation. What complicated the matter was the external aid afforded to each side, which risked a major confrontation – a sort of African Vietnam. Our intuition was that there might shortly be an outbreak in which one would not wish one's family involved. We determined not to bring Katharine home for the holidays, and drew up plans to travel to Nairobi with two cars, our own and the project one, loaded with household effects. Fergus had official permission to spend four days in Nairobi for consultations at the Epidemiological Centre, and we booked a family unit at the Fairview hotel for an indefinite period dating from Katharine's end of term. I wrote to the headmaster, asking if he could transfer her to the sister school at Banda, also in Kenya, and if he could admit Mary as well. I would try to get a part-time job and a flat or small house on a short-term lease in the Nairobi suburb of Karen – named after the Danish writer Karen Blixen.

The most worrying aspect of all these plans was that Fergus had to remain at post until any hostilities actually did break out, otherwise he could be accused of 'desertion of post'. We still had heard nothing concrete about our transfer, except a wire from Brazzaville saying they supported his candidature, and another from the chief medical officer saying the same thing. Our apprehensions fluctuated from day to day, and although we thought that the situation might ultimately defuse, we did not feel justified in taking any risks with the children. Others, not so well off financially, would have no choice but to stick it out, and hope their High Commissions could be relied upon to do the necessary.

Within two weeks there was a sea-change, and things became a bit more settled – for the time being at any rate – and reconciliation was in the air, so we returned with Katharine after a week in Nairobi. We would not be convinced of any lasting reconciliation, however, until there was visible evidence of withdrawal, or at least a drastic thinning of the build-up of forces on our side of the border. In Mwanza we could count the number of military vehicles heading in the direction of Bukoba and the frontier. Then at the beginning of December, Amin accused Tanzanian troops of firing across the border and threatened to bomb two Tanzanian towns on Lake Victoria if the troops resumed hostilities. Dar es Salaam did not issue a response to this and Tanzania also officially ignored claims of terrorism, looting and shelling by its border troops.

The anxiety over Fergus's heart attack and recovery, combined with the uncertainty of his future in WHO, against the backdrop of escalating military conflict, naturally took its toll, and my dependence on alcohol deepened as a result. A bottle of Scotch, the taste of which I disliked, was by this time the first item to go into my overnight bag, and I recall once shopping for staple supplies at Mwadui and adding a 'Special Offer' case of Southern Comfort. I also remember being driven by Pa Jenset from Kisumu to Kaptagat with a carload of children returning after a half-term break; he had a flask of brandy, from which, after first offering it to me, he took periodic swigs. I declined, thinking the gesture bizarre. Such was my innocence, or ignorance, if you prefer, it did not cross my mind that both our families were being driven by a man, over the limit, on a notoriously dangerous road. Nor did I relate his behaviour to my own, although the first thing I would do on arrival would be to pour myself a generous drink.

Drink-driving was not a criminal offence at that time, and the perils of dependence had yet to become a routine subject for press and media coverage. I look back in horror at the mileage I covered first in Africa, later in France, Switzerland, and the UK, with a high level of alcohol in my system: often the car contained not only our children, but some of their friends. Like most alcoholics, I thought my reactions were, if anything, sharpened. The cunning element in addiction is that the first fix delivers a kick-start to the nervous system – ideas for poems, short stories, or the skeletal plot for novel of the year must be jotted down without delay lest they be lost; paint is applied with frenetic energy; relationships feel more profound; inhibitions lessen. The great literary and artistic surge throughout Europe in the nineteenth century owed a debt to individuals steeped in opium, absinthe and a multitude of other mind-altering drugs. Thankfully, because of my asthma, I could not smoke, though I did give it a try. Cannabis was first offered to me in Tanzania by a Danish woman; it was the threat of choking, more than common sense, that led me to refuse, but intuitively I knew it might lead to hard drugs, although a decade was to pass before I saw, at close quarters, the ravages of terminal stage addiction in a rehabilitation clinic where I was the only 'pure' alcoholic. The Danish woman sank into alcoholic depression, and died prematurely from liver failure, leaving a widower and two adolescent children.

As the year drew to a close, among the festive greetings we received was an ostentatious Christmas card from the Gnome, our secret nickname for Ansari, which we felt like returning with a note saying: 'You forgot to tell your secretary to remove us from your list.' Fergus, infuriated by a request to provide an account of the project 'outstanding in Africa' for presentation in New Orleans by a biologist from the Communicable

Diseases Center, employed delaying tactics and shelved the request indefinitely. Plagiarism was rife in the field of biological research.

16

On the Run from Amin – Goodbye to East Africa

Fergus was in Dar for the annual conference of the East African Medical Association in January 1972. By then he had been invited to go to New Orleans, but the Brazzaville office had not given authorisation, so we assumed it would be refused. He had left me with a mountain of project-related work to prepare for his return. The children had begun to press us about their next visit to Ireland, and it was impossible to explain why the country was no longer the happy place of their memories. Fergus would not qualify for home leave before July, but I could go earlier if I could get Michael and Mary into the local primary school, within walking distance of our house at Craigavad, during May and June. Again everything hung on our next posting. Geneva was still hanging fire, but it was clearer than ever that Dr Ansari was dissembling; one of his peccadilloes was to sound out several people for the same job. So the level of tension continued. I was angry and resentful, and in perpetual dread of a recurrence of last year's episode with Fergus's health. Another worry was Stephano's wish to return to his native coastal town of Tanga. He was not unhappy with his work, but restless because his wife refused to join him for more than short periods. He had been at Mwanza far too long – eight years with Webbo and now almost five with us.

In March Fergus went by road to visit Shirati Mission Hospital, which he used as a base for snail surveys, and to assess the level of lake pollution. In Mwanza, even since 1967, the level of pollution had escalated, with high quantities of oil, raw sewage, chemical waste, and fertilisers – then subject to no control – finding their way through a multitude of streams and drains to the lake. Later in the month he collected Katharine, and found her healthy, tanned, and elated to have come third in class.

We went to Mwadui for Easter: the children spent most of their time in or around the pristine pool; Fergus was invited for a round of golf and we both played some tennis. Back at Bwiru, Katharine forced the issue of ear-piercing, Mary being one up on that count, so I took her to the Asian practitioner who was known to be on the point of leaving. (I insisted on it being done properly, rather than the method favoured by Stephano's brood who, after piercing with a red-hot needle, inserted a length of thread with knots, one of which was pulled through on alternate days. It got grimy, but nobody ever got an infected ear.) I was regarded askance by other parents for giving in to such 'vulgarity' – particularly when we returned to the UK.

Michael lost, in quick succession, five of his special friends, four for ever, and one for three months on home leave. That left only two boys whose missionary parents belonged to a weird sect of The-Lord-Will-Provide sort. Having had more than my fill in Ghana of weedy brats coming to play, with me always ending up playing the role of the Lord, I dreaded the next few weeks.

The good news was that the meat trade was to be handed back to the Somalis, and the same month we had a public holiday to mark the demise of Sheikh Karume, vice-president of Tanzania and president of Zanzibar. More errant dogs than usual hung around in the vicinity of our house, and Noggin lost his innocence. He did not enter the first-round contest, being a bit slow in the uptake, but poor Blackie, low in the peck order, did, returning badly mauled, with a number of festering wounds and a bad limp. Noggin took off the next day, returning with an air of contentment before going to sleep for the best part of twenty-four hours. Both dogs were infested with fleas and ticks, despite wearing Vapona collars: the desirable damsel came from a lower socio-economic group, and lived at a mud hut complex near the shore.

I often wrote to my mother with news about our day-to-day lives, but also with growing concern about the ever-increasing violence in the North: the Abercorn bar bomb, for example, was a particularly heinous attack, killing two and injuring over a hundred; the first attack on the Europa hotel, for which the

IRA claimed responsibility; and my astonishment that none of the parties seemed to take into account Communist infiltration. One Dublin journalist had written of aspirations towards a 'People's United Republic of Ireland'. We had joined the Alliance Party shortly after it was formed under Oliver Napier in 1970, and deplored the Ulster Unionist Party, which did not help in any way to lessen the tensions, seeming on the whole to be an unproductive bunch, apart from such progressives as Terence O'Neill and Brian Faulkner. It was not until I heard David Trimble for the first time that I thought: here at last is a Unionist politician worth listening to.

Late April saw the arrival of an Irish WHO consultant, whom Fergus had been asked to assist on his trip from Dar to Bukoba, where he was to join an 'expert' meeting on the Kagera River irrigation scheme. The assistance covered facilitating him on to a small plane, feeding him, showing him the delights of Mwanza, visiting the project at Misungwi and, not least, asking one of the ship's officers to reserve a berth for the return journey. Hot and clammy again, after months of relatively pleasant weather, trips to the town had become more exhausting because an increase in petty theft meant car windows had to be wound up, and doors locked on even the shortest errand.

During the Easter holidays, we had taken the children to the Tivoli cinema in Mwanza. Unusually there was in excess of eight hundred EA shillings in my zebra skin wallet to pay the Isamilo Primary School fees. A large holdall was on the floor at my feet, but, when Katharine wanted something out of it, I had a moment of panic when I reached down and could not feel the bag, which was found to have 'slipped' down the slope towards the seats in front. I thought Michael must have accidentally kicked it. The bag had been stuffed with sunglasses, mosquito repellent and, most precious of all, an envelope of black and white negatives, but not until the following morning, when I was on the point of putting the fees in an envelope for Fergus to deliver at the school, did I realise that the wallet and negatives were missing. By late afternoon the police had three small boys in custody, and returned the negatives, which had been thrown on the ground just outside the cinema. The main perpetrator appeared to be deaf, speaking poorly or through interpreters; none looked more than eleven or twelve years old, and all were poorly dressed. He admitted taking the money and claimed to have taken it to his village. Neither we nor the police believed this, as there would not have been enough time for him to get back to Mwanza, where they had been apprehended. We thought he was probably under threat by someone older, possibly even an employee of the cinema, and was afraid to split.

After their initial display of efficiency, the police were slow to do anything more. I was summoned to attend court at eight thirty in the morning, but not until two hours had passed was I asked to confirm that I was Mrs McCullough. On hearing that this was so, the leisurely fellow indicated the dirty cement step on which I had been sitting, saying brightly: 'You will sit there.' The ironic tone of my reply that I had been doing so for two hours was greeted impassively, and no seat was offered. The 'prisoners' were present among many others, and I was interested to see the most innocent and appealing of them sporting a natty pair of bell bottoms and new suede safari boots. I had advised the police to warn both shoe shops to look out for small boys brandishing 100 shilling notes, but clearly not soon enough. At the end of the morning I was informed the prosecution case was not prepared, nor was any police representative present. We never expected to recover the money, and I bear the urchins no malice; they probably got off with a warning, and will have operated more cautiously thereafter.

In May we were already making plans for the long school holidays, which for Katharine ran from mid-July to mid-September. Our friends John and Rosemary, after a punitive two years in the highlands of Papua New Guinea, were now based at Tanga on the coast, opposite Pembe Island, north of Zanzibar, so we planned another safari to visit them, going by Nairobi to Mombasa and Tanga, and returning via Arusha and the Serengeti. Fergus had legitimate reasons to visit Nairobi, Arusha and now Tanga, where the WHO/Medical Research Council Bilharziasis Chemotherapy Centre was based, so would again be able to combine duty travel, for which he received a per diem allowance, with days off, which would be counted as local leave.

The Ruanda-Burundi affair rumbled on, with an estimated ten thousand refugees fleeing across the border to the Kigoma region. We still had hopes that Fergus's next visit to Geneva would clarify the future, despite the fact that our suspicions had been confirmed that Dr Ansari had indeed appointed an American in the post, despite the fact that he was currently doing another job – a conveniently confused situation. He may well have had all this fixed when he was last in Mwanza partaking of our lavish hospitality, talking sentimentally about his new marriage, and weeping over the plight of the poor lepers in the town, while knocking back a third green chartreuse.

While Fergus was in Geneva, I flew from Mwanza with the two younger children to spend Katharine's half-term holiday in Nairobi. We stayed at the Fairview and had the use of a car belonging to friends who were going on leave. It was a Renault 4L model with a uniquely horrible gear-change which stuck out of the steering column: I got used to it, but always feared accidentally getting into reverse. After half a day Mary and Michael started to cheer me on from the back seat: 'You're getting a lot better, now go faster' – unwise in Nairobi traffic. We did the usual dreary things, like dental checks and buying new sandals for all three, but also visited the Snake Park and the now famous Animal Orphanage.

At the end of June Fergus had an almost cordial letter from Dr Ansari, acknowledging receipt of sundry working documents and reports. The change in tone was marked, and may well have been the result of his activities having come to the notice of both the head of Communicable Diseases, and one of the assistant directors general: time alone would tell. We did consider taking the case to an ombudsman or the International Labour Organization, but that would have been drastic while some men of principle still walked the corridors of power at headquarters. We felt that Dr Ansari underestimated our joint ability to fight if sufficiently provoked.

In July a man was murdered more or less at the bottom of our garden: cut to pieces with pangas by three assailants in the middle of the night, and we did not hear a sound. Other nights were loud with the noise of drunken scuffles, and dogs giving tongue at the constantly howling hyaenas; but the night of the crime was remarkable for its silence. Compared with what was going on in Ruanda, it was a trivial incident. One European had perished in the massacres and further outbreaks were anticipated. Never known for my political correctness, I said it was one method of population control in that small, very backward country. As I write today the population has burgeoned, the demographics have changed because the AIDS virus has destroyed much that was good in tribal systems, and the mindless slaughter continues unabated in that region, not only of humanoids, but of the great apes and most other living things.

Around this time I began making enquiries about property in Scotland, where the Church was selling off old manses on the grounds that they were outdated and the upkeep too costly; new bungalows were thought more appropriate for contemporary clerical families. We were thinking eight years ahead to the time when Fergus could take early retirement at fifty-five, and had decided that Scotland, rather than Northern Ireland, would be a good choice. We did not want to commit the children to a future in a society constrained by underlying hatred and narrow prejudice. We had shortlisted the Borders, or the area around Kirkcudbright and Wigtown, but one house at Carsphairn in the Rhinns of Kells, near Castle Douglas, sounded so beautiful I was sorely tempted to take a trip to investigate further. To settle in Scotland would merely reverse the journey made in the mid-eighteenth century by my paternal great-great-great-grandfather Stevenson, who, with many other Scots, left Ayrshire in search of a better life at Ramelton in County Donegal.

Late in July we collected Katharine from school on a morning when blue-black rain clouds were massing in every direction and even a short shower would have reduced the fifteen-mile track from the school to the main road to a morass. The nightmare, however, was reserved for the 'short cut' we took down to Sondu on the Kisii–Kisumu road – the main Kericho–Sotik–Kisii road being murderous and subject to numerous diversions. It began all right, but when we went down a very steep gradient and found a mud-slide at the bottom, we knew there must have been a downpour the night before. Turning back impossible, there was no option but to bore on like the worst scenes in the East African Safari rally. Sliding and jolting, a deep narrow ditch on either side, Fergus drove out of skid after skid, keeping the engine revving because to stop or brake would be fatal. I could not have driven under such circumstances because it demanded a mixture of physical strength, experience, determination and courage. Despite all we had endured in Ghana, nothing had been so terrifying as this, and I had not realised he could drive so well; later he admitted that neither had he. In all, it probably took no more than forty-five minutes, but near the end we narrowly missed a tractor, before rounding a hairpin bend where women were washing clothes in a roadside pond – I remember a fleeting vision of our vehicle in the water, but it didn't happen. Thereafter, all went smoothly, apart from a bit of unpleasantness at the border post, where two officious policemen were unaware of the diplomatic privileges usually accorded to UN personnel. Fergus found a letter from the regional commissioner in Mwanza, which did the trick in the end, or maybe it was his threat to take their names and numbers for reporting to a superior officer that did it. We reached Bwiru just before darkness fell.

In our absence the long-suffering staff at the institute had sent an ultimatum to the East African Community headquarters in Arusha, saying they were going on strike unless Dr Eyakuze was removed from his post. The dispute had yet to be resolved, as the decision rested with the secretary general of the EAC. The situation was farcical, in that there were by that time three typists at the institute, none was competent, and all, including the latest appointee, were hugely pregnant. So my workload expanded to include typing a few letters for the director. As mentioned previously, he was a brilliant clinician and good administrator, but lacking in 'people skills'. Many colleagues felt that Fergus deserved a medal for having survived, with only two major altercations, for as long as he had. My belief is that, in his own quaint way, he respected us both. More than twenty years later, on hearing that Fergus had died, he wrote me a very sincere letter of condolence.

In August, we spent the first night of our trip to Tanga at Lake Lagarya, where Jane Goodall and her husband made their first studies of hunting dogs, jackals and hyaenas. The last crooked wooden sign had underestimated the miles from Naabi, the red-ball sun had started to sink below the horizon and the track could no longer be distinguished from surrounding scrub when we drew up, in clouds of dust, at George Dove's Ndutu camp. George was a reformed white hunter with a magnificent waxed handle-bar moustache: he was a glorious extrovert, but his warm welcome was genuine, and he had an inexhaustible store of anecdotes about people and events. Each tent had a Heath Robinson shower and thunderbox at the rear, and the children were thrilled to have their own tent beside the one we occupied. They slept soundly, but Katharine complained in the morning that something had been scratching at the canvas of their tent, trying to get inside. We dismissed this as having been a loose bit of dry grass stuck in the roof, but later in the day large paw marks were found not far from the tents. The antelopes were more varied than we had seen in other parts of the Serengeti, with herds of topi, hartebeest and a few gerenuks. We had also seen areas where large trees had been damaged by elephants, although none were to be seen, apart from a few stragglers crossing the road at the point where the track down to Ngorongoro crater begins its tortuous descent.

To keep costs down we broke the journey to the coast by staying overnight at a new YMCA hostel in Moshi. As we drove past the North Pare Hills the next day the views of Kilimanjaro were superb: like many other peaks, the mountain is often obscured by low cloud and mist. That my pictures have survived is little short of a miracle, because on projecting them in Tanga, the dreaded Newton's Rings appeared, contracting very slowly under the heat until they disappeared. Some had developed a fungal growth, and the desiccators I had hoped to find in the laboratory in Tanga were nonexistent.

After initial shyness, the children resumed the happy relationship they had formed three years earlier, but we were surprised to find the McMahon lot had, in the interval, lost their fluency in Swahili. We stayed in a guest wing of the main house at the Medical Research Council centre, where John was director, and Rosemary worked on a WHO health and nutrition project. Fergus spent most days working with John at the laboratory, while I looked after the children. I took them through the mangrove swamp to the beach, and explored the town, dead after the recent exodus of Asian shopkeepers. But between shuttered premises a few hung on, selling ancient stock, collections of second-hand books, old records of American origin, a few quality model railway carriages, and an exquisite Scandinavian green celadon stoneware pot, which is now in my sitting room. The locality was also in recession because of a slump in the sisal industry, on which it had been over-dependent. Arusha and Moshi too were sad reminders of what they had been when we had first visited them three years earlier: by comparison Mwanza was a centre of abundance. Fresh seafood could be bought daily, and by trial and error I learned which were the best, and to avoid anything exotic-looking that the stall-holder would waft temptingly under my nose. We were introduced to snorkelling, which Katharine and Mary took to immediately; they swam out to an offshore raft, around which myriad small multicoloured fish, including the angel fish they had seen in their grannie's tank, teemed. Even I, who have always loathed having my head under water, managed some tentative viewing. Michael, who had not yet dispensed with rubber wings, had to be taken out on adult shoulders: his breakthrough happened at Christmas in the pool at the Kericho Tea Hotel.

We returned to Mwanza to find new Dutch families installed on the compound: a biochemist with wife and three children of five, four and eighteen months; and a young doctor and his wife, whom Noggin and Blackie had adopted in our absence, finding they got the kind words and pats they did not get from Stephano, who did no more than dish out their daily food. That the new children spoke not a word of English was no deterrent to Michael, who disappeared soon after lunch on our first day back and was not seen again until I went to collect him and introduce myself to the new neighbours.

Shortly after Katharine returned to Kaptagat, there was a marked change for the worse in relations with Uganda after Amin fulfilled his threat of taking punitive action against Tanzania. We awoke one morning to the sound of low flying aircraft, followed by the unmistakeable *wump* of bombs landing, which I recognised from the air raids on Belfast in April 1941. The noise grew fainter as the two planes dropped more bombs on Mwanza town, before fading to silence. Several of the bombs had landed in the Bwiru area, and one made a hole in the roof of Jarockij's prison, unoccupied at the time. In the town the only fatality was reported to have been a beggar who had been sleeping under a mango tree. This action galvanised all sorts of dormant groups, and the embassies were inundated with enquiries from nationals about where they stood in the event of full-scale warfare. From the safety of the coastal region the

Swedish and Dutch embassies took a detached view of the incident – 'Oh, is there some trouble in the Mwanza area?' Our lot took a more realistic approach, having got it wrong the previous year when there had been an incipient crisis, but the official line was that one was on one's own until one reached Dar es Salaam. Rumours were rife that not a gallon of petrol could to be bought between Mwanza and Arusha, owing to the exodus of practically the entire Asian population.

We packed bags, ready to depart should the situation worsen, though some people with numerous dependants fled the next day, and many in the town moved to their families in outlying villages, leaving a ghost town with all the shops shuttered. Fergus was due to fly to Brazzaville – also liable to violent outbursts – early in October, so it was out of the question for him to leave me and the two children in Mwanza. Dr Eyakuze advised him to evacuate us to Tanga when we heard that Libyan reinforcements had reached Uganda and had crossed the border near Bukoba, where heavy fighting was in progress. This was later denied by both sides, but in truth total chaos reigned, and nobody had the slightest idea what the situation really was.

Despite Nyerere having said that such infringements were not to be tolerated, no official statement or condemnation of the action was forthcoming. Our decision to get out was strengthened by the fact that we could be completely cut off if Ugandan forces were to arrive by air. Situated as we were on an offshoot of the road to the airport, the local authorities had only to declare the closure of road, air and steamer services for us to be isolated. So, in convoy with one of the Land Rovers driven by a Canadian, Steve, whose car had been found at the last minute to be unroadworthy, we left on the same route to the coast we had covered little more than a month before. Stephano, whose daughter Elizabeth was in the last fortnight of her second attempt at the final examinations for upper primary school, was left in charge of the house and dogs. We were particularly sorry for the Dutch biochemist, a nervous type at the best of times, having survived internment by the Japanese in Indonesia. His car was the same model Renault 4L that I had driven in Nairobi, and they had set off through the Serengeti to Dar the day before us. Steve, his wife, two children and another childless couple, had crammed their baggage and camping equipment, plus several large containers of petrol, into the Land Rover. These, which Fergus and Steve had spent sweaty hours filling and lifting, were later found superfluous; the rumours had been panic-driven, and we were able to fill up at intervals on the journey to Tanga.

Fergus left us in Tanga and travelled on to Brazzaville via Dar and Lusaka, and during his absence the news blew alternately hot and cold – indeed, the day we arrived the air-raid we had witnessed was being publicised as almost a nonevent. Then Amin resumed his tactics: he finally sent his delegate to the peace talks – a week late – and a Tanzanian source reported that he had agreed with Mobutu to delay the final date for departure of any remaining Asians. This was not broadcast on Radio Uganda. He continued to claim that forces were poised to invade his territory and that he was taking sole command of the army. I believed that his end would undoubtedly come soon, and I hoped it would be a sticky one. My intuition let me down on that one. We had a friend who was to receive a higher degree from the hands of the dictator, but the investiture was postponed when it was announced that the vice-chancellor of the university had 'gone into hiding' – probably a euphemism for liquidation by Amin's undisciplined troops.

A good aspect of the situation was that neither Mary nor Michael was missing school, as all the Mwanza schools had closed soon after the bombing of Bukoba, and they were in any case heading for the six-week holiday period that began at the end of September. In the meantime, I taught them both in the mornings, but found it hard to cope with that on top of cooking, washing and the variety of insect life, which peaked now that the climate had turned humid. Mary worked without complaint, but Michael's ploy was to make the exercise so unrewarding that in frustration I would release him to play outside. That, however, was not without its risks: there were quite a lot of snakes around, and one morning a tall tree crashed without warning to the ground, narrowly missing a corner of the house.

On the day that the wind rose in sporadic gusts and the first heavy rains fell, Fergus returned from Brazzaville. No decision had been made about our future with WHO; both assistant directors general were on leave and nobody had been officially appointed to the controversial post. We felt they were probably waiting until Ansari's retirement at the end of March before taking any action. Accolades continued to come from all quarters about the project, but no job offers. Fergus was getting a number of requests for references from fellow scientists wishing to escape from Uganda. Forty-five expatriate lecturers at Makerere University resigned in protest against the treatment of some of their African colleagues, including the vice-chancellor, who had disappeared without trace.

The last time we had returned from the coast through the Serengeti I had said, 'Never again', no matter what the circumstances, despite the great game viewing and stupendous scenery, and here we were en route again, heading back to Mwanza five weeks later. There was a sort of Marx Brothers unreality about the peace talks. Amin said they would form a good basis for future improved relationships, and one got the impression that a treaty may have been signed hastily by the foreign ministers who then rushed to their respective bosses to see if they would agree to the conditions.

January 1973 would be devoted to finishing Fergus's final assignment report. It was vital not to jeopardise the report, or delay its production, and I knew I could finish it, provided I could get peace in the mornings. The two competent typists at the institute, recruited when the pregnant trio left, had resigned saying they could no longer put up with the rude and inconsiderate behaviour of the director, so I was left with no choice. Fergus had asked to defer his local leave until 1973, but the regional office, in its usual gracious way, refused his request: so it was either use it up in December or sacrifice it.

Before beginning this leave, we decided to give a party for the fourteen supporting staff who had worked for Fergus since the start of the project in 1967. When the wives and partners were included, the head count was more than thirty. I calculated we would need two legs of goat, a large variety of fruit and vegetables, samosas and six cups of dry rice, as well as thirty-six bottles of beer, local gin, a few bottles of wine and a variety of soft drinks. After a shy start, it turned into a really good party with 'loud music', as they say in *Noggin the Nog*, including 'African Safari'. I showed slides of the staff, the project area, and some pictures of the Serengeti and its wildlife, which many present had never seen. The effort was much appreciated, which made it worthwhile. Stephano helped me, but clearly he did not approve: his position was anomalous as the father of the librarian's ex-'wife'. Periodically he let drop uncharitable remarks about one or other member of staff at the institute; sadly some of the gossip was well based. One talented technician had died from acute alcohol poisoning having drunk 100 per cent proof wood alcohol. Fergus had seen him a few times with woefully reddened eyes, never suspecting the cause, because his work was irreproachable.

We began our two-week holiday, spending the night at Thomson's Falls, north-east of Nakuru, en route to Mount Kenya, which Fergus said I must see before leaving East Africa. All effort was in vain, as it was invisible under a pall of bluish-black cloud. We stayed in a pleasant old house perched near the top of the falls. There was not much to do except take walks, do some riding and descend the 261 steep stone steps to the bottom of the falls. I would happily have settled for the view from the top, but the children were determined to go down, so I had to accompany them lest something untoward should happen. Thomson's Falls village sewage was discharged into the river at the top, and the water supply was taken out at the bottom: local health authorities claimed it was treated and quite safe to drink, but the lodge manager told us that she boiled and filtered it. Hot and sweaty when we returned to the top, all agreed the view was better from there. We then went to Nairobi, where the Christiansens had managed to get us a house to stay in rather than at the Fairview Hotel, thus saving some cash, but not as much as one might wish, if you take into account a token gift of gratitude to the owners, and supermarket bills for five. I got through Christmas shopping and dental appointments after three days, but at the end began to feel distinctly odd and very cold, and took to my bed on arrival at the Tea Hotel in Kericho. I ran intermittent fevers of mounting severity which lasted till Boxing Day, each time, after a heavy sweat, feeling a bit more normal, and able to eat a little; but full value for money was not enjoyed.

On the other hand, the children had a hell of a good time, which would not have been the case had we stayed at Mwanza without Stephano to help (he had gone to Tanga, and the dogs were being looked after by our Dutch neighbours). A high point of the holiday was Michael excelling himself by learning (a) to dive, (b) to do the breast-stroke, and (c) to pick things off the bottom of the heated pool, all in one afternoon. He had just watched and waited till he was ready, which is what he always told us. Donald Gilchrist, now working at a mission hospital in Kenya, came for lunch during our stay, and told us that he had been appointed surgeon on the oil pipelines in Abu Dhabi: a lucrative post, undertaken to fund boarding school fees for the boys at Fort Augustus on Loch Ness. We had agreed to meet the McMahons for Christmas at the hotel, and their youngest, Andrew, developed viral pneumonia; he had to be hospitalised, so it was not the relaxing break we adults had anticipated. I was tested for typhoid and brucellosis, which proved negative, and after a few days, I was on the mend. But on our return home, a nasty cold developed – it must have been a judgement on me for having remarked to Fergus that we had all been remarkably healthy for almost a year.

We did not send Katharine back for the next term: a new headmaster was taking over, and many of her favourite teachers and friends were leaving. Isamilo Primary School agreed to take her for the few weeks remaining before it would break up for a five-week holiday at the beginning of February. As it turned out, it was fortuitous that she had not returned to Kaptagat, as she, too, developed viral pneumonia and was confined to bed for a full seven days. Response to drugs was minimal and recovery was slow, with a danger of relapse, so we had to discourage a tendency to get out of bed and horse around with a hula-hoop.

Now the packing began of the detritus we had accumulated over the last six years. Much would have to be sent to the United Nations Development Project storage unit in Dar until we heard where the next duty station would be. Very few things were worth taking to Ireland, though the meat grinder and mixer were still going strong after almost daily use. I warned my mother to await the next delivery of cockroach eggs. There was no trouble in off-loading any other electrical gadgets that were in working order. We were officially informed that each of us would be entitled to 25 kilograms of unaccompanied air freight, which meant that I would be able to bring home things such as the sewing machine, projector, carvings and better books, rather than have them stored in coastal climatic conditions, prior to going by sea to an, as yet unknown, destination. (Good news for the books, as any sent to Dar were badly foxed when we saw them again three years later in France.) While all this work was going on at home, Fergus was still churning out papers on mollusciciding, obligatory quarterly reports, as well as a few photographic requests. He now thought we should defer our departure until late March.

It was no surprise when Mary and I both developed a persistent cough, aches and pains, a high fluctuating fever, periods of shivering and heavy sweats: we were not as ill as Katharine had been, but it was untimely, and delayed my work programme. Mine took hold the night before the arrival of a professor from the London School of Tropical Medicine and Hygiene, who was accompanied by an eminent paediatrician, and his wife, a family planning consultant. In the morning, after preparing the first stages of the evening meal, I was forced to admit defeat and palmed them off on the Dutch doctor's wife. The next day I had recovered enough to have lunch ready when Fergus brought them back from a tour of the project area. Afterwards I took to bed again. Whatever the bug was, it was by far the most unpleasant we had suffered since coming to Mwanza in 1967. Mary was a cheerful, uncooperative patient who refused to remain long in bed despite having a temperature as high as 103 at times. The only thing that knocked her out was a paracetamol tablet plus a dose of Benylin – which we all referred to as Grannie's *dawa* (Swahili for any medical 'cure' – Grannie became addicted to it).

Before our departure I had a final job to do for Fergus. A trip to the Misungwi project area was necessary to photograph all the 'Wazee' (respected senior citizens, in our parlance), or ten-cell leaders of the TANU party organisation, which ensured that each ten houses or households appointed a leader whose job it was to bring any complaints to the right authority. It was pleasant to drive, very early in the morning, through the thirty-nine miles of sporadically settled Sukumaland south of the lake to Misungwi and beyond. On arrival I was met by the most senior of Fergus's field team, who had done his best to assemble everyone involved in the photo-shoot; however, we had a three-quarter-hour wait before the latecomers put in an appearance. There ensued, with the aid of an interpreter – Sukuma is a separate language – protracted discussion as to how best to position them into a practical shape for the group picture. Much good-humoured banter accompanied the bringing of benches, stools, chairs and an odd assortment of stones, on which the youngest perched themselves. Failure to understand the concept of depth of focus led to further complications, such as not realising that if one lurks behind someone taller in the front row, one is not going to appear in the picture.

About a year previously, WHO had sent an official photographer to record the project. We had entertained him, but neither of us liked him, and I had predicted that he would not send copies of anything he had taken. This proved the case, so the only satisfactory pictures taken were by me; likewise, the only villagers to get copies of their photographs were my victims. This took up a lot of time, as I had to do all the processing, including mixing the chemicals. After such a long delay that I thought it had been lost, the Kodachrome film of pollution sites in and around Mwanza came back from processing. It shows the shades of shit, tan, yellowish white and purply brown effervescent contaminants that were being poured into the lake at Mwanza South; mainly by the detergent and textile factories, but some by the East African Railways and Harbours division. The level of pollution augured ill, for the local population as well as fish and other wildlife, and needed to be emphasised at a conference in Nairobi, which the regional office had refused Fergus permission to attend. The paper on pollution of the lake and other water-bodies was instead presented by the director, with slides by yours truly.

Inevitably Michael got a version of the super-bug, and was disappointed to miss the conjurer who visited the school: the girls said he did not miss much as his tricks had been limited, but he had eaten fire and wiped a piece of cow-hide across Mary's face – to what purpose, nobody knew. When Fergus felt a sore throat developing, he immediately began a course of the strongest drug then available, an experiment not tried on any other victim. Alone of us, he did not succumb. Michael's illness took three weeks, having had a relapse during which his temperature soared. We took him to a Danish paediatrician, whose X-ray showed a patch on his left lung, so he was put on tetracycline. His muscular little legs had become stick-like and his complexion pallid, but like Katharine, when he began to eat again, recovery was rapid.

Brazzaville had not replied to a cable Fergus had sent some weeks previously requesting travel authorisation for his dependants, without which no reservations could be made, but refused to let us buy our own tickets. We had made this request in order to use up some of the currency gained by the sale of household goods. The currency restrictions prevailing in Tanzania at that time could not have been better designed to frustrate the individual, complicate existence, create jobs for the boys, and generate maximum confusion. Wires were to-ing and fro-ing and, as our travel dates approached, the scene at home was one of total chaos, the house being littered with half-packed boxes, little heaps of as yet undesignated stuff, toys and books that suddenly became 'favourites'. The poor dogs were not experienced enough to know what it all signalled, though they knew well enough what suitcases meant. Our Dutch neighbour had agreed to take them; they liked her and were very much at home in her house. But I did not know how the cats would take our disappearance. The Indian vet refused to put animals down, arguing, 'You just leave it in the bush and someone will give it a home.' But I knew that the bush was full of starving cats and dogs, which had been abandoned by expatriates as the easiest thing to do.

Our travel authorisation came by wire on 12 March, and we made the final arrangements for our departure. Fergus had requested a two-day duty stopover in Geneva but was refused. He planned to go anyway, footing the per diem costs himself, with time deducted from home leave. He fulminated at the meanness, but as we had predicted refusal, I told him he was wasting his already depleted energy.

The children and I travelled ahead; Fergus left at the end of the month, driving the project car to the coast, to call at the lab in Tanga, say goodbye to the McMahons, thence to Dar to arrange for the storage of our heaviest boxes. He spent a few days in Geneva, before joining us at Craigavad.

17
From Drumlins to Alps via Congo Brazzaville

Sybil, now returned from West Africa and living in London, had offered to accommodate me and the children at her home in Mill Hill for a few nights before we flew to Ireland. This was a magnificent gesture, and would allow me to stock up with Marks & Spencer clothing, and take the children to visit museums and galleries. Sybil had a part-time teaching job, and we had even more shared interests now that she had completed two tours at the Medical Research Council centre at Fajara in the Gambia.

By 1973 street violence in the UK was on the increase, and one might be mugged even in Mill Hill. I found the London scene radically changed from when I had stayed in 1966: now there were more black faces, more elegantly dressed Asian ladies, and for the first time entourages of affluent Arabs in flowing djerbahs cruising Cromwell Road, Knightsbridge and Harrods. I was, and remain, inefficient and apprehensive where bus, train and tube transport are concerned, so it is hard to believe that alone I took five children (mine and Sybil's two, Angus and Dougal) into central London, where they enjoyed the Science Museum, and in particular an expensive visit to the top floor restaurant.

Back home in Craigavad, it never ceased to astonish me how Michael and the girls adapted within days to the change, trotting regularly between the two houses to visit Grannie, and renew friendships made two years ago. The primary school accepted all three for the summer term, so one of the first things to be done was fit them out in the uniform, thankfully an unpretentious one. There was no need to go to Belfast, because Holywood had an excellent store which stocked all the local school uniforms, in addition to the latest fashion range from Ladybird. There were at least two greengrocers, two fish shops, two butchers, two home bakeries, two chemists, a hardware shop, two antique shops, two small cafés serving home-made food, two Chinese restaurants, at least three off-licences, and several pubs which served palatable food. The Palace Army Barracks was situated on the outskirts of the town, churches of every denomination were represented, and the train station was within walking distance of the maypole at the town centre.

The main reminders of what was going on throughout Northern Ireland were the sandbags and coils of wire around the RUC barracks. This peaceful town was only six miles from battle-scarred central Belfast, with its security gates and armed patrols, but the fear was of a different order from that in areas where warring factions terrorized all citizens irrespective of race or religion – Falls Road, Shankill Road, Andersonstown, parts of the Antrim Road, Ligoniel and Ardoyne were zones one entered only when there was no alternative choice. Prior to the opening of motorways, the route to what is now Belfast International Airport went through Ligoniel and past Ardoyne, up a steep tortuous road past Divis, before it joined the main road to Antrim near Templepatrick.

I registered with the medical practice in Holywood which my mother attended. One of the first subjects I raised was unease about my drinking. The avuncular doctor asked how much I drank, and I gave a truthful estimate. His reply was jocular: 'Sure I drink as much as that myself, you've nothing to worry about.' But intuitively, I knew that I *had*. An RUC night patrol later found him asleep in his car in central Holywood. At the trial he pleaded guilty of being 'drunk in charge of a motor vehicle', with the excuse that he thought it preferable to driving under the influence. Not long afterwards he retired, still a well-respected, much-loved family doctor.

Nothing concrete emerged from the talks Fergus had at headquarters, so prospects for the next year were bleak. The only post on offer was for a specialist on schistosomiasis based in Brazzaville. From a family viewpoint this was unacceptable: the climate was debilitating, the French schools unsuitable, and staff housing inadequate – a characterless concrete apartment block, in which Roger Lyonnet, now in a situation not unlike our own, had a two-bedroom flat. Fergus had his suspicions about what had provoked Ansari's change of attitude. At a party during one of his visits to Geneva, he had been propositioned by Ansari's mistress, a notoriously rapacious woman, with a yen for tall, good-looking, fair-haired men. The incident had not gone unobserved, and shortly afterwards the vacancy notice within Ansari's unit was withdrawn, effectively 'freezing' the post.

When Fergus joined us early in May, the shadow of imminent separation detracted from enjoyment of home leave. However, the province is at its best during May and June, so we went to Inishowen, this time renting a chalet near Goorey Lodge. Sunny blissful days passed for the children, who tobogganed once more down the slopes of fine sand at Lagg, flew their kites, and at a small cove near Malin Head, collected pebbles of quartz and carnelian, for polishing in the stone tumbler I had bought. Katharine and Mary were avid collectors, but on one of the few drizzly days Michael was heard muttering, 'I don't see the point in all this' – he was suffering withdrawal symptoms from TV. Fergus also was in withdrawal, finding little pleasure in a pipe, on which he argued he would not become dependent, because he could neither inhale nor keep it alight for long. Attacks of bronchitis had become more frequent, and of such severity that doctors were unanimous in warning that if he did not stop smoking cigarettes, the next attack might well be his last. Parallels with Alcoholics Anonymous philosophy are clear: 'Some of us tried easier, softer ways, but the result was nil till we let go absolutely.'

We were on holiday, therefore it was normal to relax in the evenings in front of the peat fire, with a glass or two of whiskey. Doherty's stores in Malin, where I bought groceries, would have a replacement bottle if necessary – it wouldn't do to run low when visitors dropped in. All quite normal, responsible drinking, on which nobody had occasion to remark, but a furtive element had infiltrated our marriage; I would unload the shopping so that Fergus would not see the bottle, and store it in an inconspicuous place. At home it would just go in the drinks cupboard, modestly stocked compared to the variety we had kept at Mwanza, where the constant stream of visitors demanded all tastes be catered for. Bristol Cream sherry was popular with the north Down ladies; Amontillado for the more sophisticated among them. I had worked on my mother's well-founded distrust of drink to the extent that, at social functions, she would now accept a token glass of sherry, though she said it had an immediate effect on her, and she dreaded being in any sense out of control. San, too, regarded drink with caution: one of the reasons for the failure of Murray's garage business had been his 'getting into bad company' in the York Street pubs. Now she enjoyed a glass of Bristol Cream when she came to visit for the day, or sometimes to stay overnight. I would drive over the Craigantlet hills to Dundonald, collect her from the flat to which she had become resigned, and take her for lunch and shopping in Newtownards, Holywood or Bangor, getting home in advance of the children's return from school.

November 14 of that year is memorable, because I collected San early on the day Princess Anne married Captain Mark Phillips. San had long revelled in the pageantry surrounding royalty, while my attitude to the princess, who had entered 'the hearts and minds' of the great British public, was not uncritical. We sat, San, my mother and I, in front of the screen, watching the footage, listening to Richard Dimbleby's comfortable commentary. Before our lunch, which I served on trays, I gave them both a glass of sherry, while, out of sight in the kitchen, I drank two or three. I was still eating normally, had abundant energy, and had not yet begun to gain weight; nor was I drinking in the morning. Notwithstanding, the insidious disease was making a classic relentless progression towards the next stage.

Fergus had no choice but to accept the job in Brazzaville, but he contrived to negotiate a two-month course in Geneva to improve his French. This coincided with school summer holidays, so we rented a top-floor apartment near the InterContinental Hotel from a colleague who was going on leave. There was a swimming pool on the roof and a shopping mall nearby; the WHO headquarters, the UN building and other international organisations were within walking distance and public transport regular, clean and efficient. So much could be done on foot or by tram, that we did not really miss having a car. We visited the old town, the Bauer museum of oriental ceramics, jade and lacquer, the Russian Orthodox Church with its golden onion dome, the National Gallery and the Jet d'Eau. We found an excellent Italian family restaurant, inexpensive by Geneva standards, where the waiters were friendly and the children could watch their pizza of choice being prepared.

When we returned to Ireland, the children settled well in Glencraig Primary School, and despite household chores, I found time to join a pressure group fighting successive planning applications from developers to build on an unofficial greenbelt adjacent to the foreshore and what is now the North Down Coastal Path, directly in front of our house. The Reverend Ian Paisley, though remote, was behind a proposal to build a reform school beside Rockport Preparatory School. I also made contacts within the Alliance Party, and our car was covered with electoral stickers; a Catholic labourer working on our house remarked: 'Sure, yer wasting yer time, dear' – in many ways he was right. I met some congenial people such as Jack Calvert, his wife, Anne, and Bertie McConnell, all of whom did sterling work within the Down County Council, and a group of us formed a delegation to meet the minister appointed by Westminster to the Northern Ireland Office to explain our misgivings about the threat developers, including Paisley, posed to the coast, and the suspicion that hardline unionists backed repeated applications to the chief planning officer in Downpatrick.

When Fergus returned to Brazzaville, he was sent on a succession of short-term assignments to Gabon, Cameroon and Equatorial Guinea. The plus point was total immersion in an all-French-speaking society, but it was a punishing schedule under enervating climatic conditions, living in a series of run-down ex-French colonial hotels and *pensions*. I cannot recall if he came home for Christmas, as few letters from that period survive, but it would not have been surprising had it been Fergus who turned to drink. The only person in our family to profit from the situation was my mother. She enjoyed having the children so near, and either joined us for meals or I would take a helping of our meal through to her. Like many elderly people living alone, her diet lacked variety and I suspected she was anaemic. She suffered from eye spasms, which affected her eyesight, but she drove well into her eighties, when the condition became so bad she was forced to admit defeat and sell the Austin A40 to which she was very attached. This was a major psychological blow for someone accustomed to driving some sort of vehicle from 1914 onwards.

As a special dispensation, Fergus was allowed to take his local leave in 'the country of origin', rather than the Congo, so in the spring of 1974 we took the car via the Larne–Stranraer ferry to Galloway, and thence by a winding route through Moffat, Edinburgh and the Borders, to visit a Quaker school in Yorkshire, which we had shortlisted as a possibility for Katharine, who would be eleven plus at the start of the autumn term.

Roger, still in limbo and also waiting for a transfer from the African region, offered us his flat for July and August, when he would be on leave in France. So it was agreed that I would fly to Brazzaville with the children via Charles de Gaulle Airport. Of all the airports I had been through, this was by far the largest, noisiest and most confusing. At the check-in desk an inscrutable, heavily made-up woman, in a shiny red plastic jumpsuit, acknowledged me in ultra-rapid French. After scrutinising our tickets with obvious suspicion, she checked the passenger list and informed me that we were not on the list for the midnight flight, which was fully booked. Our 'chariot', piled high with luggage, blocked the baggage conveyor, beside which the children stood in a defensive clump. That we were unwelcome to Air France, and the growing queue behind, was only too evident. I stood my ground, brandishing WHO documents, my British passport, and a letter from the UN representative who would accompany Fergus to meet us. She told the other passengers to join another queue, as she was closing the desk. I gathered she had decided to consult her supervisor. After a long interval, she returned, gesturing at us, saying: 'Vous restez ici.' No apology, no explanation. We were the last group to board the throbbing aircraft a few minutes before midnight.

The flight was indeed fully booked: this was West Africa again. The women were heavily built market-mammy types, many wearing long dresses in the missionary-inspired style with a little frill above the waistline. Their gold earrings and bangles indicated status, as they swayed up and down the centre aisle searching for space in the overhead lockers for their duty-free purchases. The majority of the men were dressed in sharply tailored suits, worn with flashy ties and Mobutu-style sunglasses. Among them was a scattering of dignified Muslims in flowing white robes and intricately embroidered headgear. At first nobody took the slightest notice when told to return to their seat and fasten seat belts, but eventually all settled. As we roared down the runway, I counted to nearly sixty buttock-clenching seconds before the plane was airborne; the children were already almost asleep.

At six-thirty in the morning Fergus and the WHO representative, both freshly shaven and crisply dressed, met a crumpled, bleary-eyed, grubby and underslept group of four. They 'facilitated' us and our baggage – which, to my relief, came through quickly – to a chauffeur-driven UN limousine, in which we arrived at the residential compound and Roger's flat. The air was hot and humid, the sky sunless, and we were not to see the famous River Congo until some days later.

Roger's cook/steward, a rascally-looking scoundrel if ever there was one, greeted us unsmilingly. I reflected on how fortunate we had been in our house-servants. We sized each other up, and Emmanuel saw a promising victim: my French was inadequate, therefore there would be scope for misunderstanding – genuine or contrived. His main job was to look after the laundry, take it outside to hang limply in the sunless yard, iron and stack it away. Beds were to be made and floors swept, but I made it clear that I would do most of the cooking. That, however, would mean familiarising myself with local stores, the UN commissariat, and the market. There was none of the relaxed badinage of Ghanaian communities, and compared to the peoples of East Africa, this lot were inscrutable, even sinister. I had yet to read Joseph Conrad's *Heart of Darkness*, or Graham Greene's *Journey Without Maps*, but they got it right. When we made an excursion to look over the wide expanse of river towards Kinshasa, it was a depressing scene: the river was grey-green and at this point sluggish, though rapids and the Livingstone Falls, further downstream, barred direct access to the open Atlantic. Scarcely any birds populated the marginal undergrowth, in which rusting carcasses of camouflaged military vehicles, tractors, even a few tanks, were scattered. We were all badly bitten by the omnipresent sand-flies. The swimming pool was uninviting, its yellowing tiles cracked, the metal railing rusty, and few other children used it; rotting vegetable matter floated on the surface of the murky water, and snakes, many of them venomous, were common in the surrounding vegetation.

Fergus was not alone in his disillusionment about working

under the aegis of the regional office. Virtually all staff, from the lowest general service grade to the assistant directors, were depressed, apprehensive and intimidated under the rule of Dr Quenum. Nepotism was widespread: the director had a dozen children by different wives, and could legitimately claim staff benefits for all of them; any favoured acolyte – they were few and short-lived – would also get away with milking the UN to the hilt. Retirement age was a nominal sixty, but many educated Africans did not know their real date of birth, so it was common to see professional staff at a high level continuing in post, and reaping benefits in one form or another. At a ludicrous level, staff were precluded from displaying personal objects such as family photographs on their desks, while the national flag was obligatory; desks should be at right angles to the walls, and only the director could place his diagonally across a corner. My politically incorrect hypothesis is that an errant gene exists in Africa, manifesting itself as megalomania in those who gain power. It equips them with magnetic personality capable of arousing the uncritical masses to support blatantly undemocratic policies under the guise of freeing themselves from the shackles of wicked colonialism. Sierra Leone, Liberia, Zambia, Zimbabwe, Angola, Mozambique, Ethiopia, Somalia, Guinea-Bissau, Nigeria – the list is endless of fragmentation, over the last fifty years, of the existing infrastructure in countries capable of growing sufficient crops to sustain a populace above starvation level. Now global warming, repeated failure of rains, the proliferation of families composed entirely of AIDS orphans, added to famine on an explosive scale, compound the misery of vast swathes of the population.

All of our acquaintances were unhappy with their lot – this was a hell-hole in which few flourished. Fergus maintained the pretence of being only a transitory resident, staying in a succession of *pensions*, and buying a bicycle rather than a car. When we left, he moved to share a bungalow with Vernon Bailey, an Australian consultant, with whom he shared many interests, including art and ornithology. Vernon had designed a series of stamps of indigenous birds for the Republic of Congo and was proud of the designs, about which we both had reservations – many looked stiff, and not in the same league as the plates in *Bannerman's Birds of West Africa*. He was a kindly man, who took us on a number of excursions to his hideaway hut deep in the hinterland, and his advice helped to stabilise Fergus at a time when his spirits were at an all-time low.

We had bought an apartment in Divonne-les-Bains, a spa town at the foot of the Jura almost on the Franco-Swiss border. Within a half-hour drive of Geneva airport and the headquarters building, it was to be completed by late 1975, by which time we were convinced that Fergus would have escaped from Brazzaville. I was determined that the transfer should not be further complicated by a frenzied search for suitable accommodation. Property in France, though not constructed to such a high specification as that in Switzerland, was cheaper. Our decision to live in France provoked dire warnings from colleagues who regarded it as unwise and 'not quite the thing'. Minus points were that vehicles registered in France would not bear CD (Corps Diplomatique) plates; that charges and restrictions relating to use of the autoroute would be punitive; and laws relating to snow tyres were complicated and would entail endless expense (the colleagues were right on that one). The Swiss police were not to be trifled with, but were less feared than the French gendarmerie – no less ferocious, but volatile and unpredictable.

Our parting at the end of August was one of the saddest of our life. The demijohn of Chianti I had bought was found to be nearly empty, and Fergus blamed Emmanuel for the excessive inroads. I let that pass, erosion of moral principles having now entered the equation, justifying my silence in the knowledge that, if not responsible for that particular theft, he had been caught out in several other instances. From time to time I would calculate how much my drinking cost, but it was too uncomfortable to face, so I put it to the back of my mind. Nobody yet suspected how excessive my drinking had become, and many regarded me as a tower of strength in the circumstances.

Shortly after we returned to Ireland, I flew with Katharine for her first term at Ackworth School in Pontefract – one reason we had chosen this school was the short flight between Belfast and Leeds. She seemed happy to return to boarding-school rules, and quickly made friends with a girl who had spent some years in the Sudan: her father was a UN consultant at the Food and

Agriculture Organization based in the south of the country not far from the border with Kenya. Mary and Michael continued at the local primary school, and my mother was relieved to see us again.

Most people, rather than employ decorators, did their own house painting. After a series of lettings, the house needed a face-lift, so I began a number of projects, from painting the sitting room ceiling, to hanging wallpaper of a bold 'contemporary' design on the chimney wall, laying carpet tiles in the bathroom, and painting doors a 'designer' shade of air-force blue from the architects' range. By this time, in addition to sherry, the drinks cupboard contained red and white Cinzano, Campari, Dubonnet, Bols Advocaat, Cointreau, crème de menthe, green chartreuse, brandy, gin and a selection of malt whiskies. The brandy was for Aunt Rosemary, the chartreuse for the Pharmacist, both infrequent visitors – but it wouldn't do not to have their favourite tipple on hand. San and my mother grew fond of Advocaat, which I argued was good for their health – in the quantities they drank, it probably was.

A number of incidents can, in retrospect, be attributed to drink. Often I started a job on impulse, so rather than wearing overalls, I wore the fashionable flares of the time. It was such a pair of red cotton bell-bottoms that overturned an open can of Dulux, which quickly spread beyond the limits of the newspaper protecting the living-room carpet: no amount of cleaning ever quite removed the stain. Protecting surfaces was not my forte. On one occasion, such was my confidence with a blow-lamp that I decided to strip the bathroom door, but a coil of burning paint fell on the newspaper that was protecting the carpet tiles, and I was choking on black smoke by the time I managed to extinguish the flames with a wet bath-towel, and open the window. While this was going on, my mother was working in her garden, and the children were at school. Another incident, potentially more dangerous, concerned the airing cupboard where bedding was stored. A naked low voltage bulb, which lit the interior, had been left on overnight: in the morning there was a smouldering hole in a duvet that had been in contact with the hot bulb. I did not tell anyone about that.

Basic items of furniture had to be bought for the flat in Divonne, and a local firm found which would be willing to store items in advance of shipping them as part of a container load destined for Italy. The firm I selected was willing, but inexperienced in dealing with shipments to continental Europe; none of them knew a word of French, German or Italian, and all spoke in a broad Belfast accent. I scoured antique shops and auction rooms and at a clearance sale in Hanna & Browne, Belfast's most prestigious furniture shop, I bought some large items. The list of 'alcoholic' purchases was also growing – most notably, a black-lacquered Edwardian upright piano, which meant the family in which nobody was more than an occasional strummer, now had two pianos. (It went to France, where I sold it to a jazz club.)

In October Michael appeared, wearing a sheepish expression, with a dog he claimed had followed him from the school gates. It had an instantly appealing personality, was neither cowed nor underfed, so I suspected it had a loving owner. It was agreed that it should stay the night, but an effort had to be made to reunite it with its owner. Michael reluctantly agreed that this was only just. He need not have worried because nobody came forward, and we came to the conclusion that Oscar had been dumped at the top of the estate, just off the main Bangor road, by someone who knew he would find a good home. He was of medium size, probably a mix of boxer and foxhound, of high intelligence, and had few faults, apart from a tendency to disappear for long periods in pursuit of some desirable bitch. Michael adored him, as did we all, but his arrival further complicated plans for 1975.

That I cannot recall the Christmas period of that year may be due to the fact that Fergus remained in the Congo, and we were both deeply depressed. He was also angry, tired, resentful and lonely: all reasons to seek refuge in a haze of alcohol. But he did not, or only rarely, as when, under cover of darkness, he put sugar in the petrol tank of a particularly unpleasant colleague. He was with us during the school holidays at Easter 1975, when we went to Malin and stayed in a recently restored schoolhouse. I have a picture of Auntie Dodi, Katharine and Oscar sitting on a rock, hair windswept by an arctic gale, which soon afterwards delivered pea-sized hailstones.

In September of that year Mary joined Katharine at Ackworth, while Michael remained at Glencraig until the October half-term when we left Northern Ireland to move to France. Once more we stayed en route at Mill Hill with Sybil and Iain, who fortunately are dog-lovers, because this time we brought Oscar, who, under sedation, had been flown over in a crate. The plan was to cross the channel from Folkestone to Calais where a duty-free Renault awaited collection.

The taxi we hired from Mill Hill to Folkestone broke down on the journey, with the result that we missed the afternoon ferry, and spent a chilly, windy afternoon killing time in steamy cafés, while the channel turned more choppy by the minute. It was late in the evening when we docked, to find the formalities we had dreaded because of Oscar were nonexistent; he went through without arousing any comment, and soon we were outside in the dark, looking for a taxi to take us to the hotel. Next morning we collected the car. For some reason the choice of vehicle had been left to me, and I had discussed our needs with the main Renault dealer in Belfast who was plugging the latest hatchback. I had ordered the de luxe model with bronze metallic paintwork, but what greeted us was a standard model with dreary beige paintwork; worse still, it had a 1.2 diesel engine. Fergus's remarks on seeing it are unprintable, particularly when he heard that he should not exceed 50 kph until it was due for its first service.

It is a very long drive to Divonne, and few details remain on my memory stick apart from Michael insisting on sleeping overnight in the car with Oscar because the *pension* had refused him entry. The nights were getting colder, and we had not calculated that the last lap of the journey through the département de l'Ain would be on Armistice Day. Most of the hotels we passed were *fermé*, and the Auberge du Vieux Bois on the road from Gex to Divonne, where we had hoped to find a room, was shuttered, displaying the notice 'Fermeture annuelle'. We were exhausted, it was late in the day, and for the first time the momentous nature of our decision really struck home. Fortunately the Auberge du Beau Soleil near the *thermes* and casino was open, and M. Buffon, with flat black shiny hair, thin moustache and striped apron, would be delighted to show us a family room on the top floor. Oscar was already in the bar mingling with red-faced *fermiers*, who patted him, agreeing he was a fine *chien de chasse*, while Michael played table football.

Filet de boeuf and frites were on the menu, followed by fruits, a cheese board and vanilla ice cream. We ordered a carafe of the house red, and Fanta for Michael. Without our asking, a plate of kitchen leftovers and a bowl of water was brought for Oscar, who slept that night on Michael's bed.

We collected keys to the flat from the *notaire*'s office before going in search of the concierge. The approach was by an unsurfaced cul de sac off the main road near the cemetery, the bicycle shop and the *église protestante*. The car park, which had been asphalted, was shared with another *bâtiment*, where the concierge lived. M. Rossi emerged from his lair, bald, unsmiling and rotund, and we both found him difficult to understand. He spoke rapidly in an unfamiliar argot – think Marcel Pagnol films and *Jean de Florette*. Neighbours reassured us that even the French found him difficult to understand; he was Italian, and had learned his French in the Pyrenees. He escorted us across the entrance hall on the *rez-de-chaussée*, from which a lift descended to the *sous-sol*, where each apartment had a storage unit, and refuse bins awaited collection by the council lorry. A chute from the kitchens above discharged into a huge container, which it was his duty to wheel out to the roadside. All this we ingested as we passed a wall of metal postboxes, to a flight of marble stairs leading to our *1er étage* flat.

The living room faced south with a view over Lac Léman to the Alps and Mont Blanc, the bedrooms faced the Jura, and the kitchen and bathroom overlooked the car park. Naked wires and a hook hung from each ceiling, the entrance hall and sitting/dining area had wood-block flooring, the kitchen was red tiled – Cardinal polish again – the bedrooms acrylic carpeted in crude colours that were not what I had specified. The bathroom was small, and tastefully tiled in pale turquoise, while the WC was so small its door opened outwards, forcing one to enter sideways.

We also owned the adjacent studio flat, which had a large bed/sitting room, kitchen – which we planned to use as a utility room – and a bathroom. Fergus and I would use this as our bedroom/study, leaving a room for each child in the main flat. The tiles above the sinks in both kitchens were large and dingy cream, so one of the first DIY jobs I undertook was chipping them all off, and sending them down the chute to the *sous-*

sol. This provoked a wrathful visit from M. Rossi: culpable, I should have realised that rubble would have to be disposed of elsewhere. I was being sucked into the world of *bricolage*, where a whole new vocabulary had to be learned, and would learn the hard way that in France they do most things differently. Even hanging pictures and mirrors safely on our nail-resistant walls was not straightforward.

Two days later, as promised, the lorry from Belfast arrived. The driver and his two mates complained bitterly about the bloody-mindedness they had met at many points on the journey. To an extent our sympathy lay with the French: the paperwork involved was in triplicate, and our team was scarcely literate, so they cannot have been easy to deal with. French patience will have been sorely tried. On the other hand, once we embarked on the process of getting *cartes de séjours* and *d'identités* and a *permis de conduire* for me, our sympathy reverted to the Irish when we found that several trips to Bourg-en-Bresse were involved, and one, connected to the importation of the car, took us as far as Lyon.

Fergus was on a three-month assignment based at headquarters, and would not be around much of the time; in any case, DIY was not his strong point. So it lay with me to find a TV and electrical shop, curtain-makers, and a hardware store, which did not exist in Divonne, so I had to cross the border in my search for many items. Compared with Holywood, the town was ill-served by local merchants, despite boasting two *notaires*, three *agences d'immobilière*, and two *bijouteries* catering for the super-rich visitors to the casino – after Monte Carlo, it was the largest in France, and one morning I met Omar Sharif face to face coming out of the *maison de la presse*. There was much to be done in the six weeks before the girls would join us for the month-long Christmas break: their rooms should at least have ceiling lights, and Michael would have to be enrolled at one of the international schools if he was to start in mid-January. In the meantime he was happy walking Oscar down to the little port on the artificial Lac de Divonne, where the dog loved to swim and retrieve sticks. Having known no more than a few basic words of French, Michael quickly became at ease with boys of roughly the same age who played football around the *bâtiments* – the concierge's son, Roberto, among them. There being no official play area, this was a contentious subject, provoking constant complaints about noise and danger to windows. Mme Bernier, who had the misfortune to live directly below us, despite having grandchildren was particularly intolerant and given to knocking on her ceiling if we made too much noise, as we did on Michael's ninth birthday. Her husband, a pleasant, even timid, retired doctor, had specialised in nervous afflictions at the *thermes*, to which patients were referred from all over France.

At Christmas the weather was sunny, with a light dusting of snow, and ski slopes above 1,000 metres were already open. Fergus had booked a table for our festive luncheon at the Cheval de Bois in a tiny village halfway to Gex, which, while not Michelin-starred, had a good reputation. A roaring log fire blazed in the comfortable lounge, and the two gay owners made us welcome, but the children felt the constraint of having to be on best behaviour, and were unimpressed by chestnut stuffing, lack of bread sauce and the inferiority of French bacon and sausages; a tower of choux pastry balls, however, got full marks, as did the *îles flottantes*. Afterwards they went tobogganing on the red plastic sledge last used on the sandhills at Malin. Oscar loved sliding on his front in the snow, and the children had a riotous time. Fergus, however, complained that despite fur-lined gloves his hands were cold, and I felt strangely distant from the classic Christmas card scene, wishing we had drunk more wine with our meal and counting the time till we would be back in the flat where I could top up. Never noticeably drunk, I needed a certain level to give me a kick-start, and keep functioning throughout the day. I had by this time become what is properly known as a 'high functioning alcoholic'.

Winters were cold in the 1970s and 1980s, and the football field at Saint-Cergue was always flooded and turned into an ice rink. The girls had their own skates, Michael to my disgust insisted on buying hockey ones, and my own pair, last used in Boston, still fitted. When Fergus could be persuaded to take to the ice, we had to hire skates for him. On one of our visits, a middle-aged man, in knickerbockers and fur hat, did an impressive hockey stop beside us, excused himself to Fergus, who was holding Oscar on a lead, and begged me to join him for a waltz. 'The Skater's Waltz' floated over the air, and although it was twenty years since I had last danced, I managed not to bring him down. A small group of admirers had gathered, and the children were mortified.

There was a café overlooking the rink in the pavilion from which the music had come: it served soup, chips, hot chocolate and, of course, wine. They did not object to the presence of dogs, so I was able to slope off to the pavilion on the pretence of taking Oscar for a walk and having a hot drink, while Fergus stayed with the children who were reluctant to leave the ice before the temperature plummeted in mid-afternoon. The drive back down to Divonne was a dramatic one with twenty-seven hairpin bends, dangerous at the best of times, but in winter, despite constant salting and gritting, perilous. Quite often we would pass a vehicle that had slid off the road and come to a standstill, its bonnet crushed against a tree trunk.

I can remember precisely what I wore the day that I danced: the costly ski pants we had bought for our two ski holidays at Verbier had survived storage. Worn with my black Cossack hat and a natural wool Aran sweater, they looked chic, but had become uncomfortably tight around the waist. I was almost forty-eight and was in danger of turning into what my mother scathingly termed 'thick in the middle'; she disparaged females who 'let themselves go' once respectably married. The menopause had begun, and that combined with the sugar content in alcohol, was a recipe for weight gain. There was not the widespread obsession with healthy lifestyles that exists today, so I rarely weighed myself, although I was careful to watch Fergus's *ligne* since his heart attack. I no longer had time for dressmaking, and while acceptable clothing could be bought for Fergus and the children, garments for myself were difficult to find. Entering a boutique in France was a sure step to humiliation; the most popular sizes were UK 8 to 12, 14 was in the danger zone, and 16, 18 or 20 almost unheard of. Eventually I learned to look for Swedish, Dutch or German makes with greater success, but styles were safe rather than fashionable. French feet being to scale, my search for 7+ (or French size 42) raised some exquisitely shaped eyebrows.

The girls returned to school in Yorkshire and Michael went to the International School in Versoix, near Geneva, where he was unhappy. Why, we never really discovered, but after we moved him to the International School La Châtaigneraie at Founex, just across the frontier in Switzerland, he never looked back, remaining until he had done his O-levels, then transferring to The King's School in Canterbury.

Fergus had access to bilingual secretarial help while he worked at headquarters, so demands on my secretarial skills were now confined to editing and personal correspondence. WHO continually updated its typewriters, so I always bought the last model to be discarded. Radical changes were under way, and by the early 1980s all professional staff were encouraged to familiarise themselves with digital technology. Most were too advanced in their careers to learn keyboard skills, and a few were technophobes, so the full benefit came to the next generation, who wrote their theses on computers. Photocopiers were less temperamental, and laser printers saw the end of the carbon-copy era and the need for stencil cutting. But Fergus remained under the aegis of the African regional office, and worked from Brazzaville during much of 1976. The wheels of change ground slowly into motion only after Dr Ansari's retirement at the end of March 1976. The summer of that year was exceptionally warm and sunny all over Europe, and I remember looking out from the kitchen sink to yet another cloudless day, nostalgic for the unpredictable Irish weather.

Some of the UN wives advised me to join the American Women's Club, assuring me it had been the salvation of many newcomers to the Canton de Genève; of course, it would be difficult for me, having chosen to live in the outback. I was ungracious, and will have been dismissed as cold and unfriendly – but their consciences were salved, having made the gesture. I remember saying I knew few better ways to waste a morning than at a coffee party: a view I still hold. Cocktail parties with messy little canapés and small objects on sticks which inevitably fell to the floor were equally abhorrent. The noise, the mindless chatter, loathed by the saner of both sexes – I knew as a supportive wife that I must make a token appearance from time to time, particularly as Fergus would soon be working at headquarters. I was never drunk, nor did I behave in an unseemly manner, but I did not circulate well, sometimes finding an equally miserable loner – always male – to talk to. I had a tendency to get into 'lively debates', something of a loose cannon. The fact that I had always eaten something, and tanked up before going, will have contributed to the animated exchanges. I kept a miniature bottle of something in my handbag at all times. Over the years, fashionable handbags evolved into capacious sacks, capable of containing a whole bottle.

The year, despite our separation, seemed to pass quickly because my days were busy from the time of making Michael's packed lunch, and delivering him to school no later than 8.45 a.m., until it was time to collect him at 3.30 p.m. The apartment now had a modicum of character, but we both knew that it was a transient base – neither of us was suited to apartment life. I acquired a *femme de ménage*, Janine, who came twice a week to polish the wood-block floors, apply Cardinal to the kitchen tiles, and help me with ironing. Drying the washing was a nightmare because, despite having balconies on both sides of the building, the hanging of anything on the railings to dry was forbidden: with good reason – otherwise the apartments would have taken on the look of a slum development. A discreet clotheshorse would not arouse comment, but beating rugs, or watering plants was *défendu* lest dust or water fall on the *balcon* below.

Janine came from Perpignan, but had come to Divonne to be near her elder daughter, married to the son of a local farmer. Her French was easy to understand, although, again, the accent was strongly regional. I soon gathered that her daughter had married a violent drunk who took after his florid-faced father, one of the regulars in M. Buffon's bar. There were too many children, all were undisciplined and several wet their beds. No regular income came in as Claude, her son-in-law, relied on casual work. On learning that Fergus might be persuaded to sell the Renault, Claude insisted on making our acquaintance; he was persistent and in due course did buy it.

Poor, disillusioned Janine, dark-skinned, with lovely bone structure, but prematurely aged, returned to sunny Perpignan only to be killed by a drunken motorist while out walking with her youngest grandchild.

18
Well of Loneliness

I was unwell. Having always been a good sleeper, my nights were now broken by nightmarish dreams, sweats and long periods of insomnia. On waking, I was nauseous and had been sick several times. I thought I might be pregnant, and knew that no matter how dangerous or inconvenient that might be, I could not contemplate a termination.

We were registered with a young Portuguese doctor who said I was not pregnant, and my disturbed sleep was in all probability caused by stress; he prescribed a short course of antidepressants. My blood pressure was raised and he took the menopause into account. He did not enquire about my drinking, but I concluded that the symptoms emanated from not eating adequate evening meals, and drinking a lot of whisky at night after Michael went to bed. The nausea was a form of alcohol withdrawal, and ceased as soon as I downed a stiff drink. I had yet to learn that after the initial boost alcohol gives, it acts as a depressant. Each morning I gave Michael breakfast and prepared his packed lunch before driving him to school, then stopped on the return journey for groceries and another bottle of something or other. No wonder I was gaining weight when I recall the alternatives I downed in an effort to cut back on spirits: cassis, Cinzano, Campari, crème de menthe, Drambuie, Benedictine, chartreuse – you name it, I drank it.

Nonconformists had always attracted me, and I made a few acquaintances through Michael's playground friends; one was Karen, a German girl who lived with a married Frenchman and his two children in the same block as M. Rossi. She worked from home, translating German into French, and both languages into English, sometimes having a surfeit of the latter, which were passed to me. My school French was adequate to translate French to English, but not the reverse. I learned a great deal about cattle-breeding in Honduras, Nicaragua, Panama and Belize – all the Panamanian isthmus countries in fact.

Through Karen I met Eva, who had a flat at the end of our corridor. She was Austrian, tall, red-haired and strikingly good-looking; of a certain age, she could well have modelled for a Gustav Klimt painting. She had an office job in Nyon but supplemented her income by doing translations; her weekends were spent with a French national who lived in an ambitiously designed villa near Gex. From what I gleaned from Eva, their drinking began every Friday and ended late on Sunday, in order to sober up for the next week's work.

On a misty early autumn walk near the yacht club, I was calling the heedless Oscar when a voice rang across the water asking if I was English; on hearing that I was Irish, he answered: 'So's my wife.' A working-class lad, Jim had a first-class Oxford degree in political history and three boys at the International School, and his wife had spent her formative years in Brazil. He worked for the International Labour Organization and lived near Ferney-Voltaire. Expansive in the way of an alcoholic who has drunk just enough to prompt generous impulses, he was determined his wife and I should meet.

Shortly before Fergus returned to the Congo, we had met the owner of the apartment whose entrance door was nearest to our own. Horst was an Austrian in his early sixties, who came to Divonne twice a year for 'the cure'. He spoke impeccable English, was clearly from the upper echelons of society, and insisted we join him for dinner at one of the more exclusive local restaurants. He drove us there in his immaculate Mercedes, which outclassed all the other vehicles in the car park. It was a pleasant evening, despite the food being unremarkable. That, however, was of little concern to Horst, who concentrated on the wine list.

What did this succession of encounters with alcoholics mean? Did Fate, about which I was ambivalent, have a hand in this? Was some alien force trying to tell me something? Or was it simply that drinkers gravitate to drinkers?

Regular drinking since Fergus's heart attack in 1971 had led to dependency and I wanted to put a stop to it, so I decided to conduct an experiment. On returning from the school run and Oscar's morning walk, I put a bottle of whiskey in the centre of the dining-room table, resolving not to touch it until noon. Like a scene from the film *Woman in a Dressing Gown*, I walked around it, intoning: 'I'm not going to open you, I can resist you, I hate the taste and smell of you, and I'm not going to drink you ever again.' At eleven o'clock I downed a gin and tonic. Thereafter, as gin too could be detected on the breath, I changed my allegiance to vodka, in the false belief that it was odourless.

Something radical would have to be done. I knew that AA had groups in every country of the world. Only a degree of courage was needed to ring the number given in the Geneva telephone directory. A gravelly male voice answered in an East Coast American accent. His name was Dick, and he would be happy to meet me on Tuesday evening at seven thirty in the foyer of the Intercontinental Hotel, before escorting me to a meeting. I did not have anyone to stay with Michael, but told him to go to Eva if he was worried about anything. He had a load of homework to do, always worked independently, and did not seem at all fazed by this arrangement. Only long afterwards did I realise how irresponsible it had been to leave him alone: Fergus was in Thailand, my mother in Ireland, and nobody knew where I would be in Geneva. Worst of all, there was always alcohol in my bloodstream, and I kept a miniature bottle in the glove compartment of the car.

I knew immediately it was Dick when a tall, middle-aged, weather-beaten man in a dark blue blazer appeared in the vestibule. He ordered two bottles of mineral water, and said I did not look like a terminal drunk. I replied that this was not a positive factor, probably even encouraging me to continue on the slippery slope. When I told him that Fergus was not aware of my dependence, he asked caustically: 'Something wrong with his nose?' I said that on his return for Christmas, I intended to confess the extent of the problem and my resolve to tackle it by attending AA meetings on a regular basis.

Meetings were held in a quiet backwater of the old town. The entrance was unobtrusive and the atmosphere thick with smoke. Dick led the way to a room with a billiard-sized central table, over which hung a low lamp with a faded, pleated silk shade, evocative of scenes from early films where Mafia men gather to play ruthless card games. He introduced me to the man who was to chair the meeting, another American, and his subdued wife, who had seen better days. Their accents were southern, and his manner crude, peppered with unnecessary epithets, but they said in harmony: 'Glad to meet you, you are in the right place.' Framed exhortations hung on every wall – 'Let Go and Let God', 'Keep it Simple', 'One Day at a Time', 'First Things First', 'Live and Let Live', 'Take it Easy', 'Keep coming back, it works if you work it'. A giant photograph of Bill W., the Akron stockbroker who with his friend, Dr Bob, had founded the fellowship in 1935, dominated one wall. I hated the word 'fellowship' – it smacked of joining something and I was essentially a loner. I was soon to learn that this was characteristic of many alcoholics.

People were filtering in, perhaps a dozen men of assorted ages and half that number of women. None appeared the worse for wear, but a few were withdrawn, in contrast to the rest who were laughing and relaxed. Dick whispered to me: 'Try to keep an open mind, and take the cotton wool out of your ears and stick it in your mouth.' The chairman rose and asked us to 'Stand for a moment of silence, to remember why we are here.' Next, he asked one of the men to read the preamble, which said that Alcoholics Anonymous was a fellowship of men and women who shared their strength, hope and experience, and hoped to carry their message to others less fortunate. So far, no mention of God. A women was asked to read something called 'How it Works', to which Dick advised me to pay particular attention. God came on the scene then – referred to as 'One who has all power', it was hoped that we would find him now. When she read the Twelve Steps to Recovery, I could see immediately that Step 3 – I was to turn my life over to the care of God, as I understood him – was going to be particularly sticky, as I had no spiritual foundation on which to build, vacillating between atheism, agnosticism and humanism. (Much later, by replacing the dreaded word with 'Good', I made some progress.) When all the steps had been read out, there followed a paragraph:

> Rarely have we seen a person fail who has thoroughly followed our path, those who do not recover are those who cannot, or will not, adopt a manner of living which requires rigorous honesty. There are those too who suffer from grave emotional or mental disorders, there are such unfortunates, they seem

to have been born that way, but many recover in time if they
have the capacity to be honest.

It shattered me to the core.

The meeting was then declared open and several hands were
raised, indicating a wish to speak: each began with the formula
'My name is —— and I'm an alcoholic', with the exception of a
small mousy woman who substituted 'and I am powerless over
alcohol'. They spoke of blackouts, of memory loss so severe that
whole days had been erased. In one case the speaker had landed,
after an overnight flight, in another country. One woman had
lost her sight for several days, and hair loss was common. Some
were medically qualified and had continued to practise until
shopped by colleagues. Less dramatically, others woke in the bed
of a stranger, or found themselves in police custody – these were
all professional people, many multilingual. The Geneva groups,
for some incalculable reason, were seldom attended by what
were known colloquially as 'skid-row bums'. It terrified me to
contemplate the fact that the corridors of world politics might
be crawling with active alcoholics, whose fingers, metaphorically
speaking, could press the Red Button.

Shortly before the meeting closed, the chairman asked me if
I would like to say something, so I followed the pattern, giving
my name followed by the declaration 'and I'm an alcoholic'. I
thanked him and the rest of the group for their varied stories,
saying, with truth, that I had learned a lot. The meeting closed
when we were asked to stand and say the Serenity Prayer – 'God
grant me the serenity to accept the things I cannot change, the
courage to change the things I can, and the wisdom to know
the difference.' As we left, a statuesque woman approached me,
saying she hoped to see me at the next meeting, 'by which time
your brain should have cleared a bit'. I found her implication
offensive and her manner overbearing. Dick said she was a
Finnish national who meant well, but that she could indeed
be abrasive. I was handed several leaflets and bought a copy of
the Big Book – the AA bible, now dated, though the underlying
philosophy remains sound. On parting from Dick, I expressed
my gratitude, saying I had been impressed by the sincerity of
the group, and would return when I had digested the literature.
Before driving off, I took a swig from the bottle in the glove
compartment.

One of the leaflets, titled 'Who Me?', contained a list of questions for the reader wishing to confirm whether he or she was an alcoholic or merely someone who drank too much on occasion but could stop at any time without suffering withdrawal symptoms. It emphasised that nobody else had the right to affix the label – it was entirely for the drinker to decide. There were about thirty questions, such as 'Do you drink alone?' and 'Do you crave a drink at certain times?'; my answer was affirmative to all but three, so it was clear my worries were founded. I read the literature avidly, with a strong drink beside me. I had not understood the simple message that the programme demanded total abstinence. I read the horror stories in the Big Book with special attention, and concluded that my own case was mild in comparison: I had never passed out, had memory loss, hallucinations, or a car accident. I was not violent, verbally or physically. But there had been an incident when oil in an unattended frying-pan had caught fire, and Fergus had extinguished it with a damp towel: my reactions had been slow as we choked in the smoke-blackened kitchen.

Having been to several meetings, I was still drinking almost as much as before, although I remained silent about it. Nobody in the group challenged me, but they all knew and were clearly disappointed. However, one visiting Canadian, Ted Hooper, to whom I owe eternal gratitude, gave me a stern lecture. He said that it was clear I had not 'reached bottom' – in other words, I had not yet suffered enough. He was sorry, not just for me, but for those closest to me, who would also suffer unless I was able to accept, as well as admit, my powerlessness. He said: 'It may well be that you need a "convincer", and it may take some time, even years, for you to reach that stage.' He told me that he had been sober for some years before having what in AA is called 'a slip', which reduced him in a matter of weeks to a state of suicidal despair – he mentioned lying in a bath, a loaded pistol at the ready. But with the support of his family, who belonged to the Al-Anon group for relatives, colleagues or anyone who has suffered, or continues to suffer, because of someone's drinking, he had been given a second chance. He said that only a small percentage is so blessed, and that only ten per cent of people who come to AA for help attain long-term sobriety. The recovery rate for those who have had an extended period of sobriety before 'slipping' was even lower.

Now I was really frightened, particularly as I had identified myself as one 'of those unfortunates' mentioned in 'How it Works' who do not succeed. However, Ted never gave up on me, no matter how discouraging my behaviour, having a hunch that I might just make it in the end. There were aspects of the programme I could accept, on which I began work. I knew my mind was far from open, that I was intolerant and full of prejudices, that AA also stood for Altered Attitudes, but I was still treating it as an intellectual exercise, rather than a life-saving commitment to abstinence.

When Fergus returned from Thailand, I broke it to him that I had the same disease that had led to my father's premature death. He was shocked, having suspected nothing more than that I was stressed by sustained uncertainty about our future, and the onset of menopause. He was particularly apprehensive because of what he had seen during his years in Northern Rhodesia – marriages destroyed and childhood disrupted by the excessive drinking of one, sometimes both, partners. I told him how impressed I was by AA, and what I had learned at the Geneva group meetings, and advised him to join Al-Anon. He soon became a regular member of the small, largely female group, which met at the same time and in the same building as AA, thus ensuring that at least the driver of our car would be sober.

I had begun to listen with more attention to speakers I would previously have dismissed on superficial grounds. An overpowering American woman, rather showy in her manner of dress, spoke of being grateful she was alcoholic, because of the enlightenment AA had brought to her existence. She reiterated what Ted had said: 'If you're not convinced, go out and try some more controlled drinking.' But it was weeks before I noticed that 'The only requirement for membership is a desire to *stop* drinking'. I was not a member; I was merely attending meetings and learning a great deal about my condition. Still defiant, I clung to the hope that I might conquer the demon by my own efforts. I had been told to seek help, but the very idea was anathema. The word 'denial' was freely used in the meetings – a word I was never able to utter. Another American woman, who, outside the group, ran a counselling service, spoke to me with some venom across the table: 'You're in such denial, it's beyond belief.'

So parochial was the English-speaking population in the Canton de Genève and the Pays de Gex that anonymity would sooner or later be breached at some level. Failing to remember Dick's instruction to put the cotton wool in my mouth, I voiced the opinion that anonymity was unnecessary, as we suffered from a disease. It was drawn to my attention that if we were known to belong to AA and then 'slipped', it would not be a good advertisement for the fellowship. Point taken; but many months, as predicted by Ted, were to pass before the next stage in the relentless progress of the disease set in. Dick added to the horror stories in the Big Book, telling me about a woman, now confined in a Geneva mental hospital, whose drinking had led to Korsakoff's syndrome, commonly termed 'wet brain'. He had known her when she was a diplomat, renowned for her sharp wit and intellectual capacity. He no longer visited her, as she had no idea who he was.

I persuaded my mother to get a passport and she flew to Geneva for Christmas. Now eighty years old, it was her first flight since 1927, when I was *in utero* and she took pictures from a Tiger Moth of the Collon House where I was born some months later. She appeared in a wheelchair, escorted by a solicitous flight attendant, impressed by the efficiency of air travel, if not by the packaging of milk in 'fiddly' little plastic tubs that she had found hard to open. During her stay, we took her to the old part of Geneva, the Jet d'Eau, lunch at our favourite pizza restaurant, the Palais des Nations, and to see WHO headquarters, where Fergus now had an office in a new block – the original building, with its massive, gravity-defying, concrete-canopied entrance, having been found too small shortly after completion. Fergus drove her up the corkscrew road to Saint-Cergue, then into Switzerland, along the ridge of the Jura, and back to Divonne by another equally tortuous route with panoramic views to Lac Léman, Mont Blanc, and the Alpes Maritimes. I coped with preparation of a traditional festive meal, and had a rooted Norwegian blue spruce on the balcony lit by tiny coloured bulbs and decorated with baubles, some dating from the Boston days. But often I was tired and would retire to bed for a prolonged siesta, pleading exhaustion from cooking, shopping and other chores, leaving the others to their own devices. My mother remarked that I seemed to have little appetite for the delicious food I prepared, and was surprised at my burgeoning weight; my bouts of irritability, facial flushes and girth were attributed to the menopause.

In the early months of 1977 Fergus undertook a six-week mission to China to make an assessment of the schistosomiasis problem in the hinterland of both Beijing and Shanghai. By and large I was coping at all levels, and continued to type manuscripts and translations, in order – if truth be told – to earn conscience money to pay for my drinking. A rough calculation put my annual expenditure on booze level with a year's boarding-school fees. One reason I seldom had a hangover was that my system was permanently topped up. Not only was the quantity increasing, the alcohol content was also escalating. No longer did a glass of wine or Martini deliver the kick-start required – it had to be spirits. Anxiety about a dwindling supply would make me irritable and incapable of giving my undivided attention to anything or anybody until I had stashed away what I calculated would be enough. I began, squirrel-like, to secrete emergency supplies to see me through public holidays. Small bottles in the bathroom, ostensibly of nail varnish remover, might contain vodka. A few years later, when temporary loss of memory had set in, I would search fruitlessly for a hidden bottle. Disposing of the empties became a problem; rather than put them in the communal bin, I took them to a bottle bank elsewhere in the town, or into an area where I did not risk being recognised.

Fergus and I had decided to look for better accommodation and I came across a small notice in the weekly local rag: '*À vendre, Villard, dans une ferme, pied de la montagne, grande appartement, 4 pièces, cuisine, salle de bains. Vue imprenable sur lac, jardin, potagère.*' I asked Eva what '*dans une ferme*' signified and she said it was probably part of a large traditional house. On the morning Fergus returned from his trip to China, we drove straight from the airport to view En Barye, as the property was called. At the top of the town, under cliffs beside the municipal campsite, it proved to be the precisely divided half of a stone house, built in 1857 on part of a glacial gravel deposit, and in need of substantial repair and renovation. The other side was a vast *grenier*, containing straw, the remains of six cattle stalls, and three rooms on the ground floor, occupied by a retired shepherd, M. Marc-Joseph, who could be seen observing what was going on from a small, pine-topped eminence on the opposite side of the road. The owner lived in Provence but her nephew, a schoolteacher who no longer used the house as a summer retreat, had been delegated to negotiate the sale. Now retired, he was moving to Provence where his aunt lived. As we talked, a pair of buzzards circled above the house; occasionally, we were told, they were joined by red kites searching for small mammals. There were red squirrels, noisy green and pied woodpeckers, a variety of finches, and tits, as well as a busy pair of nuthatches. To an extent it was these attractions that blinded us to the house's numerous disadvantages. And on April Fool's Day, in a *notaire's* office, we signed a complicated document formalising our ownership.

In retrospect only someone touched by insanity would have undertaken this project. It demanded determination, attention to detail, and energy, and most of the decisions would rest with me, as Fergus, hitherto to a large extent his own master, was working for the first time at the hub of a giant bureaucratic machine. Headquarters staff tended to regard those who came 'in from the bush' with suspicion, as some proved difficult to tame. We engaged M. Gaston, who did not look like an architect, apart from the suede shoes and yellow waistcoat. He was rotund, rather like David Suchet's Poirot, and at our first site meeting jumped up and down on the living-room floor, plunging his penknife into floor and skirting before pronouncing them sound. He recommended contractors and subcontractors, and supervised the site in general, but even with my experience of properties in Ireland, it was a formidable undertaking. A convivial atmosphere pervaded the house throughout the summer – several of the workmen were bon viveurs with florid faces, their radios blaring incessantly. Gauloise smokers to a man, they never turned lights off during long lunch breaks, and their arrival was unpredictable, but they knocked off on the stroke of 5 p.m. As in Africa, they had honed their skills in the art of incomprehension – always with the excuse that my French was so deficient there had been a *malentendu*.

By Christmas, however, work was well advanced, and just

before the girls joined us for the Easter of 1978, we moved in with another load of furniture from Ireland, as well as what was in the apartment. It had been sold to a master butcher, who complained of a *mauvais odeur du chien*, but paid the asking price, saying there were ways of getting rid of the smell. I was taken aback by his comment, finding it unnecessarily forthright – albeit true. A dose of my own medicine, no doubt.

My fiftieth birthday had been a few days earlier, and the gnarled wild cherry tree that canopied the access drive was in full flower on the day of the move. We were told it was traditional to plant a cherry, a walnut and a lime to celebrate the completion of a house, so the cherry, the giant walnut on the Jura side of the house, and a towering lime tree outside the kitchen, had probably been planted on the same day in 1857. So there we were, an ideal family, husband secure in a UN job, three happy, healthy children doing well at school, cute dog, and superwoman mother – the struggle to settle in Europe over at last.

When Fergus was not away on duty travel, we went twice a week to AA and Al-Anon meetings in Geneva. Pride inhibited me from getting a sponsor, nor did I warm enough to any of them to ask. I might well have met with a refusal, as it was plain to see that, while I was familiar with the programme, I had not progressed beyond mouthing the truth that I was an alcoholic: about the rest, humbly seeking help, asking for protection and care – that was alien philosophy. I doggedly stuck to the view that my life was still manageable, I did not need restoring to sanity, and I had got through half a century seldom seeking either help or advice from others. So I was not a member of AA – I merely attended meetings as an interested observer. But my pride and compulsion to control situations and people ensured that the agony would be prolonged, not only for me, but for the rest of the family, including Oscar the dog, who was sensitive to mood changes and raised voices.

Sybil and Iain came with their two boys and camped in what passed for a garden, before Fergus had transformed it to what would, in the UK, have qualified for opening to the public. (The French, in general, don't 'do' informal gardens. There is little between a peasant plot and the formal gardens of a chateau, but regrettably some of the French now emulate the garish awfulness of UK suburbia, aided by most of their *hypermarchés*, which always have a garden centre.) Reminiscing years later, Sybil and Iain recalled sensing something was wrong, but could not identify what it was. I had been there in body but not in spirit, distanced by thoughts of the next 'fix'. The children, aware of my dependence, were apprehensive about how I would behave in front of their friends, and were guarded about whom they invited to stay during school breaks. By their late teens, mostly only friends with an active drinker in their own family came to stay. Once, when Michael invited a rugby fanatic for the afternoon and evening meal, I served the food all the while delivering a diatribe about the thuggish nature of the game and the mental capacity of its followers. Michael was mortified, and his eleven-year-old friend was distressed to the point of tears; he clammed up, ate little, and never wanted to come again. He told his mother, a nice woman, who confronted me when next I met her at the school. I was genuinely ashamed, and when apologising confessed to a drink problem which I was dealing with by attending AA meetings. I trusted her discretion not to broadcast this fact, but suspect she did, knowing that often children other than my own were in the car with me and would have been at risk.

An appointment was made to consult a liver specialist in Geneva. The vibrations, as they say, were not good: he was a shrivelled, diminutive man who made no attempt to hide his disdain for people, women in particular, who drank to excess. In his opinion it was all a matter of strength of mind. The liver function tests were normal, and he advised me to pull myself together while my liver was still intact. Shortly after that I gave it a real bashing, called our Portuguese doctor to the house, and asked him to help me dry out at home rather than occupy a hospital bed. He gave me an intramuscular injection, and prescribed a short course of muscle relaxants and tranquillisers. Not in the least censorious, on leaving he said: '*Courage, madame, c'est une maladie difficile.*' Michael came and sat on my bed, the first of many times, hoping that this time I would succeed in stopping drinking. Oscar lay on the floor, or, if he could get away with it, beside me on the bed. Fergus returned from work anxious to know how I was feeling. Somehow I managed to crawl down to the kitchen and prepare their evening meal.

Repeatedly, after sobering up, I would return, shamingly soon, to drinking. Five days were spent in the psychiatric wing of one of the Geneva hospitals; another time I was admitted to hospital in Annemasse for detoxification. I was taken to a private room at midday, but by three thirty no member of staff had appeared, I had no supply of alcohol with me, and time was running out before the tremors would start. So I panicked and called a taxi, for which I did not have enough cash. The driver, pleased to have such a long run, and assured that he would be paid on arrival, drove me back to Divonne, weak with lack of food and shaking, to be met by a grim-faced Fergus, who was preparing the evening meal. The drying-out process was better conducted in nearby Nyon hospital. The message was the same: my liver was functioning normally, but from what I had told them, total abstinence would be the only cure. Medical costs for the treatment of alcoholism were not then covered by WHO health insurance. The organization was soon to review its policy on the treatment of what in the US was recognised as a disease, and footed the bill for my later incarcerations in Bristol and Surrey.

Most social occasions were agonising. During the Christmas and New Year break of 1978–79, we were invited to stay for two nights at a chalet near Martigny, owned by Inge, an Austrian woman in Al-Anon whose American husband, Terry, like me, was supposedly 'in recovery'. The scene, when we got there, was an amalgam of every festive card ever printed. In dazzling sunlight the temperature was sub-zero, and thuds and scrapes of skaters echoed over the ice of a small lake, fringed by snow-laden conifers. Inge's dog, a spayed bitch not unlike Oscar, welcomed his company, and our hosts' two children got on well with ours. Inside the chalet a roaring fire had been lit, and preparations for the evening meal were under way. Fergus, who always suffered from cold extremities, was glad to be inside, but an element of caution inhibited adult exchanges, and bonhomie was not entirely spontaneous. The chalet was decorated with berried holly and mistletoe, there were crackers for the children, roast suckling pig, a large boiled ham stuck with cloves, many seasonal dips and nibbles, as well as thin frites of the sort I shall always associate with the Café de Paris in Geneva. Terry and I were offered a choice of mineral water, apple or cranberry juice, but for Fergus and Inge there was wine. (Early in the AA programme we are told that what other people drink should be no concern of ours: they are normal drinkers, entitled to drink whatever they choose. Most newcomers to AA fear their abstinence at social functions may bring unwelcome attention, but in reality few people, other than those who have a problem themselves, will attempt to force alcohol on others.) The truth was that Terry groped his way during the night to a cupboard where he knew Inge stored bottles of schnapps and other liqueurs, while I had to ration a small bottle of vodka concealed at the bottom of my grip. Not until a decade later, with four incarcerations in rehabilitation clinics between us, did Terry and I feel ready to share the memory of our misery that night at a group meeting. The children and the dogs had really enjoyed themselves, however, which must have rewarded Inge to some extent for the herculean effort she had made to maintain a normal lifestyle.

In the summer of that year, no discernible change having taken place in my behaviour, Fergus, two friends from Al-Anon, two AA members, and the children organised a confrontational meeting to take place at home. The aim was to convince me that my recalcitrance was such that they thought I should go to the Broadway Lodge rehabilitation clinic in Bristol for at least one month. At a practical level Katharine, who had just sat her O-levels, would be at home and could take care of the house, the two younger children and the dog while Fergus was at work. I put up no resistance, having come to the same conclusion, and encouraged by the recent return to the group of a woman with multiple dependencies who had undergone a radical transformation. I was so confused that even packing a suitcase was a challenge; simple decisions were daunting, and I remember gyrating with twitching fingers in the middle of a mess of disordered clothing. Fergus flew to London with me, and by the time we landed at Heathrow withdrawal symptoms had begun. Reluctantly he agreed to buy a half-bottle of vodka to sustain me on the journey to Bristol. I took periodic swigs from the bottle in the juddering, insalubrious lavatory of the train to Temple Meads.

Not far from tears, we clung to each other in the pillared entrance foyer of the clinic, aware that options were running out and that survival of the family was at stake. A nurse appeared to fetch me, and informed Fergus that on no account was he to telephone me, nor was I to telephone him, for the next month. Letters were permitted. Fergus then left for his return flight to Geneva.

I was taken to a long room reminiscent of a school dormitory, in which there were ten beds, each with a locker, and a curtained hanging space for clothing. Familiar AA literature, a flask of water and a glass were on top of each locker. At the far end of the room, where the bathroom and lavatories were, was a desk at which a patient sat scribbling diligently. One or two women sat on their beds reading notes; none looked at me until the nurse had left, saying: 'One of the girls will help you unpack; then the doctor will see you in about an hour.' My fellow inmates then came to life, asking where I came from, and how I was feeling, because I did not look too bad. True to form, I had done a good cover-up job, but knew the shakes would soon begin, and very little vodka remained. The bottle was found when a skeletal woman about my own age opened my case. 'You'd better get rid of that pronto,' she said. 'I'm surprised the nurse didn't ask if you had any alcohol in your baggage.' So I took it to the bathroom, wondering if I could gulp the remainder without being discovered in the act, but decided to play safe and pour it down the loo. Besides, there was not enough to stave off the tremors for more than a short time.

A crisply mannered doctor remarked, as had all the others, that I did not look as if I had reached the terminal stage of alcoholism, asked if I had ever smoked, tested my motor reactions, prodded the area around my liver, and took a blood sample. I told him how much I had drunk over the last few hours, and my dread of acute withdrawal symptoms. He assured me the nurses would look after that, before ushering me out of his office with the words: 'Good luck. Listen, learn and try to do as you are told.' Then the nurses took over: their attitude was censorious, and small talk was discouraged, so I was snubbed when I admired a ring worn by the one who was injecting me. Further 'medication' would be given later, and I was now to go downstairs for the evening meal. Prison guards came to mind.

The male dormitories were in another wing of the house,

but at meetings and mealtimes the sexes mixed. In the dining room it was clear that a pecking order had been established for preferred seats and neighbours, so, as the last to arrive, I had to fit in unobtrusively. A square-set woman, with cropped, iron-grey hair, said grace in an upper-class drawl. Conversation was limited to the barest civilities and please-pass-the-salt level. I had little appetite, and had begun to feel distinctly woozy; later I thought I was going to faint in the bath. Some nameless pills, which I had to swallow under supervision, were brought just before I lay down on a very hard bed in the muffled atmosphere of the dormitory. Fergus would by this time be back in Divonne, probably mowing the grass in the fading light – it all seemed very distant.

After breakfast, at which each morning a different member of the group read 'Thought for the Day', one of the counsellors gave me a folder containing more literature, a lined pad of foolscap paper and a questionnaire to complete. It asked if I had ever imagined voices, had hallucinatory dreams, suffered memory loss over an extended period, lost bladder control, vomited in public, lost consciousness or been physically violent. Was my drinking of the binge variety or did I drink on a daily basis? Was I a social or a closet drinker? The IQ test was of such simplicity I wondered if it contained a hidden catch. Then the entire group was summoned to the smoky common room. At that time it was thought too much to ask inmates to give up cigarettes while they were being weaned off alcohol, heroin, cocaine, sleeping pills and tranquillisers, glue sniffing, and in a few cases food and sex. Most of my fellow patients were multiple addicts; my addiction was to alcohol.

A blackboard, with the Twelve Steps written in coloured chalk, hung over a late Victorian marble fireplace. One of several counsellors, most but not all of whom were themselves in recovery, addressed us. First, we learned it was not acceptable to refer to a recovered alcoholic – an addict remained 'in recovery' for the rest of his or her life. The first thing I wrote on my pad was the danger of replacing one addiction with another. The warning was clear; the risk of shifting from one panacea to another was high. I learned that many substances lingered in the system, detectable in the nails and hair for months after a period of abstinence. We should be alert to hidden risks in substances such as cough mixtures, mouthwashes, tonics and painkillers.

The role of heredity in alcoholism was not proven, but I had drawn my own conclusions from observation of groups in Geneva. A head count over many months, in groups averaging eighteen people, revealed at least two-thirds had a close relative who was alcoholic, and that an astonishingly high proportion were of either Irish or Scandinavian stock. At one meeting of ten people, seven were of Irish extraction. One Dublin woman came from a family of five boys and three girls, whose father had been alcoholic; two of the girls and three of the boys became alcoholic. All had witnessed their father's battle to stop drinking, which he eventually did without the help of AA, but the family consensus was that he became 'a miserable old codger, dry, but not sober' – 'sober' in the widest sense of the word. A fine line, the full implications of which I did not understand until many years later. I kept quiet about my studies, knowing they would provoke more accusations that I was intellectualising my problem and should concentrate on getting to grips with this 'simple programme for complicated people', that I should look for similarities rather than differences, and rid myself of the delusion that I was in any sense special or different. Protests that I had never done this or that were invariably parried by 'No, not yet'. There was much wisdom in those despised American exhortations. 'Keep it simple, Stupid,' I told myself.

We had been cautioned about the perils of lying about how much we had been drinking, or the level of drugs we had either been swallowing or injecting, as this would result in under-prescription of medication, with possibly fatal consequences. A few days after this warning we had a demonstration of what could happen. I was talking to a middle-aged, tall, sinewy, undernourished-looking American who was unsteady on his feet, attributing this to 'that damned medication they've gotten me on', when he pitched forward, striking his forehead on a sharp corner of the marble hearth. He was having an epileptic seizure and nurses came quickly to the scene. Cross-examined the following day by his counsellor in front of the assembled patients, he confessed to having grossly understated his alcohol intake. This was his third incarceration in a clinic. He worked for a major international drug manufacturing company and should have known better.

Some male inmates were there at Her Majesty's expense, having been offered the choice of a jail sentence or entering a treatment facility; most came from mining or fishing communities around Cardiff or Swansea. My counsellor, Ed, was also Welsh, and of those who helped me over the years, it was his judgement I came most to respect. The wide spectrum of social background among the patients surprised me, though one of the tenets of AA is that alcoholism is a great leveller. I found the Welshmen sensitive, highly intelligent and articulate, regardless of the fact that many left school at fourteen. Roughly half of them were serious in their commitment to kick their dependency; the others regarded treatment as a soft option. One man, the visible parts of whom were so finely tattooed in red, green and blue oriental dragons, birds and serpents that little natural skin remained, had spent years in the French Foreign Legion; later, during a heatwave, his entire upper body was seen also to be tattooed.

After the evening meal, on completion of written assignments, a period was set aside for socialising. This took place in what had been an elegant drawing room with early nineteenth-century plaster cornices and ceiling roses. Now it had acquired the same institutional atmosphere that pervaded the entire building: chairs covered in uncut moquette were grouped around low tables with overflowing ashtrays in the centre – an indication that someone had not done the house task allocated to them, which would come under scrutiny at the next group meeting. These meetings were chaired by one of the counsellors, who, after summarising what had been covered the previous day, would ask each patient to give a short account of what stage they had reached in the programme, what step they were working on, and how they felt their handwritten life story had been received by the group. The opinions expressed were always to be respected, no matter how hurtful, as they were made in a spirit of love and hope that the author would achieve sobriety. This generality was idealistic and far from true: after a week I could see that some patients took a fiendish delight in the discomfiture of others. Two in particular, nearing the end of their stay before going for 'extended' time in a halfway house, would set traps for an unwary newcomer, who would then be grilled by a counsellor, as well as by the rest of the group. In retrospect, I am sure their behaviour was recognised by their counsellor, and was one of the reasons they were going to remain under observation. Without warning, the spotlight would switch to another victim, the accusation often being of trying to keep a low profile, wearing a cynical expression, not contributing enough to discussions, or continuing to be in denial.

The life story had to be given to one's counsellor, who then passed a copy of it to each member of the group. Each patient's task was to write a letter to the author, giving their comments, and listing defects of character detected from the story, or perceived at group meetings. Having listened to the letters written to other patients, I prepared for a vitriolic response. Most letters to me were censorious, and several emotional: my story read like a Barbara Cartland novel; it was pretentious to mention living near Geneva; my accent was affected; I was full of anger and resentment, and had fabricated much of the story; I was vain, attaching too much importance to my appearance; I talked too much and didn't listen; I was inordinately proud. On the positive side, I was seen to be generous, helpful, essentially good-natured, and possessed of a saving sense of humour. Several implored me to 'Let the barriers down and show your vulnerability', 'Get out of the driver's seat', 'Get honest with yourself and others', 'Stop the denial and face reality'. Nobody seemed to have detected my intolerance and inflexible attitudes.

At evening gatherings several nurses, and a trainee counsellor, sat on the sidelines observing the behaviour of the animals in the zoo. I was not alone in resenting this, as it was clear that among them, a few saw us as inferior specimens of the human race. Their observations were passed to the counsellors, who would discuss them in group the following day. It was not long before I came under fire for having stuck throughout the evening with an all-male group, perceived to be my social equals. In fact, we had discovered many common interests. As for social exclusivity, I had little in common with the hunting, shooting and fishing females. The women belonged to the landed gentry, with few interests outside shooting parties and the sporting achievements of their husbands. Talk was of house parties, dogs, horses, estates, boarding-school holidays, and periodic forays to Ascot, Henley and Cowes, who had married whom, and whose marriage appeared to be on the rocks. Passing reference was made to stately homes and members of the aristocracy whose exploits had exposed them to the savagery of the tabloid press. A subtle form of name-dropping prevailed – 'When I was a page at the Coronation', 'When we attended my brother's investiture at Buck House', 'My uncle, the High Sheriff', and so on.

Periodically minor royalty appeared at the clinic, supposedly incognito, as did pop idols: it was emphasised that these individuals suffered the same affliction as ourselves, and their anonymity must be respected. Particularly poignant was an ashen-faced withdrawn young woman, wearing a shabby raincoat, nondescript jumper and skirt, with shoes so worn the soles were holed. She scarcely exchanged a word with any of us and was transferred to a more exclusive retreat within a few days. There was much whispering among the county set that she came from the Scottish Borders, and was a distant relative of the queen.

Twice during my stay house rules were seriously breached. The first incident was the discovery of an empty vodka bottle in a flowerbed under a window in the men's dormitory. An emergency meeting was convened, at which my counsellor, slamming the offending bottle down on his desk, demanded that the culprit confess. There was no point, he added, in keeping quiet, as the staff knew not only his identity, but how and where the bottle had been obtained, as did several of his room-mates, a few of whom had taken a swig. This was also an exposure of group guilt, and the chief culprit was told to leave within two hours.

The next incident involved a young woman I had got to know quite well. A heroin-addicted, alcoholic, chain-smoking call girl from London, she confided to me what had triggered her deterioration. I was appalled when she showed me the extent of scarring on her arms and inner thighs – a preferred injection site. Some male patients took a delight in exhibiting their scars, but it seemed bizarre in a woman who had not yet lost all interest in her appearance. She told me the cost of her treatment was being borne by an Arab benefactor in the hope that she would soon be well enough to join him in Saudi Arabia. (I have to admit that I rather doubted this part of her story.) She confessed to having been on the game, but now intended to go straight. I was therefore further shattered when four patients, who had been out on day release, reported seeing her, carrying nothing more than a handbag, trying to hitch a lift from drivers heading in the direction of London.

At the end of three weeks I had completed the written part of Steps 1 and 2, but was firmly mired in the third, which required me to hand my life over to the care of God, as I understood him. Ed told me how he, too, had been stuck on Step 3, but had been 'enlightened' while sitting under an apple tree in the grounds at Broadway. This was so preposterous that I had difficulty suppressing a giggle; given Ed's down-to-earth personality, this revelation was hard to credit.

At this point in my recovery I broke the house rules. I decided to telephone Fergus. Early one morning I crept furtively from the dormitory, and down to the telephone in a niche near the kitchen. He answered immediately, shocked that I had broken the rule he too found hard to observe. I told him I was genuinely stuck in the programme, and felt I could make no further headway. A male patient, up equally early, was in the kitchen and overheard the call; no doubt in a spirit of love and helpfulness, he reported my transgression. I was given the statutory two hours in which to find a room at a nearby guesthouse, and leave. After a late breakfast at my new abode, I met a couple who mentioned they had come to visit their son who was in a nearby clinic. From what they said, I deduced it was the one I had just left. I told them what a good reputation it enjoyed, and how its success rate was above average. 'Honest with themselves and others'?

Ed did not delay in telling Fergus that I had not 'reached bottom' and warned him of worse to come, expressing sincere regret that he and our children would continue to suffer. Almost word for word what Ted, now back in Canada, had foretold. Ed wrote a long letter to Fergus stating his opinion that I would ultimately come to accept the fatal nature of the disease, and abandon all reservations about the Twelve Steps. He hoped only that my mind and body could withstand further punishment, writing: 'Unbelievable as it may seem, she's not yet ready.'

That hot, dry summer was almost at an end. The girls had

coped well in my absence, and would soon return to school, while Michael would start his O-level year. I was ashamed, subdued and withdrawn when I got back. My mind had cleared to the extent that getting a flight back to Geneva had gone smoothly, despite my now more restrained need for the odd fix. The children must have longed for those happier times when I had been stimulating company, before I began to see myself as little more than a domestic drudge, before I had hurled an iron casserole from the terrace into the garden, narrowly missing a car, screaming, 'Food, food, fucking food!' They were glad to see me, but conversation was guarded – there were too many unspoken fears for it to be otherwise. Fergus sought refuge after work in his garden, and I resumed the role of housekeeper. We still attended meetings, but I did not speak openly about what had happened during my treatment, nor could I bring myself to share my impasse at Step 3. Had I done so, it might well have helped me, and other defiant individuals new to the AA programme of recovery. Sober AA members sensed that I was still drinking furtively, and that it was just a matter of time before there would be a serious incident.

Mary invited a boyfriend to stay for the last week before the autumn term began. My reaction to this young man was one of scarcely concealed horror. Unhealthily pallid, James was tall, lanky and unkempt; he had a Mohican haircut with a thin pigtail, wore grimy plimsolls without socks, and the rest of his clothing was greenish-black, reminding me of Oxfam shops or the RUC uniform. One fingernail was repulsively long, arousing the unspoken question – was it for scratching the Mohican or plucking an instrument? In his favour, he spoke well and was mannerly. Fergus better concealed his dismay, enquiring what subjects James studied, but found himself lost for comment when the answer was Caribbean poetry and music.

I went to Nyon in search of fresh fish for our evening meal. Despite all I had heard about the risk of mixing drugs at times of particular emotional stress, I occasionally took some Librium capsules prescribed for Fergus (which he never took), in the hope that they would calm me and lessen the urge to drink. On this day I mixed them with vodka. Emerging from a side road near the frontier post at Crassier, I put my foot on the accelerator instead of the brake. The Volvo shot into the path of an oncoming vehicle driven by a Swiss woman who had been speeding. Neither of us was injured, but the passenger side of our car was crumpled, and the bonnet of her tinny Fiat concertinaed. The gendarmerie was quickly on the scene to take measurements, and a statement from the Swiss woman, who stood fulminating by the roadside. I was driven to the police station in Divonne, to be cross-questioned by the officer in charge. On his desk stood the half-bottle of vodka they had found on the passenger seat of the Volvo. Incriminating evidence, if ever there was, making my protest that the other driver had been speeding inconsequential. A blood test was taken. When Fergus came to collect me, the officer told him the law would take its due course. We drove home in a silence rare between us. Negotiations ensuing from the accident involved both insurance companies. Despite looking all right, our Volvo's chassis was said to be so distorted the car was deemed a write-off.

I watched our postbox for weeks, waiting for a letter summoning me to appear in court at Bourg-en-Bresse, but when at last an official letter came, it contained only the results of the blood test, sent to me in error. After some deliberation, I burned the evidence and was never called to court. The Swiss woman got a new car to replace her ancient Fiat and was placated. Fergus ordered a replacement for ours, which would not be available for some weeks, so I was reduced to a bicycle, a sedate model with a wicker basket, unearthed in the basement when we bought the house. Its brakes were worn, and it was heavy, reminding me of the Hercules I rode to school during the war. It was a two-mile downhill run to central Divonne, but a stiff climb back no matter which route I chose. Michael went to school with Fergus and got a lift home with a family recently moved to the town, whose children attended the same school. For large scale shopping I could hire a taxi once a week, but this imposed a limit on the number of bottles that could be bought without arousing comment. Disposing of empties was now even more difficult: it looked odd taking a clanking bag with me on walks with Oscar to the nearby quarry, where there was a small lake. It was a popular area with local people, so the likelihood of being seen flinging bottles into the water was high. It did not occur to me that the water level was seasonal, and in spring, as millions of tadpoles lost their fight for survival, many bottles would be exposed when the water dried up. There was a bottle bank on the road between Villard and the town centre, but a limit to how many I could take on the back of my bike, and any passing car or pedestrian would spot me. My life had become little more than a haunted existence – an insult to the many people who cared for me.

One bicycle trip to town was particularly eventful. On the way down I managed to let a deep pothole unseat me, and on the way back I subsided into a ditch to escape a speeding lorry which passed perilously close. Neighbours rushed out having seen the incident, unanimous in loud condemnation of the driver. My bicycle was slightly damaged, the contents of the basket – including two bottles of vodka – were strewn at the roadside, and I felt a sharp pain in my right shoulder. Michael, who was studying at home, was summoned to the scene. From his expression it was clear that, while concerned, he knew the real purpose of my shopping expedition. He escorted me home, where I collapsed shocked and exhausted on our bed. Then he put the sensible purchases away and hid the bottles, in contravention of all he had been told about the ineffectuality of trying to control an alcoholic's drinking. In truth, he was nearing the end of his tolerance, and later confessed that despite his love for me, he could have wished me dead rather than witness the protracted destruction of his mother and family.

The shoulder was broken, though this was not confirmed for several days. It was a complicated break requiring an operation to knit it together with metal pins; this was done at Nyon hospital, where I was known, having had liver tests and a dry-out. Several AA members visited me; they did not mince their words and some were running out of patience. Now, when Fergus was away, I had to ask an AA friend to drive me to meetings. Once, after a meeting at which I had not spoken, my withdrawal symptoms were so severe I was shaking by the time we got home, and was sick on getting out of the car. My driver was sympathetic, having been at that stage himself, despite the example of two alcoholic parents, both of whom had died in their mid-fifties.

My behaviour had become more bizarre, particularly when Fergus had to leave on an overseas tour. I knew his absence was inevitable, and that he enjoyed visiting such places as St Lucia, the Philippines and Beijing. I was also aware of his concern that I was an unfit guardian of Michael, now fourteen, while he was away. One winter evening I threw his briefcase containing travel documents and passport out of the kitchen window. Worse, another time I stuck hairpins in the locks of his car, before hiding in the back of the other one in the car port; I was not far from hypothermia when Fergus found me, drowsy and incoherent, curled up on the back seat. The following morning he took a taxi to the airport rather than risk being driven by me. Full of remorse, I vowed never to behave so badly again. When he rang from Beijing, the call came late at night, and he knew instinctively that I had been drinking. I had sounded insouciant, assuring him we were both well, missing him, and looking forward to his return and the arrival of Katharine and Mary for the Easter holidays.

The shooting of Oscar triggered probably the most deranged act of my drinking career, leading me, much later, seriously to question my sanity. It was a beautiful Saturday morning in early summer. I was sober and busy preparing our midday meal; Fergus was working in the garden with Oscar as company. Only when the dog appeared beside him wounded and bleeding did he realise that he had sloped off in pursuit of Vinette, M. Ganeval's bitch, with whom he was wont to take off into the forest. M. Ganeval, a retired *chasseur*, and his tiny crippled wife lived in a roadside farm, just over the hill from us. Marc-Joseph feared him, saying he was a trigger-happy alcoholic, and that he never went near that house. We had not taken much notice of this, as Marc-Joseph himself spent every weekend boozed up with his card-playing mates. Fergus telephoned the vet, who knew Oscar well, and was told to bring him straight to the surgery. I sat in the back of the car with Oscar, now in shock, cradled in a blanket. I do not remember where Michael was, but we were glad he was not there. They sedated Oscar and told us to ring in the afternoon when they would know the extent of his injuries. He had been shot through the bladder, and never regained consciousness. I insisted on going to see him, curled up like a hedgehog, and broke down hysterically in the surgery. Michael was devastated; he adored that dog.

Not long after, I saw a gun lying on top of the woodpile outside the entrance to Marc-Joseph's room; noises of merriment came from within, where his friends had gathered to play cards and down several bottles of red. On impulse I grabbed the gun, put it on the back seat of the replacement Volvo and drove up the narrow corkscrew road from Vesancy, past a little pond where we had skated during the previous winter, almost to the foot of the cliffs above. Here I hurled the gun into the undergrowth and returned home. When Fergus enquired where I had been, I was evasive. When Marc-Joseph's party began to disperse amid much cackling, the theft was discovered. The owner came to ask Fergus if he had seen any stranger passing, as the precious gun, which had belonged to his father, had disappeared. Fergus truthfully said he had not seen anybody suspicious, and suggested that one of his friends might have taken it as a practical joke.

Fergus knew intuitively that I had taken it, and when asked, I did not deny it – my unbalanced mind associated all guns with dog slaughter. Michael and he found the weapon after a long search; then the question was how to 'find' it without arousing suspicion of complicity. The hedge surrounding our garden was thick along the roadside and Fergus had been cutting it back, so he contrived to come upon it a few days later, stuck in a particularly dense bit of thicket. It was generally agreed that a passing prankster, knowing the owner was inside, had put it there. The thought that the gun might have been loaded had never crossed my mind.

Worse was to follow. A window in Katharine's bedroom overlooked the road leading to M. Ganeval's farm; glancing out one night when the moon was full and a dusting of snow had fallen, she saw me walking up the road. Sensing trouble, she put on her boots, and followed my footprints. She caught me preparing to stick a bundle of something into the ventilation hole of M. Ganeval's *grenier*. There was a box of matches in my pocket. Ever since, I have searched my soul, and do not know to this day if I would have carried out the plan. Probably not, as I am a coward when it comes to taking radical action.

Writing this more than a quarter of a century later, I begin to lose patience with myself, knowing that were I an outsider, I would be tut-tutting about total disregard for other people's feelings and their safety, irresponsibility, no moral fibre, lack of ethical standards, and how could she have been so stupid.

Wise, sober, old timers in AA have been heard to say, 'It took every drink I ever had to get me here'– they are among the 10 per cent who made it in the end. Ironically, family members sometimes say their lives have been enriched by the experience of living with an alcoholic, and that familiarity with the Twelve Step programme has helped them to cope with problems and find serenity in their own lives.

Each New Year's Eve I confronted the face in the mirror and asked: where are you going to be this time next year? Dead? Much the same? Destitute? In a mental hospital? Suicide was not an option – I would be inefficient, and officious people would resuscitate me. I had been around AA long enough to see a few members die. One of my drying-out sessions had terrified me because, for the first time, I had a hallucinogenic experience. Lying in bed shivering and shaking, despite the heat of the day, I was convinced drops of water were coming through the ceiling. I could touch them, and called Fergus to touch them too; he said they were imaginary. Then I pointed to a climbing plant winding its way around one of the beams that supported the roof. The list of things on the 'not yet' list was shortening. I no longer tinted my long, grey and untidy hair, though from time to time I would try a new style. My face was puffy and my complexion almost permanently flushed; I now looked the part. Fergus said I resembled my contemporaries Simone Signoret and Jeanne Moreau, both raddled and wrinkled caricatures of their former selves. I remember a sunlit cobbled square in Calais, where we sat waiting for the ferry. Two scruffy figures of indeterminate gender came to sit nearby, between them a sack and a bottle, from which they drank in turn. Little divided us – I could easily have ended up a bag lady, had it not been for the love and support of my family. Sober members of AA would say: 'There but for the grace of God go I.'

My mother's health was in decline and her eyesight was failing. While in treatment, to excuse handwritten letters to her, I had resorted to deception, saying my typewriter was out of order. Later, when I confessed to having the same disease as my father, she merely said: 'That explains a lot.' I assured her I was dealing with the problem by attending AA meetings, even quoting from the literature, and implying it might help her deal with her addiction to Valium. I spoke of the lack of a spiritual element in her life, and suggested she get in touch with the local minister, a Derry man, who had known my grandmother and knew something of our family history. I gave him a partial version of my own predicament, and asked him to call on my mother. The poor man was out of his depth, and I cringe at the duplicity. However, a subtle change was taking place: I was less dogmatic, no longer switched off *Thought for the Day* or the Sunday service. I wrote to several speakers whose writings on different faiths interested me. That they had wrestled with lapses in belief throughout their lives impressed me, as did their frankness about the inner turmoil they suffered. In that era such an approach was rare; soul-searching at every level of society, before Facebook, Twitter and reality TV, was in its infancy. Austin Williams, then vicar of St Martin-in-the-Fields, wrote me a long, thoughtful letter, expressing his hope that I would eventually find a philosophy that would bring a degree of serenity and sobriety.

I now recognised that alcohol was inimical to friendship, and that loving relationships withered when one partner continued to drink compulsively. Our circle of friends had dwindled, and I no longer made the effort to go to concerts or the theatre. A family outing to the famous Knie circus was a disaster: I berated the ringmaster of eight beautiful, all-white, ostrich-plumed geldings, ridden by a sequin-encrusted female. So audible was my criticism of the cruelty involved in their schooling, people sitting nearby hissed '*Shsshh*'.

Michael, whose O-level results were good, was offered a place by The King's School in Canterbury to study for A-levels: he was the second boy only to be accepted who had not come up through the junior ranks. Katharine came back to Divonne after her A-levels to do an intensive secretarial course at a college recommended by Eva, while Mary was in Bath about to begin a foundation course in book illustration and design. We took the elegant Mercedes that Fergus had bought from Ted to Plymouth to collect Mary at her digs in Bath and visit the McMahons, now in semi-retirement near Cheddar Gorge in Somerset. I told Rosemary, a devout Quaker, about my affliction, and her verdict was that 'something' would have to replace the void left in the absence of alcohol. My intake was reduced, but steady, and I felt hollow within.

We travelled on to Canterbury to coincide with the end of Michael's first year at King's, and to meet my mother at Gatwick. The wheelchair contained a tiny brown, owl-like figure in a crocheted woollen hat, clutching a capacious handbag. She would soon be eighty-six, and the spark had gone. In her prime she would have been thrilled to examine the Mercedes – I hated it, too big, with a fiendish hand/foot brake – and explore the cathedral precincts. Even the quaint streets and Tudor architecture aroused little comment, and her remarks tended to be negative. No mention was made of having enjoyed the flight, or how well she had been looked after. She said the airport was noisy and confusing, and the town too full of tourists, the stairs in the pleasant seventeenth-century guesthouse were difficult for her, and she certainly did *not* want a 'full English breakfast'.

We sailed from Dover to Zeebrugge, and thence to the Ardennes region of France, passing on the way many well-maintained war cemeteries. I feared my mother might become tearful on passing through battlefields of the 1914–18 war, but if she was thinking of Jack and his death at Passchendaele, she showed no emotion. This visit, which I had taken so much care to organise, was doomed to failure – quite simply, it was too late. Shortly after we got back to Divonne, she became unwell, and preferred Mary's help and care to mine. That reveals a lot about our relationship, and I fear that she had become afraid of me. Not surprisingly, considering I had hidden her Valium capsules in a crazily wrong-headed effort to control what I believed to be *her* addiction. They were returned, but only after she had pursued me, brandishing her walking stick. Confessing to alcoholism, rather than improving behaviour, removed inhibitions, and to my shame I aired a list of long-held resentments, upbraiding her for my solitary childhood and feelings of being unloved. I should rather have concentrated on the good things she had done, and how dutifully she had reared an inopportune child born at the end of a disastrous marriage. Once, in a reflective mood, she said: 'San was really more of a mother to you than I was.'

She now had stomach cramps and wanted merely to escape from me and return to Ireland. Katharine managed to get her ticket altered and drove her to the airport. Rosemary met her in Belfast, and shortly afterwards she was admitted to hospital with a strangulated hernia so severe an emergency colostomy was done. I argued with the surgeon, pointlessly, as it was a fait accompli, that this had been draconian, and the gut should have been disentangled. Another example of how alcohol loosens the tongue. But I was genuinely upset, knowing that my mother would find it hard to bear the indignity of living with that procedure. Rosemary, now well into her seventies, and a martyr to asthma, said my mother was adamant about remaining at home, that a carer visited morning and evening, a home help gave her a midday meal, and the district nurse kept a close eye on how she was coping. Rosemary and her husband visited frequently, and Dodi, now retired from active social work, also keep a professional eye on her progress.

Meanwhile, Katharine would graduate soon, Mary was still studying art, and Michael would remain at King's until he was nineteen, so the children were at home only during the holidays. The following year Fergus had commitments ranging from the Caribbean to Thailand and the Philippines, and I continued to attend AA meetings, never achieving a significant stretch of sobriety. Throughout the early months of that year, I wrote to my mother, never referring to what led to the truncation of her visit to France. I do not know what she told Rosemary, but suspect it was a watered down version of the awful truth.

19
Rock Bottom to Release

That summer I went to stay with my mother, and found her resigned to a much restricted life, seeming to enjoy more than ever the superb view over Belfast Lough to Greenisland and Knockagh war memorial, with her parents' old house clearly visible on the opposite shore below. The Liverpool boat passed close inshore on its daily voyage, as did naval vessels, tankers, cargo ships and an occasional oil rig. The shoreline was hidden by a wilderness of gorse, through which a narrow track led to the beach, but it was years since she had been able to walk that distance. Once an avid reader, her eyesight had continued to worsen, and I suspected she no longer saw clearly the television to which, after initial rejection, she had become addicted. Her doctor thought she had suffered a series of minor strokes, and there were signs too that dementia was setting in. She enjoyed the improvement in diet that came with my presence, and loved to see pictures of the children and to have me read their letters to her – they were good about writing. There were quiet times when I cut and filed the nails of her once beautiful, now knotted and blue-veined hands, while we shared memories of Donegal. But each day brought a series of humiliations. Her carer came at eight in the morning to get her up and washed. I had learned to change her colostomy bag when necessary. I prepared her breakfast, though had I not been there, the home help would have done that as well.

I worried about what would happen to her when I returned to France. My loyalties were divided; in effect, I felt trapped. But the decision about what to do next was taken out of my hands. After giving my mother lunch one day, I left for a walk along the coastal path towards Helen's Bay, saying I would be back in time to prepare our evening meal. When I got back, her chair was empty. I was aghast, and my first thought was abduction of a defenceless old woman. Her handbag was gone, but there was no sign of disturbance. I went to her bedroom, where a suitcase had gone from the top of the wardrobe, and some clothes were missing; her hairbrush and hand-mirror were not on the dressing table. In the bathroom the toothbrush mug was empty, and a sponge was missing from the bath-rack. A lump settled in my stomach, which I treated with a glass of almost neat vodka. I rang Dodi, who was equally shocked. The doctor's surgery was closed, so I rang her carer, who was evasive. When, by process of elimination, I tracked down the name of the nursing home my mother was in, the proprietor said: 'Your mother doesn't want to see you.' I was unable to discover who arranged my mother's admission to the nursing home, and why it happened the way it did. Only recently has it become obvious it was probably Rosemary's decision to take such drastic action. She was later transferred to a local authority care home at Crawfordsburn.

I cleaned the house, booked my flight to Geneva, and arranged to stay for a couple of days with a Quaker friend, Harold Sidwell, on the other side of Belfast. I was on the carriageway approaching Holywood when a police car brought me to a halt. At the barracks, breath and urine tests were required, and my car was impounded for three days, but I was allowed to take a taxi to Harold's house. He was sympathetic in the trustful way of nice people who have no conception of what the alcoholic suffers and is firmly convinced that all that is needed is a bit of willpower. He also found it hard to believe I was as desperate as I claimed, because a few weeks earlier, when he had cycled to Craigavad to visit us, he had noticed nothing amiss. I was ashamed of having bought a bottle of vodka from the off-licence nearby, while Harold went further afield to buy food for our supper.

I decided to find out where I could be admitted for yet another detoxification, so that at least I would arrive back in Divonne in a sober state. The choice was between a mental hospital in Downpatrick, or the psychiatric unit of Purdysburn Mental Hospital, on the outskirts of Belfast. I decided on the latter. The doctor examining me thought I exaggerated the severity of my condition, and was merely suffering from depression; I was too coherent to be in the late stages of alcoholism. He agreed, however, to keep me under observation for three days and treat me for the withdrawal symptoms I knew were inevitable, considering my intake over the last emotionally charged week.

So that the three days should not be boring, the medical officer took me to a large room devoted to occupational therapy. Groups of dull-eyed women sat at tables making objects ranging from barbola work to felt flowers and coiled clay pots. A Bechstein grand piano stood alone at the centre of the room. I was introduced as Elizabeth 'who will be with us for a few days only'.

A good-looking woman about my own age approached saying she felt we might have a lot in common and that I looked interesting. She then told me that she was interested in traditional Gaelic lyrics and songs and was a professional pianist. I said how much pleasure it would give me to hear her play. So she sat down at the keyboard and began to sing, in a smooth contralto voice, a selection of songs and lyrics from all over Ireland. Some were long, but she was word perfect. At the end the group responded with a round of applause.

Then she joined me and the MO and without any preliminaries lay down on the floor, exposing her unclothed nether regions as she did a few floor exercises. This was the Korsakoff's syndrome about which Dick had told me. 'Very sad, she used to run a legal practice and was much in demand to give recitals.' At home, however, her behaviour had become intolerable so her family arranged to have her 'sectioned'.

Witnessing this spectacle should have provoked an accelerated 'rock bottom' in me but it did not. Some wit in AA said 'some of us reach the bottom of the bucket, then dig a hole in it.'

I made a court appearance in Bangor, at which the magistrate, who had a reputation for imposing savage sentences on persons convicted of driving under the influence of alcohol, imposed a fine of £500 and loss of licence for six years. When this news reached Divonne, the family decided unanimously that it was time for yet another confrontation. I was told that, unless I agreed to go for further treatment, I would find myself alone in the house. Katharine had graduated and was planning to teach at a high school for girls in Tokyo; Mary was in Bath; and Michael, after a gap year, would go to Edinburgh to read geology. Fergus was exhausted, often kept awake at night listening to my introspective ramblings. He could no longer stand the strain of living under the same roof, and threatened to move to a flat near the WHO building. He did spend a few days with Katharine in Canterbury without telling me where he had gone. I was furious and went berserk. This approach is known in AA terms as 'tough love'. I was not surprised, feeling guilty, particularly when he was away on duty travel, for the anxiety that accompanied him wherever he went. Apart from this, I had come to an independent decision to go to another treatment centre, this time in Surrey, in a further attempt to kick my dependency. I had been thrown out of a clinic five years earlier for not being ready, now surely I must have 'reached bottom'. My family certainly had.

This time, just after Christmas 1986, I was able to pack my suitcase in an orderly way, but the parting from Fergus at Geneva airport was the most poignant yet: my choices, it was clear, had finally run out. Sober on the flight, I could not resist the opportunity to buy a flask of vodka at Heathrow. It was after dark when my taxi drove up the drive to Farm Place. I had become garrulous on the journey, chatting to the driver, whose mirror will have reflected my furtive swigs, and who probably knew what type of ailment was treated at this clinic.

My arrival coincided with the evening meal of the director, and she left me in no doubt how inconvenient the interruption was. The nurse who checked me in asked if I had any alcohol, so I confessed, and was directed to the cloakroom, where I poured the remainder down the handbasin. The large room I was to share with five other women had a capacious Victorian wardrobe, with shelves, hanging space and drawers, and an en suite bathroom. The only injunction given that night was to forget I had previously been in treatment, lest I should feel in any way superior; soon two of my room-mates revealed they too had been in rehab.

The director, to whom I had taken an instant dislike, interviewed me next morning, all the background information lying on her desk. I was in no position to be other than totally co-operative. I kept reminding myself of the importance of keeping an open mind, and that principles should always outweigh personalities. Notwithstanding, I could discern few redeeming features in this cold, charmless woman. I wondered if perhaps a generous spirit lay within, but so far could not detect any sign of humanity. It was an inauspicious start. I hoped the other counsellors would be more sympathetic – most of them were.

At the first group meeting the director turned to me: 'In over twenty years working with alcoholics I have met only two women as sick and steeped in denial as you, and both are dead,' she said. I believe it was a calculated attempt to break my pride, but it merely provoked antagonism. Anyone unwise enough to protest against such tactics, however, was accused of self-justification. Like practices at other clinics, we were told to voice direct criticism about our immediate neighbours: this was regarded as a healthy exercise in honesty. We also had to list their good points, an exercise so excruciating for some – particularly newcomers – they broke down in tears.

Domestic chores were legion, and each morning a rota list, which it was our duty to read, appeared in the hall. Personality conflicts were rife, and character defects revealed in consequence of petty disputes were subjected to open discussion: thus providing malicious members of the group a heaven-sent chance to vent their 'honest' feelings. Triumphs, however, were mostly short-lived when the spotlight settled on the accuser rather than the intended victim. From many of the stories I heard, I felt that addiction to hard drugs resulted in a more rapid and profound decline in moral standards than did alcohol dependence alone. When it came to manipulation, theft, deviousness and cruelty, both mental and physical, the 'pure' alcoholics were, in comparison, paragons of virtue. It hurt me that any effort I had made to help others was interpreted as 'people pleasing' – an attempt to curry favour.

I went through Steps 1 and 2 again; this time there was no question that life was unmanageable, or of my need to be restored to sanity. I rewrote my life story and read it aloud to the group, afterwards analysing their written comments. They were painfully similar to those made five years earlier, one letter accusing me of being an attention-seeking drama queen.

Now that many reservations I held about the existence of a higher power had been resolved, Step 3 was proving less difficult. My research on theological matters was superficial, and my studies no more than basic, but I was starting to overcome some prejudices, was less judgemental, and more open to compromise. Step 4 demanded the taking of a 'searching and fearless moral inventory', and I enjoyed this task; but brutal comments from my peer group indicated the need for further fearless searching.

Step 5 was seen as vital, without which there was little or no hope of recovery: 'Admit to God, to ourselves, and to another human being, the exact nature of our wrongs.' In the outside world it was considered wise, if one was religious, to do this step with a minister of religion; otherwise a trusted friend or, rarely, a total stranger. At this clinic it was the director's husband Heinz, a lapsed priest, to whom what amounted to a confession was made. He would never have been my choice, and he sensed that. Some patients emerged tearful from the ordeal; others beaming with relief, and glowing with satisfaction at having 'passed'. When my turn came, I failed, accused of being full of unresolved anger and resentment. This had not been the case, but after such misjudgement, it became so. I was angry at not being offered a choice of person with whom to share such an intimate and critical step. It was suggested that I remain a further month, at the end of which I would repeat Step 5, and thereafter – assuming I had 'passed' – would go to a halfway house for three months before returning home. I knew this would not work and that if I were to agree under duress, I would merely accrue further resentments. So, having informed a very disappointed Fergus what had happened, I discharged myself.

Many of the patients were sympathetic, sharing my dislike of Heinz's role as father confessor. Some gathered in the porch to say goodbye; a few hugged me with genuine affection, saying they were sure I would make it in the end. The director, arriving on the scene, said sharply that this was not an approved discharge, and ordered them to go about their respective tasks forthwith.

When I returned to Divonne, the atmosphere was subdued, and our relationship cautious. It was like the first days in Ghana – we were in love, but an element of the unknown inhibited total commitment. I felt drained by what had happened at the clinic, withdrawn and incapable of spontaneous gaiety. I was not drinking and did not feel the urge to do so, despite the usual stock of alcohol being in the house. There was an indefinable change in my attitude at every level, but I still had a sense of not belonging, being a soul apart – maybe it was always going to be that way. I recalled what Donald Gilchrist, a devout Catholic who experienced long periods agonising about the future of mankind, had said: 'When it comes to the crunch, you're on your own.'

Spring brought the usual riot of conflicting colours – short-lived mauve magnolias, proximate to garish yellow forsythia, deep blue grape-hyacinths, daffodils and tulips – and in early June the glory of the mountain meadow outside. From the kitchen window I could see young nuthatches, on the point of fledging, peeping out of their nest box; then each sat for several minutes on the windowsill, before flying off to various bushes, from which their chirruping would attract the parent birds bringing food. Soon it was high summer, hot and humid, with the threat of violent storms in the air. Early one morning, while I was making tea to take up to our bedroom, an overwhelming urge for a drink to boost my energy struck. When a bottle of strong ale lurking in the fridge did not give the required boost, I drank some neat brandy. Retching violently into the sink, I exclaimed, 'That's it!' And it was.

Immediately I felt a sense of release, and Fergus said: 'What's come over you? I heard you singing this morning, and I haven't heard that in years.' Not long after, when I laughed at some trivial incident, I realised how long it was since I had laughed spontaneously. Ideally, the miracle should have coincided with Fergus's birthday on 25 July, but it happened exactly one week earlier on 18 July 1987. Later he told me he had sensed something radical had happened: was it possible I had gone through a spiritual awakening, as described in the AA literature? I returned to regular meetings, where the transformation was also noticed, though some members, who had followed my antics over the years, found it scarcely credible. Those who delighted in clichés were comforted by 'another miracle in AA'.

Katharine returned from Japan for Christmas, and on 12 January 1988 we celebrated Michael's twenty-first birthday with a large party attended by friends of all generations, some 'normal', but a number we had made through AA and Al-Anon.

Epilogue
Soaring on an Updraft

I returned to Ireland in the summers of 1988 and 1989 to visit my mother. She had been told by Dodi and Rosemary that I had stopped drinking, so there was no question of not being allowed to see her. The tiny figure sat in a wheelchair, wrapped in a rug, staring out to sea from a bay window. The view over Belfast Lough was very similar to the one from her own house: from here the panorama stretched as far as Larne, Ballylumford Power Station and Black Head at the beginning of the Antrim Coast Road. Her sight was hazy, and she could only guess at what I was wearing, liking the colours and stretching a hand towards my long string of pearls. No reference was made to the past, and I shall never know if she derived any solace from my sobriety. On my last visit, accompanied by Dodi, Rosemary joined us, looking sprightly in a floral dress she had made herself. Together we tried to entertain her by speaking of people and places she had enjoyed, but it was impossible to know how much she understood. Her attention would wander to the chocolates we had brought, and sometimes she would nod off in mid-sentence, but from time to time she would interject a pithy comment, interspersed by flashes of frustration at being unable to express herself – 'It's all inside, it just won't come out.'

The nurses came to say supper would shortly be served, then they took Rosemary and me aside to tell us the patient now had little appetite and had to be spoon-fed if any significant amount were to go down. They added that sometimes she had to be sedated at night to prevent her from trying to climb out of the bed, which had side bars like a cot. The thought was unspoken – we shared the hope she would soon die in her sleep, which is precisely what she did ten days after I returned to France. She would have been ninety-three in two months' time. Rosemary, thirteen years her junior, died little more than a year later from the asthma that had plagued her throughout life.

Over the next six years I became an active member of AA, as was Fergus in Al-Anon. He had also become a serious golfer with a handicap of ten. I took lessons until I became proficient enough not to shame him on the course. Katharine married in 1992 and had a daughter, Caitlin, the first and only girl of our seven grandchildren, and the only one that Fergus got to know. Katharine had been six months pregnant with Rory when Fergus died on 1 May 1995. So he never knew we have six grandsons. He was at Michael's marriage to Gelise in 1994, but the first of their three sons was not born until 1997. Mary married the year after his death, and has two sons born in 1997 and 1999.

Ted died sane and sober in 2000. Despite his efforts to fight it, the disease got Terry – with whom we shared that uncomfortable New Year's Eve – in the end: he was one of the 'unfortunates', but many members of AA believe the patient hours he spent listening to them were a major factor in their own recovery.

I moved to Scotland, and Michael, who works at the WHO headquarters, now lives with his family in the old house in Divonne. I bought a cottage on the Isle of Raasay in 1997 but had a stroke two years later, after which it was downhill all the way healthwise throughout my seventies – gall bladder, shingles and osteoarthritis – but now in my eighties, taking Winston Churchill as a model, I keep 'buggering on'.

Maps

Northern Ireland and Donegal

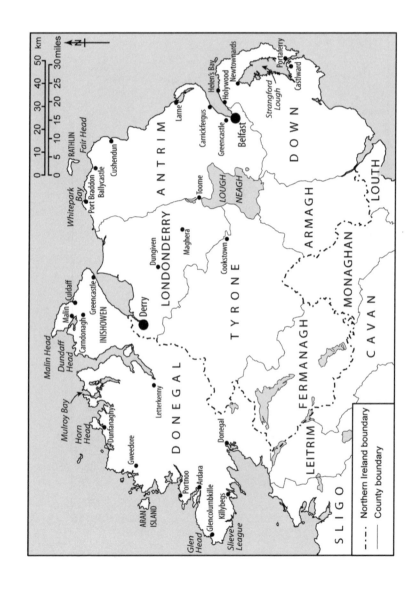

Ghana

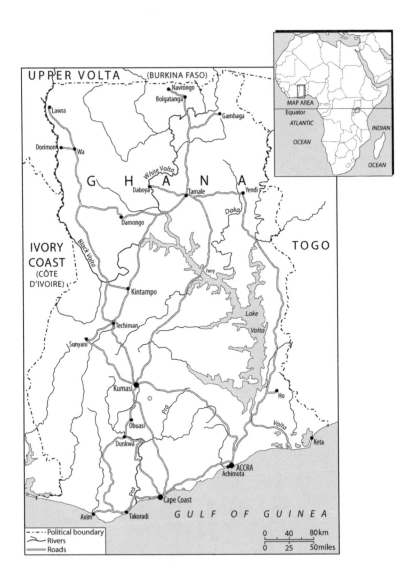

The Game Reserves of East Africa

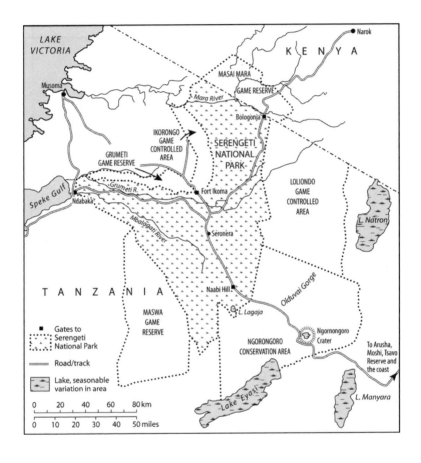

The East Africa Community Countries:
Kenya, Uganda and Tanzania

Franco-Swiss Border

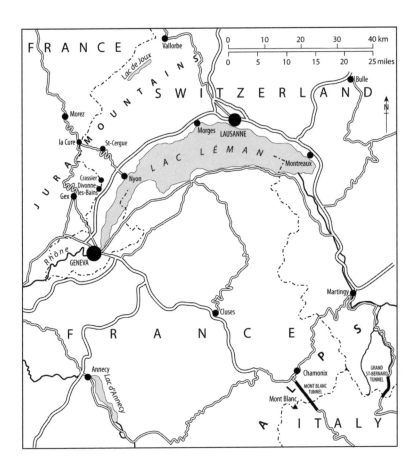

Family Tree

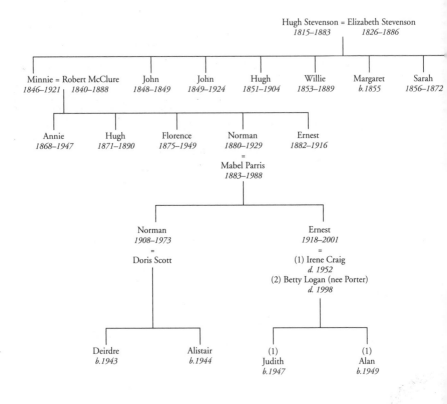

Hugh Stevenson = Elizabeth Stevenson
1815–1883   1826–1886

Minnie = Robert McClure | John | John | Hugh | Willie | Margaret | Sarah
1846–1921 | 1840–1888 | 1848–1849 | 1849–1924 | 1851–1904 | 1853–1889 | b.1855 | 1856–1872

Annie | Hugh | Florence | Norman | Ernest
1868–1947 | 1871–1890 | 1875–1949 | 1880–1929 | 1882–1916
=
Mabel Parris
1883–1988

Norman | Ernest
1908–1973 | 1918–2001
= | =
Doris Scott | (1) Irene Craig
| d. 1952
| (2) Betty Logan (nee Porter)
| d. 1998

Deirdre | Alistair | (1) Judith | (1) Alan
b.1943 | b.1944 | b.1947 | b.1949

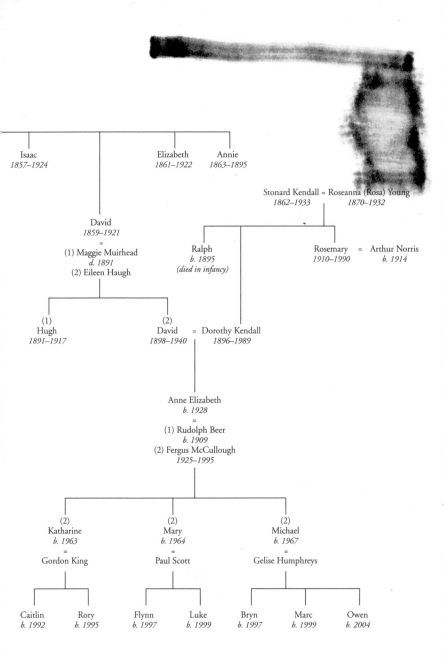

Isaac
1857–1924

Elizabeth
1861–1922

Annie
1863–1895

Stonard Kendall = Roseanna (Rosa) Young
1862–1933   *1870–1932*

David
1859–1921
=
(1) Maggie Muirhead
d. 1891
(2) Eileen Haugh

Ralph
b. 1895
(died in infancy)

Rosemary   =   Arthur Norris
1910–1990   *b. 1914*

(1)
Hugh
1891–1917

(2)
David   =   Dorothy Kendall
1898–1940   *1896–1989*

Anne Elizabeth
b. 1928
=
(1) Rudolph Beer
b. 1909
(2) Fergus McCullough
1925–1995

(2)
Katharine
b. 1963
=
Gordon King

(2)
Mary
b. 1964
=
Paul Scott

(2)
Michael
b. 1967
=
Gelise Humphreys

Caitlin
b. 1992

Rory
b. 1995

Flynn
b. 1997

Luke
b. 1999

Bryn
b. 1997

Marc
b. 1999

Owen
b. 2004